W9-BDB-685

Evaluating and Treating Adult Children of Alcoholics

EVALUATING AND TREATING ADULT CHILDREN OF ALCOHOLICS

VOLUME TWO: TREATMENT

Timmen L. Cermak, M.D.

Edited by Pamela Espeland

A Johnson Institute Book
Professional Series
Minneapolis

A JOHNSON INSTITUTE PROFESSIONAL SERIES BOOK

Published by the Johnson Institute
7151 Metro Blvd., Suite 250
Minneapolis MN 55439-2122
(612) 944-0511

"In Their Own Words: How Clients Experience the Five Characteristics of Co-Dependence" in Chapter 3 is quoted from the Johnson Institute video, "Co-dependence: The Joy of Recovery." Used with permission from the Johnson Institute. Appendix II: A Time to Heal is reprinted from Timmen L. Cermak, M.D., *A Time to Heal* (Los Angeles: Jeremy P. Tarcher, Inc., 1988), pp. 1-8. Used by permission of Jeremy P. Tarcher, Inc.

Library of Congress Cataloging-in-Publication Data

Cermak, Timmen L.
    Evaluating and treating adult children of alcoholics :
a guide for professionals / Timmen L. Cermak.
        p. cm. — (Professional series)
    Includes bibliographical references and indexes.
    Contents: v. 1. Evaluation — v. 2. Treatment.
    ISBN 0-935908-64-1 (v. 1) — ISBN 0-935908-66-8 (v. 2)
    1. Adult children of alcoholics—Mental health.   2. Psychotherapy.
I. Title.   II. Series: Professional series (Minneapolis, Minn.)
RC569.5.A29C47   1991
616.86′1—dc20   90-5057
                                                                            CIP

ISBN 0-935908-66-8

PRINTED IN THE UNITED STATES OF AMERICA

10   9   8   7   6   5   4   3   2   1

For
Mary, Elizabeth, and Katherine

CONTENTS

ACKNOWLEDGMENTS

It is impossible to acknowledge all the people who have been my teachers. There are those whom I have met, those whom I have heard speak, and those whom I have only read. There are those who considered themselves my teachers, and those who considered themselves my peers, students, clients, friends, relatives, and probably even my enemies. There are certainly those to whom I have already expressed appreciation, and those to whom I have not. To you all, I owe a debt of gratitude for teaching me most of what is written in this book. At the same time, I accept full responsibility for all that I have chosen to write, and for what I have still failed to understand.

There are many who have supported my writing of this book. Carole Remboldt, of the Johnson Institute, is a master at wading through the morass of my first manuscripts and discovering what value lies hidden within. Her endurance deserves to be recognized. Her editorial comments and pleas for clarity and simplicity have also contributed immensely to my work. The text was then masterfully edited by Pamela Espeland, who is largely responsible for whatever ease of reading may exist.

I am indebted to the staff at Genesis Psychotherapy and Training Center (San Francisco) who, by their refusal to accept anything simply because I said it, have continually pressed me to develop my thinking. Thank you, Mary Brand Cermak, M.F.C.C., Walter Beckman, Ph.D., Marcia Bradley, M.F.C.C., Roger Lake,

M.F.C.C., Debra Muse, Psy.D., Lisa Rood, L.C.S.W., and Jacques Rutzky, M.F.C.C. Administrative help at Genesis has always been professionally provided by Marilyn Meshak Herczog and Gloria Ruiz.

Without support on the homefront, little of value would happen professionally; and little professionally would be of value. To my wife and colleague, Mary, I express special appreciation. And to my daughters, Elizabeth and Katherine, I say, "Thanks for not understanding how any of this could be more important than getting down on the floor and playing."

EDITOR'S NOTE ON LANGUAGE AND ABBREVIATIONS

The term "alcohol and other drugs" is used throughout this book to emphasize that alcohol *is* a drug, just like cocaine, marijuana, valium, uppers, downers, or any other mind-altering drug. Too often, people talk about "alcohol or drugs" or "alcohol and drugs" as if alcohol were somehow different from drugs and in a category by itself. The consequences of addiction are essentially the same for all these mind-altering drugs, and the need to find ways to prevent or intervene with their use is equally as urgent.

The term "chemical dependence" is used because it covers addiction to all these mind-altering drugs, and because it's short and simple.

Also for reasons of brevity and simplicity, these abbreviations are used:

- "AA" refers to Alcoholics Anonymous.
- "ACA" refers specifically to adult children of alcoholics, those beyond the teen years.
- "Adolescent COA" refers to COAs in their teen years.
- "CD" refers to chemical dependence.
- "COA" (children of alcoholics) refers to all offspring of alcoholics, of any age. It is the most general category.
- "FAS" refers to Fetal Alcohol Syndrome.
- "NA" refers to Narcotics Anonymous.

- "NACoA" refers to the National Association for Children of Alcoholics.
- "PT" refers to psychotherapy.
- "PTSD" refers to Post-Traumatic Stress Disorder.
- "Young COA" refers to COAs from birth to adolescence.

VOLUME TWO: TREATMENT

INTRODUCTION

This is the second of two volumes meant to be read and used together. Although each is designed to be complete and coherent on its own, their subjects are intertwined. Treatment of adult children of alcoholics, the subject of this volume, is inappropriate without a full psychological evaluation of the client. And evaluation, the subject of Volume One, is meaningless unless it points the way toward appropriate, individualized treatment for those clients who need treatment.

Volume One: *Evaluation* presents a cohesive framework for evaluating ACAs. The data obtained from applying this framework must then be organized into a diagnostic impression of each client. The process of diagnosis involves selecting information from the evaluation which both encapsulates what has been learned about the root causes of a client's current problems and begins suggesting treatment strategies which are most likely to be effective.

As noted in Volume One, *ACA and COA are labels, not diagnoses*. The proper treatment of adults from alcoholic homes demands an assessment along each of the axes outlined in that volume. Is the client chemically dependent, in addition to being an ACA? Are there stress-related symptoms, such as psychic numbing or reexperiencing the trauma? Is co-dependence the primary characteristic? Does underlearning exist? Are other major psychiatric problems present as well, such as schizophrenia or depression? And, has the client begun a program of recovery?

Depending upon the specifics of each individual client, therapeutic efforts should be directed toward the most appropriate goal for that individual. Volume Two outlines the treatment implications of data obtained on different evaluation axes. These general implications help us to prioritize and guide the individualization of treatment for specific clients.

For example, a chemically dependent ACA should have his addiction addressed first, rather than beginning with trying to unravel family of origin issues. In the same vein, clients who dissociate frequently due to psychic numbing are poor candidates for insight-oriented psychotherapy, since they will tend to go numb whenever their anxiety begins to rise. And co-dependence will have to be treated differently, depending on whether it is primary, childhood onset or secondary, adult onset.

Oftentimes the initial decision facing therapists is whether a specific client will be served best by a referral to individual or group therapy. To make these decisions a bit more rational, separate chapters outline the different principles and techniques for treating ACAs in individual and group settings. The concluding chapter then explores issues of countertransference and the training of therapists for working with ACAs.

Finally, I wish to reiterate that the subject matter at hand is far too vast to be covered in a single work. Because we are at an early stage in our understanding of COAs, I ask the reader to tolerate the folly of my trying to cover as much as I do.

Timmen L. Cermak
November, 1990

1

TREATMENT AND
HEALING

Both the chemical dependence (CD) field and the psychotherapy (PT) field have developed expertise which is valuable to the therapist treating adult children of alcoholics. This expertise only partially overlaps. While the non-overlapping areas differ, they are not incompatible with each other, even though members of each field have tended to take this view. Before outlining the specific treatments recommended for stress-related characteristics, co-dependence, underlearning, and the chemically dependent ACA, it helps to understand the different approach each of these two fields takes toward treatment.

The human body and mind possess specific, and limited, mechanisms for healing themselves. Whatever treatment is provided can only work through activating and facilitating these inherent mechanisms. For example, immobilizing a broken bone promotes its healing only because bone cells can slowly knit the pieces together and harden the new growth with calcium. When the bone cells are unable to perform their function, no amount of immobilization alone can heal the break. To draw a parallel example within the mental realm, expressing feelings is valuable when old traumas are gradually being remembered, but accomplishes much less healing when critical memories remain covered by denial. Unless the process of remembering is active, no amount of expressing current feelings can heal deeper wounds.

Where the CD and PT fields differ is in the techniques used to activate the natural processes of healing. Recognizing these differences improves our chances of developing an affirmative relationship between the chemical dependence and mental health communities—between recovery and therapy.

THE PROCESS OF HEALING

The human body is constantly balanced between the processes of damage and repair. Physical health is enhanced in two ways: either damaging processes are diminished, or reparative processes are amplified. For example, surgery can bypass narrowed cardiac arteries (removing the pathology), and exercise can develop new collateral arteries (increasing cardiac tone). Obviously, the two approaches are not mutually exclusive, although one may be more appropriate than the other at different points in time. Increasing exercise to build collateral circulation may be contraindicated until dangerous arterial constrictions are removed.

Most of the advances of modern medicine have been within the realm of understanding and removing pathology, thereby permitting the natural healing forces to catch up and win the day. For example, penicillin does not "cure" pneumonia. Rather, it poisons the bacteria that cause the disease, weakening them enough to give the upper hand to the body's own efforts to kill and remove them. If the body's immune system is compromised (as in AIDS and advanced cancers), no amount of effort to fight infections can ultimately prevail.

The maintenance of physical health exists on a continuum, with the two ends so far apart that they seem to have become qualitatively different. At one end is the mechanistic manipulation of pathology through surgery and tiny biochemical tools (i.e., bits of matter on the molecular level such as drugs, hormones, genetic material, etc.). At the other end are efforts to optimize the quality of life through nutrition, physical conditioning, and meditative and spiritual practices. The one end of the continuum focuses on pathology and attempts to remove it. The other end focuses on health and attempts to maximize it.

The continuum is no different in the psychological realm, and accounts for many of the distinctions between psychotherapy and recovery. Some forms of psychological treatment focus on identifying and resolving pathology; others focus on identifying and developing an individual's strengths. However, just as the only avenues capable of producing true physical healing are inherent within the body (e.g., the immune system), the only avenues capable of producing true psychological healing are inherent within the mind. Medical doctors cannot produce substitutes for the immune system; psychotherapists and CD professionals cannot produce substitutes for what the mind can do on its own. Our best efforts are those which cooperate with and facilitate the mind's natural healing powers.

To draw a simplistic analogy, let's look at gardening. The gardener doesn't create the seed or invent germination, cell division, photosynthesis, and pollination; these are givens in the process of growth that the gardener must learn to nurture and understand. At one end of the continuum is the elimination or removal of damaging forces (bugs, sunburn, freezing temperatures, weeds). At the other end are efforts to optimize growth (tilling the soil, fertilizing, adjusting pH, watering). Throughout the summer, it is not the gardener who "makes" the plant grow; this happens because of the natural forces inherent within the seed, given the right conditions.

We are far from truly understanding the natural forces of healing within the human mind. In Chapter 7 of *Volume One: Evaluation*, I suggest three activities which appear to promote these natural healing forces: 1) honesty, 2) experiencing feelings (specifically, the willingness to receive them non-judgmentally), and 3) entering into community. These three forces work synergistically, with each becoming most powerful in the presence of the others.

Honesty

Honesty is the antidote to denial. It cleanses psychic wounds and gives the mind a bedrock of reality upon which to stand. Without honesty, one's very sense of identity becomes disconnected from the specific details of history and fact. Authenticity becomes impossible. Life is conducted in the vague world of infinite possibility. Honesty ties life down within narrower limits, but simultaneously gives it indisputable substance. While fantasies of healing may comfort clients, true healing only occurs in reality.

Many techniques of counseling and the disciplined commitment to "rigorous honesty" embodied in the Twelve Step way of life promote healing by activating this first force. They inspire and praise the courage necessary to become increasingly honest. They confront retreats from the truth and exude confidence that truth is inevitably healing. And, perhaps most importantly, they assume that the ability to achieve greater honesty is inherent within each client.

On the other hand, some clients are blocked from the truth, despite great courage to face it. These blocks may be constitutional, or they may be aspects of their identity which crystallized into psychic blindness during early development. Psychotherapy attempts to find and resolve such blocks in order to allow honesty to flow freely again. Psychotherapy accepts that such blocks can be crippling, and must be directly addressed before the ability to be honest can be unlocked.

Experiencing Feelings

Experiencing feelings is a form of honesty—a form which necessarily moves beyond any tendency to keep the truth contained in the intellect. It moves out of theory and into the field, in the same way that digging one's hands into the soil to plant seeds makes gardening more concrete than merely reading about it.

When feelings are experienced, they are treated with respect as living beings. As a client becomes increasingly able to experience feelings, they become reanimated and juicy. They begin to squirm, and their spontaneity must be contended with in some way other than by squashing it. Experiencing feelings means allowing their reality to become *present* reality. It means allowing them time to rumble around in your chest, vibrate through your spine, twist in your gut, and heat or cool your groin.

Again, counseling techniques and recovery programs encourage people to lighten their grasp on life. They provide new access to feelings and strengthen a person's resolve to tolerate the experience of emotion. The assumption is that people have greater capacity to experience life than they believe. By allying with what hopefulness does exist in people, feelings gradually thaw out and reenter daily existence.

On the other hand, psychotherapy accepts that the capacity to identify and tolerate feelings can be crippled early in life beyond the point at which they can be coaxed back into the light of day. Sometimes the nature of this incapacity must be explored directly before healing can proceed. Other times, efforts to experience feelings inevitably lead to being so overwhelmed that containing them again is the real issue. Counseling techniques work to strengthen the ability to express and contain, while psychotherapy ferrets out and works with the blocks to such expression and containment.

Entering Into Community

Entering into community extends honesty to qualitatively new levels. It calls upon us to be realistic about our identity as one member of a larger whole. It exposes our real feelings to public scrutiny, even as the feelings are present and active. This light of day transforms a person's identity, deepening and purifying it. The aspects of ourselves which exist only through exercising our nature as social animals come alive and must be integrated into the reality of being, on some level, separate individuals as well. When entering into community is combined with deep levels of honesty and a willingness to experience feelings, the soil has been properly tilled, fed, and watered. Healing naturally ensues, at the maximum pace and to the greatest extent possible within each of us.

Recovery programs provide safe and predictable communities to enter. They also encourage meditation upon one's relationship with whatever concept of a God (or Higher Power) is acceptable. Such spiritual pursuits call into question our relationship with the whole of the universe, often humbling any grandiose fantasies we might still have of ourselves. Effective counselors can also create safe environments, either in one-to-one or group relationships with clients. Trust is nurtured in order to gently elicit and encourage an individual's faltering willingness to be vulnerable to others once again.

On the other hand, psychotherapy accepts that individuals are capable of locking themselves into secluded corners with no possibility of discovering the keys to freedom. Trust cannot be nurtured when fear is too great. Psychotherapy techniques attempt to reach back into the original experiences of fear in order to explore how these experiences permanently affected a person's developing sense of self, and to provide an opportunity to reexperience the fear in a new context. The goal is to foster development of the very sense of self beyond the points where it froze in fear.

COMPARING CHEMICAL DEPENDENCE AND PSYCHOTHERAPY MODELS

Before going any further, it's important to emphasize that the comparisons made in this chapter between the CD and PT models are *not*, repeat *not*, meant to imply that these two approaches are mutually exclusive or contradictory. In fact, I believe the direct opposite—so much so that in my own practice, both approaches are continuously present, although in different proportions at different times.

The purpose of conceptualizing their distinctions as clearly as possible is to achieve even greater integration of the two. This is the same paradox faced in human development: Only through the recognition of separateness can true relationship be achieved.

In my experience, the following six distinctions between the CD and PT treatment perspectives are the most relevant to the special needs of ACAs.

1. CD focuses on health; PT focuses on pathology.

For years, I resisted the charge that psychotherapy is more interested in what is "sick" in a person than what is "well." This implies that there is something wrong, even demeaning, about such a focus. The reality is that it is sometimes useful for therapists to have well-honed techniques and a sophisticated framework for uncovering and removing the blocks to healing that exist in their clients. The entire diagnostic endeavor is our public, communal effort to come to terms with what we believe are the common ways human mental health is disrupted.

The process of attending to and enhancing healthy aspects in a client (i.e., CD counseling) is a different experience (for both client and therapist) and follows a different dynamic than the process of attending to and resolving unhealthy aspects (i.e., psychotherapy). Counseling techniques directly facilitate a person's ability to be mature, while psychotherapy techniques focus on, and often begin by eliciting, a person's immature tendencies. Both approaches are valuable.

2. CD works predominantly with conscious material; PT works more with the unconscious.

In working with practicing alcoholics, CD therapists seek clients' conscious participation in dismantling their denial systems. Counseling techniques seek to clarify values, explore alternative behavioral options, and raise awareness of feeling states which are silently affecting behavior. In this sense, a good deal of therapy with every client is counseling. When the therapist works more within the client's unconscious, comes into relationship with it, develops that relationship, and engenders changes in the personality structure at a depth that only gradually gives rise to conscious manifestations, this is psychotherapy. Both approaches are valuable.

3. CD works to prevent transference; PT works within the transference.

The treatment of alcoholics in the early stages of recovery involves efforts to keep them within their adult experience as much as possible (i.e., focusing on their strengths). When a client begins to transfer inappropriate past experience into his relationship with the therapist, this is often met with a direct clarification that the therapist is not the client's mother, father, etc. When childhood memories (e.g., of abuse or abandonment) begin to well up, therapists are apt to help put these on the back burner in order to concentrate on the concrete decisions and plans necessary for the client to get to an AA meeting that night. The focus is on behavioral change.

Psychotherapy requires the presence of transference, for it is here that distortions from the past unconsciously intrude into and disrupt current life. The very structure of the psychotherapeutic relationship is consciously intended to permit and foster transference. For this reason, CD treatment is perceived as being more egalitarian, while PT treatment is more often perceived as hierarchical. Since many clients experience problems within hierarchical relationships, there is clearly a legitimate place for treatment which deals directly with issues of inequality. Both approaches are valuable.

4. CD encourages use of supports outside the therapy relationship, while PT remains self-contained.

The CD recovery model is open to clients' involvement in a variety of healing practices beyond the therapy itself. Clients are directed toward self-help programs and guided in their working of the Twelve Steps. Resistance to these resources is confronted. The fact that spiritual practices are central to recovery also illustrates the clear, concrete image the CD model has of the goal of treatment: a way of life which continuously activates the natural forces of healing.

The work of psychotherapy is more confined. The focus is on the relationship between therapist and client, for this is the primary tool for promoting change. Outside influences on this relationship are minimized. The goals of PT are also more varied. While the CD counselor strives to help the client achieve a way of life which will transform her experience, the psychotherapist works to transform the identity of the experiencer, thereby enabling new ways of life to emerge. Both approaches are valuable.

5. *CD and PT approach resistance differently.*

Concerning resistance, CD takes both a human potential view (that resistance comes from ignorance which can be overcome by education) and a transpersonal psychology view (that it stems from spiritual disconnection which can be overcome by nurturing a person's natural tendency toward healthy development). PT focuses on internal conflicts, characterological deficits, identity disturbances, and developmental arrests in the sense of self as among the causes of resistance. By working within the transference—by symbolically retracing developmental steps toward a more successful outcome—the original causes of resistance are mitigated by the addition of new experience.

The important distinction may be that CD attempts to "get beyond" resistance, while PT validates the resistance as a potentially necessary defense. Both approaches are valuable.

6. *CD thinks developmentally about the process of problem resolution; PT thinks developmentally about the origins of problems.*

CD often discourages clients' efforts to explain the source of problems. Such efforts are seen as draining energy away from discovering current behaviors which perpetuate the problems, and from searching for new behaviors to promote health. The recovery process outlines a series of specific issues and steps which are encountered along the pathway back to health. This permits treatment tasks and modalities to vary greatly along a predictable continuum during an individual client's course of therapy. By understanding the stepping-stones toward healing, each therapist can conceptualize the role he or she must play to facilitate a client's move to the next stage of recovery.

For psychotherapy, it's important to explore a problem's origins because this throws light on the specific developmental tasks which were affected, and on the disruptions to the sense of self which are likely to still be present. When the psychotherapist discovers historical data consistent with the transferences being observed in the present, this confirms the developmental steps which therapy must focus on retracing. Both approaches are valuable.

Summary

We can draw many other distinctions between the CD and PT treatment perspectives. For example:

- CD begins with behavioral change and allows attitudinal changes to follow; PT begins with attitudes and looks for evidence of change in behavior.
- CD relies heavily on self-diagnosis; PT depends heavily on therapist-determined diagnosis.
- CD is continuously vigilant against the tendency for "individualized treatment plans" to collude with a client's resistance by validating his need to be treated as "special"; PT individualizes treatment plans.

We could go on, except that additional distinctions begin to overlap with what has already been said. And all can basically be summarized by the first distinction made above: namely, *CD focuses on health; PT focuses on pathology.*

The CD model is a model for living a healthy life. The PT model is limited to being more reparative—to helping remove the barriers that keep a person from living a healthy life. Once the PT model has done its job, a client is more free to pursue the CD model (or an alternative) and more likely to succeed with it. Paradoxically, many clients require treatment through the CD model until their symptoms have diminished to the point where they are capable of entering into psychotherapy. Once again, it's important to understand that both models are valuable. The strength of each lies in its essentially "generic" nature: Each applies to a wide range of people.

The most effective therapists are those who are versed in both treatment models, who know when to emphasize one more than the other, and who can shift emphasis from one to the other as individual clients make progress in their treatment. In order to understand how both the CD and the PT models facilitate the process of healing, despite their different perspectives and approaches, it will be helpful to outline each of these frameworks in more detail.

HEALING THROUGH THE
CHEMICAL DEPENDENCE MODEL

An Overview of the
Chemical Dependence Model

The essence of chemical dependence treatment is understanding sobriety as a continuum which begins with abstinence and leads to progressively deeper behavioral and characterological changes. Progression along this continuum is referred to as "recovery." Every aspect of treatment is guided by understanding where a client falls along this continuum. Sobriety is viewed not as a state, but rather as movement through a predictable sequence of developmental tasks facing any abstinent alcoholic.

There are three distinct components of recovery: the chemical; behavioral concerns (such as changes in living situation, job, friends and social activities, and the emergence of depression, suicidal feelings or emotional disturbances which emerge once abstinence is attained); and characterological changes.[1] These components must be addressed sequentially. Until abstinence exists, all of the alcoholic's interactions with the environment revolve around the drinking. Then, until relationships with family, friends, and job become stabilized and supportive of the alcoholic's healing, deeper characterological shifts remain difficult. Recovery is seen as a gradual building process, with "first things first." For most alcoholics, a willingness to be methodical and patient is, in itself, a new strategy.

The CD model of treatment reinforces the steps a client has to make at her particular stage of recovery, while simultaneously planting the seeds of the next stage. This process is well illustrated in the CD therapist's approach to active alcoholics. The assumption is that, once active alcoholism is established, it becomes an immensely powerful force in favor of the status quo. Therapeutic efforts geared toward introspection, uncovering feelings, or behavioral change generally require a client to tolerate mounting anxiety. But, when the client uses alcohol to relieve this anxiety, the therapist's efforts are easily counteracted. The motivation for change is lost.

The emphasis of treatment must always return to square one—the fact that alcohol is the primary impediment to change in a person's life, as well as the primary source of pain. In this sense, the initial stages of CD counseling are similar to psychotherapy. The goal of each is to remove a block to healing. The difference is that, in the CD model, the block is seen as external rather than as part of the client's personality structure.

Abstinence Versus Controlled Drinking

Because the current chemical dependence model of treatment *begins* with abstinence, it is imperative to understand the controversy between this approach and those who espouse a strategy of controlled drinking. I place controlled drinking approaches, and behavioral approaches geared toward achieving abstinence through willpower, in the same general category. Both attempt to encapsulate destructive drinking, compartmentalize it, and label it as either a "habit" or a "symptom." Neither considers chemical dependence to be a primary disease. The one maintains that the problem of alcoholism can be defeated by extinguishing the drinking behavior, while the other believes that drinking can often be contained at nondestructive levels.

Much of the debate between predominantly behavioral approaches (toward abstinence or controlled drinking) and AA/recovery-oriented treatment approaches has centered on duelling data regarding long-term followup studies. However, legitimate methodological problems involving definitions of active alcoholism, collection of data, and appropriate measures of outcome cause even the best conferences on this topic to degenerate into maelstroms of competing opinion. Neither side is currently able to "prove" the superiority of its perspective, and each tends to focus on discrediting and ultimately vanquishing the other. As a result, the debate generally generates more heat than light.

What separates these two perspectives is their relative interest (or lack thereof) in using alcohol/other drug dependence as a window into deeper change. Behavioral approaches view controlled drinking or abstinence as an end in itself. AA/recovery-oriented treatment views abstinence as a golden opportunity for reawakening the forces of healing, thereby affecting a person's entire life for the better. Arguments that such an approach is *necessary* for the long-term, comfortable maintenance of abstinence may or may not be valid; and even if they are valid, such arguments may or may not be scientifically verifiable. The fact remains that, in contrast to controlled drinking approaches, AA/recovery-oriented treatment is consciously and specifically geared to improving the quality of a person's life across the board, not just those aspects directly affected by alcohol consumption. The CD model approaches abstinence in ways designed to have implications for clients' entire course of recovery.

Toward this end, the CD treatment model focuses on establishing abstinence in a way that simultaneously affects the alcoholic's identity and the thinking that supports it. The goal is to alter the core belief about being alcoholic (or, perhaps more clearly, to alter the core belief about who one is, from "I am NOT an alcoholic" to "I AM an alcoholic"), and to propel clients into exploring the meaning of this new identity. Behavioral abstinence alone does not stimulate a shift in identity, nor does it promote an awareness and exploration of the rationalizations, projection of blame, and denial which have generally permeated an alcoholic's life.

The real fight between behavioral approaches to controlled drinking or abstinence and the CD treatment model, which is AA/recovery-oriented, involves the question of whether "drinking alcoholically" constitutes a behavior or an identity. To date, no research data supports one view over the other. In fact, it's possible that either might be true in specific, individual cases. I suspect that this accounts, in part, for George Vaillant's finding that spontaneous return to abstinence or controlled drinking sometimes does occur.[2] Those people for whom alcoholic drinking is more a destructive habit may well be able to achieve controlled drinking or abstinence without having to undergo changes on the identity level. But for those in whom the denial of their alcoholism has been incorporated into their very sense of self, nothing less than a rebirth of that self is necessary.

The debate between abstinence and controlled drinking would have a chance to begin generating more light than heat if we realized that we are not truly debating the essential nature of "alcoholic drinking" as much as we are focusing on differences brought about by the extraordinary complexities of human personality, which can lead to different levels of harmful involvement with alcohol. Humans can drink excessively out of habit. And humans also can, and frequently do, entangle their very sense of identity in denial of their excessive drinking. Since it is rarely possible to determine any particular client's level of involvement (particularly while he is still actively drinking), and since the consequences of continuing to drink alcoholically are so potentially devastating, the CD treatment model has chosen to take the prudent approach of assuming the deepest level of involvement, and shooting for the best outcome, with all clients.

The Identity of Being an Alcoholic

The question is not whether every person who drinks alcoholically will benefit from accepting the identity of being alcoholic. Instead, the question is why so many clients seem to be greatly helped when they do.

I suspect that many in this category are genetically prone to alcoholism, and taking on the identity aids them in recognizing this. Many others have taken it on because of the enormous impact the experience of actively drinking has had on their lives. Like being a hostage to terrorists, the longer the experience lasts, the more it becomes central to one's very identity. Finally, there is the powerfully positive experience many clients have when they first try on the identity of being an alcoholic. They find this identity to be more in tune with the realities of their life than anything they have known for the past several years, or decades. Often, it is a welcome, stabilizing influence, the first solid sense of themselves they have felt for some time. It also opens them to the pleasure of being accepted by and belonging to the recovering community.

The CD treatment model thus treats alcoholism, if not as a rite of passage, then at least as the eye of a needle. Passing through the eye can be a transforming experience. Recovery is not simply the mirror image of the downward progression into the disease; you don't go back to being the same person you were before you started drinking. As Stephanie Brown emphasizes, "Abstinence involves the addition of *new* experiences."[3]

Abstinence can be the first step toward significant and permanent changes in identity. It is paradoxical only to people outside the CD field tradition that this first step involves accepting the "negative" and "demeaning" identity of being an alcoholic. Within the CD field, this identity opens clients to the "positive" truth that they are humans, with human limitations. While this can be narcissistically wounding—to the extreme, for some clients—such deflation of grandiosity may be necessary for profound healing to have a chance. Ultimately, as intoxication becomes less compatible with one's identity, it grows more apparent that the only limitations the identity of being an alcoholic imposes are those that involve the consumption of alcohol! As recovery proceeds, the identity of being an alcoholic becomes more deeply integrated and, at the same time, less relevant to one's self-esteem—certainly far less relevant than one's identity as a *recovering* alcoholic.

Techniques for Supporting Sobriety

By approaching the task of abstinence with a view not only toward the behavioral level, but also toward fostering changes on the identity level, CD treatment sets the stage for profound events to take place within clients. Most clients have a long way to go before these events can come to pass. Often, new friends must be found and age-old drinking friends left behind. Families must be reestablished, jobs found or repaired. Anxiety may abound; sleep may be disturbed; dreams may reappear. Depression is common. The pitfalls are many and deep.

Early abstinence is not the time for contemplative introspection or the activation of old internal conflicts. Instead, it's the time to take action and find support—to attend Twelve Step meetings or seek other social reinforcements. The risks of relapse (returning to alcohol) are real. Whenever clients begin underestimating these risks, it is up to counselors to set them straight. Sometimes clients have all they can do to put one sober foot in front of the other.

To deny the difficulty of this early period of sobriety is to deny the seriousness of the chemical addiction to alcohol, and the extent to which that addiction can impact a person's daily life. CD counselors are skilled at encouraging and directing clients to simplify their lives down to a single goal: that of maintaining sobriety. Transference issues are contained. Clients are encouraged to stay primarily in their adult experience, rather than dealing with family of origin issues. And attention is paid to the concrete steps needed to stay sober for the next twenty-four hours.

Treatment often takes the form of helping clients notice the fine details of their sober experience, chronicling differences between the sober present and the intoxicated past. Physical healing is noted, mental clarity is examined, and tolerance for the renewal of feelings is supported, even as clients are urged not to base their actions on feelings at this point. When introspection occurs, it is usually in the direction of exploring denial. Long a way of life, denial will reappear, often in sophisticated disguises. As AA so aptly puts it, alcoholism is a "cunning, baffling and powerful disease." To internalize this and put it another way, our minds have many clever ways to trip us up.

Introspection may also occur in the area of a client's ongoing relationship to willpower. By continuing to focus on the misuse of willpower, the counselor simultaneously accomplishes three things: continuation of the dismantling of denial; clarification of effective options in repairing family, occupational, and financial damage the client incurred during the active drinking phase; and further laying of a foundation for deeper identity changes to come.

As supports for a client's sobriety develop, time passes, and the struggle lessens, more attention can be paid to feelings. At times, clients suppress their emotions in an effort to remain sober; at other times, feelings burst out and threaten to overwhelm their sobriety. It eventually becomes useful to start exploring feelings, less from a purely supportive stance and more from the perspective of dynamic, insight-oriented psychotherapy.

If the work of early sobriety has been done well, clients should have the tools necessary to conceptualize and tolerate shifting more into the psychotherapy treatment model, if and when this is warranted. Psychotherapists can ease this transition in two ways. First, they should have the flexibility to return to the more directive approaches of the CD model whenever anything threatens a client's sobriety. Second, they should be familiar enough with the tools learned in early recovery that these can be reframed and called upon to help with the work of psychotherapy as well. These tools include such things as rigorous honesty, the willingness to relinquish strategies based on unquestioned use of willpower (also called "surrender"), being comfortable with paradox (e.g., finding greater control of one's life by acknowledging the lack of control over how alcohol affects one's brain), and the experience of taking a leap of faith as part of healing. This latter tool is frequently all that a client has to cling to in choosing whether to respond to a psychotherapist's invitation to enter into a deeper level of therapy, one characterized by a more intimate and vulnerable client/therapist relationship. It takes a true leap of faith for clients to cooperate with examining the transference, and recovering alcoholics/addicts often have the tools to take this leap successfully, if the psychotherapist knows how to call upon them.

Much of the value of the CD treatment model lies in its ability to conceptualize something more sophisticated than an eclectic collection of techniques to accommodate a particular client's current needs. Embedded in the model is a continuum of tasks and awareness of how each step of recovery can be accomplished in a manner which foreshadows and facilitates the next steps. Such a model clearly operates in the faith that health lies dormant within many clients, waiting only to be evoked and given form.

Activation of the
Natural Healing Forces
by the CD Model

If healing results from the natural forces of honesty, feelings, and community, then it should be possible to identify how the CD treatment model activates these forces. This is not difficult, since the CD model is literally a prescription for making the activation of these forces a way of life. The process of recovery is a daily discipline designed to promote rigorous honesty, the humble acceptance of feelings, and reliance on those outside ourselves (i.e., the recovering community and our Higher Power) for sustenance. The genius of CD treatment lies in how powerfully it is able to activate these forces in people who have lived in denial, out of touch with their deep experience, and isolated from others.

The beginning of recovery always involves dissolving the darkness of denial with the light of reality. Alcoholics must break through the denial that their drinking is adding to their pain before abstinence can be *chosen* (as opposed to being accepted as an imposition from the outside, to get people off your back). In most cases, alcoholics must also accept the reality that every effort they have made to limit their drinking or to stop it on their own have eventually failed. In taking on the identity of "being an alcoholic," the truth of an essential limitation is being acknowledged. Living in this truth permits healing to begin. Continuous awareness of this truth permits healing to be continuous. To be human is to have limitations. Accepting the reality of one's own unique limitations does not get rid of them. Rather, it permits the healing force of honesty to help us transcend the power that these limitations have to lower our self-worth.

By encouraging abstinence to be attained in ways that highlight a shift in identity, the CD model stimulates clients to ferret out denial wherever it pervades their lives. Inappropriate uses of willpower, whether in regard to trying to control the effects drinking alcohol will have, trying to will away one's grief, or trying to maneuver other people into having certain feelings, gradually come to be seen as rejecting the reality of limitations. Rigorous honesty becomes a way of life at all levels, deepening the channels through which a growing river of honesty can flow, carrying the waters of healing to the deserts within.

The renewal of feelings with abstinence is the second natural healing force, and it stems from two sources. First, abstinence itself is necessary for feelings to be present in their true forms. Intoxicated feelings are distorted feelings. They come from the bottle, and the chemical effects of alcohol on the brain, rather than from the heart, in response to one's deep experience. Intoxicated feelings do not flow toward resolution. They stand up like rocks in the middle of a river, or they submerge beneath the alcohol and fester in hiding. Sobriety is necessary for one to experience the truth about one's feelings.

Second, once recovering alcoholics surrender efforts to control their feelings, they are in a better position to experience them. The essence of feelings lies in their spontaneity, and willpower destroys spontaneity. Recovery supports an openness to experiencing whatever feelings one truly has. And thus the second natural healing force is activated. The river of truth is no longer abstract, but now becomes a surging, pulsating force that can be felt flowing through one's chest, whirling in one's groin, or beating against one's stomach. When the intensity of feelings becomes too much to bear, the CD model works to activate the third natural healing force—entering into community.

The initial community promoted by the CD model is AA. Their meetings surround us—morning, noon and night, next door and around the globe. AA members are at the other end of any telephone. They will come to your home to pick you up for a meeting. Sponsors will share their experience, strength, and hope at the drop of a hat. No one is more welcome at a meeting than newcomers, for they are held to be the lifeblood of the fellowship. The invitation to belong is pervasive, alluring, and real. Those clients who can be encouraged to enter the recovering community have accepted the ultimate limitation—the fact that none of us is an island. No one can get truly sober alone, because full sobriety means developing relationships with others in which we allow ourselves to be seen as we truly are ("rigorous honesty"), including our feelings in the very moment.

The CD model also stimulates clients' spiritual impulses. It assumes that spirituality is a normal human experience, and that those of us who are truly receptive to our spontaneous feelings will sooner or later encounter spiritual longings and a sense of awe. Clients are encouraged to expand the exploration of their actual relationship to others to include their relationship to the whole. Even a mote of honesty quickly brings most people to the conclusion that they are not God. Limitation is part of the human condition. The universe is not of our making, and it is a worthy endeavor to make conscious efforts to come into contact with the immense forces which have given rise to all that surrounds us. Whether you choose to call these forces "God," your "Higher Power" as you understand it, or something else does not matter. Healing occurs because, as you seek contact with these grand forces, you are actively being honest about your limitations, accepting the feelings of awe within you, and developing a willingness to belong to something which is so immense that it surpasses your understanding.

The CD treatment model was developed empirically, guided by experience rather than theory. As a result, the three healing forces of honesty, experiencing feelings, and entering community lie at its core. Its particular value is that it embodies a way of life that effectively ushers those souls which have been blinded, numbed, and isolated by chemical dependence into the light, the sensations, and the companionship out of which profound healing is fashioned.

HEALING THROUGH
THE PSYCHOTHERAPY MODEL

An Overview of
the Psychotherapy Model

The general mental health field contains a variety of treatment modalities, from supportive counseling traditions (such as

Rogerian therapy) that operate from the same perspective as the CD model discussed above, to behavior modification, hypnosis, cognitive therapy, pharmacotherapy, body work, and psychodynamic psychotherapies, of which psychoanalysis is the prototype. I have reserved the term "psychotherapy" to refer to only one of these traditions—psychodynamic psychotherapy—and do not wish to imply that it represents the whole of what the general mental health field offers. I focus my discussion on how psychotherapy works within the transference to resolve developmental arrests and distortions because I believe it is the most effective approach for primary co-dependence.

The essence of psychotherapy, as I am defining it, lies in the systematic re-experiencing of early childhood issues in order to complete developmental tasks. The workbench for this process is the flesh-and-blood relationship between therapist and client. As this relationship develops (or fails to develop), clients invariably transfer into the therapy the expectations and disappointments from their earliest experiences with their parents. The very structure of psychotherapy is designed to promote awareness of this transference, and to use it as a window both into past events and into the very structure of the client's current personality. The goal is to usher clients into healthy levels of intimacy with the therapist by helping them rework and more successfully complete basic developmental tasks, such as separation, individuation, and rapprochement.

Transference

There are many reasons for distinguishing psychotherapy from treatment modalities which do not work within the transference.

First, psychotherapy arose within the mental health tradition and has yet to be imported into the CD field. As a result, the vast majority of CD therapists have little experience with, and often little concept of, transferential psychotherapy. To be fully prepared to treat ACAs, they must add the process of psychotherapy to their current skills.

Second, training within the general mental health field is no guarantee that a therapist has experience with, or a clear concept of, transferential psychotherapy. This is especially true of therapists from schools which ignore traditional curricula in favor of more behavioral and humanistic approaches. Again, to be fully prepared to treat ACAs, they must add the process of psychotherapy to their current skills.

Third, those therapists who are skilled in psychotherapy need to understand the limitations of this approach. Otherwise, they lose flexibility and provide only one form of treatment for all clients.

Psychoanalysis represents the first efforts to conceptualize, study, and work within the transference. The predominant tradition within psychoanalysis called upon therapists to minimize their input to relationships with clients, leading to a "blank screen" as the purist approach. This blank screen was developed in a belief that therapists needed to remain relatively inactive in order not to confuse the transference by giving clients extraneous things to react to.

Forming a relationship with a blank screen is perhaps a more abnormal experience than therapy needs to be. With the rise of object relations schools and the influence within the United States of Harry Stack Sullivan's interactive style of interviewing,[4] many therapists have modified the "blank screen" to a "known screen." The artificiality of minimal responses to a client has been replaced by greater spontaneity and authenticity in interactions, with the belief that therapists should be able to maintain awareness of the contributions they are making to the relationship, and interpret the client's transference within this context.

Today, many therapists attempt to work within the transference by 1) entering into a relationship with clients in which direct human contact is established, 2) monitoring their own input to this relationship, 3) selecting this input according to clients' needs (i.e., not to meet the therapist's own needs for self-disclosure or avoidance of relationship), and 4) identifying the distortions to the relationship which are imported by the client. When these distortions result from feelings and/or perceptions which were originally formed toward a parent, but now are *transferred* onto the therapist, they constitute transference.

It is axiomatic that transference always contains an element of reality, no matter how symbolic this might be. At times this reality exists in mannerisms or behavior on the part of the therapist which are reminiscent of an actual parent. At other times it is simply the hierarchical structure of the therapy setting (i.e., the imbalance between a client's vulnerability to and dependence on a person of professional authority) which resonates with childhood feelings.

When psychotherapists allow the transference to exist and begin to actively explore the client's experience of it, transferential distortions often increase in intensity. Working within the transference means 1) using transference as data to piece together developmental arrests and distortions which explain the client's current personality, and 2) using the relationship between psychotherapist and client to address issues which stem from these early developmental disruptions.

Psychoanalytic therapists tend to work within the transference more through interpretations which, when well timed, bring previously unconscious material into awareness, are accompanied by feelings, and lead to change. Interpretations which are encapsulated by the intellect are not considered successful. More interactive psychotherapists rely less on interpretation, preferring to use the relationship itself as their primary tool for working within the transference. The evolution of greater intimacy is used to help clients successfully rework the stages of child development, on both a real and a symbolic level.

Child Development

The psychotherapeutic approach must be suffused by an intimate understanding of child development. Contrary to the counseling modality, which enhances access to a client's strengths and focuses on the client's adult experience, psychotherapy intentionally taps into more primitive dynamics. As a result, considerable regression may occur in the relationship with one's psychotherapist. It takes a leap of faith on the client's part to stop resisting this regression when most of his childhood experience has taught him that vulnerability and dependence must be denied and defended against. Or, on the other hand, childhood experiences may have taught him that excessive empathy and dependence comprise the only avenue toward relationships. In either case, the therapist must be able to recognize the specific stages of development which remain unresolved, and thus are transferred into the present. Then, not as a disinterested bystander, but rather as an active participant in the relationship, the therapist must invite the client to recapitulate these tasks, and work with him toward a more successful outcome.

Psychoanalysts tend to explore disruptions which occurred during the development of psychosexual drives and lead to issues of power (e.g., Oedipal conflicts) and conscience. Object relations psychotherapists and self psychologists tend to explore disruptions which occurred during earlier stages of development and lead to issues of abandonment and engulfment. In both cases, their work within the transference is guided by intimate knowledge of child development theory.

Once psychotherapeutic work has been entered into in depth, it often complicates a therapist's returning to more supportive treatment modalities. It is clearly necessary to return to the CD framework for counseling clients in, or close to, relapse with their chemical dependence. But, at other times, such a shift might be seen as the therapist's lack of faith in the client's ability to grow. In effect, both the client and the therapist are attempting a leap of faith when psychotherapy commences. The time for preparation is over, and a process of inevitable momentum begins. Entering into psychotherapy represents a commitment. On the client's part, it is a commitment to plunge into a new relationship with her self, through development of a mutual commitment between her and the therapist.

Although much has been made of reparenting in the ACA treatment field, some fundamental over-simplifications have been made in this area by those working from the CD model. In particular, counseling approaches to reparenting have often failed to understand that many ACAs possess an immature image of parenting, one which results from a combination of under-learning (i.e., never having witnessed mature parenting) and childhood fantasies developed from unmet needs. Until developmental tasks are completed, clients may lack the capacity to understand the nature of truly mature parenting.

Psychotherapy *is* reparenting in the truest sense. The forces involved are the unresolved elemental passions from one's childhood. The dynamics being worked out lie outside full awareness. Feelings and direct experience are far more important than intellectual comprehension. As a result, psychotherapy is a unique human experience—a second chance at child development.

The unique experience psychotherapy provides is deeply paradoxical. On the one hand, consent is given between equals to enter into the work; on the other hand, the bulk of the relationship that develops entails the experience of inequality. This in turn leads to other unique experiences available only through the therapeutic process. Specifically, clients can *experience* that they are acceptable and desirable for who they are, rather than for what they can do. They can *experience* that powerful forces and people outside their control can be counted on to be benevolent and to support the clients' best interests, rather than their own self-interests. They can *experience* the limitations within those upon whom they are dependent, and resolve their disappointment over these inadequacies. And they can enter back into and complete the tasks of child development at a deeper level than they previously attained.

Activation of the
Natural Healing Forces
by the PT Model

Psychotherapy calls upon both the client and therapist to be fully in each other's presence. This requires profound degrees of honesty. When clients are unable to move out from behind the facade of their false persona, healing is blocked. The initial positive step many clients take is to begin acknowledging their avoidance of being vulnerable to the therapist (e.g., "I could never get mad at you"). While such admissions may feel like failure to the clients, the honesty which is emerging starts the healing process.

An old psychoanalytic axiom calls upon therapists to analyze clients' defenses before analyzing the underlying emotions being defended against. In line with this perspective, the PT model encourages honesty first about a client's fears. It is often only after clients have trusted me with *why* they keep me from knowing who they really are, and *how* they do this, that they can begin addressing the underlying needs they hope I can fulfill for them. Their defenses protect them from the vulnerability of depending upon me at the deep level of these needs. Their willingness to become honest at this deep level often rests upon how it felt to be honest with me first about their fears and defenses.

In the process of exploring why and how they minimize their vulnerability in the therapy setting, clients are often called upon to become more honest about events in their childhood as well, especially those during which their most characteristic defenses developed. For some, it is the emergence of old memories which calls upon them to become more honest about past realities. For others, the call may come through dreams, through obvious distortions they make in perceptions of the therapist, or through exploring how their resistance to discussing certain topics may even be increasing.

Some of the most difficult honesty which must be practiced in psychotherapy involves exploring the feelings clients have toward the therapist. This difficulty stems from several sources. For one, the process is not reciprocal. Therapists listen, but do not make themselves equally vulnerable by disclosing their own feelings. This fact simultaneously increases clients' vulnerability and creates an element of safety, since the danger of acting inappropriately on these feelings is reduced by the therapist's withholding. Honesty about how clients feel toward their therapists is also made more difficult by the fact that many feelings stem from the regression which inevitably occurs in therapy. The feelings are a child's feelings, often stark and global. They have been transferred onto the therapist from how clients felt toward their parents years ago. And, finally, the very structure of the psychotherapy often makes it clear that therapists are going to listen to these feelings, but not respond to them behaviorally. It is extraordinarily difficult to tell a therapist that you want to go to sleep in his or her arms, when the "adult" part of you knows that this will never happen. Still, the pursuit of honesty is unrelenting in psychotherapy. And, if one has such feelings toward the therapist, it is an article of faith that being honest about them promotes healing.

The honesty in psychotherapy which matters most is primarily about feelings, impulses, and needs. For example, in telling a therapist that you desperately want to be taken care of by him, even to the point of falling asleep in his arms, you are then faced with your disappointment that such dependence is ultimately not possible. Virtually every client questions the value of expressing needs only to feel the pain of their going unfulfilled. Rather than being a resistance to therapy, this question is at the core of the developmental dilemmas being reenacted. Such disappointment is inevitable in the relationship between parent and child. The point is always reached at which the parent's love can no longer substitute for a child's maturation into an autonomous individual. Total dependence is not a reality.

Each child (and, by extension, each psychotherapy client) is faced with the question of how to deal with this disappointment. Some deny it, thereby impoverishing their sense of self, since longing to be dependent is an essential part of being human. Others castigate the parent for being limited, and relationships become warlike campaigns to subdue others into doing their unrealistic bidding, or to vanquish them for their failures. The lucky ones feel their disappointment enough to experience their parents' empathy. A bridge is forged despite the gulf which exists between separate individuals. For all of us, the reason for experiencing our feelings in the face of such inevitable disappointment is that this is the only avenue toward mutuality (as opposed to the fusion which is no longer available after awareness of separation becomes permanent). Unless a person is experiencing her feelings, others have nothing to form an empathic connection with. It is an article of faith that experiencing feelings, no matter what feelings may happen to be present, promotes healing.

Finally, psychotherapy activates the natural healing force of community by continuously inviting intimacy between client and therapist. As outlined in the above paragraph, the reason for experiencing disappointments at the hands of a therapist (as opposed to denying these feelings) is that this provides the only avenue toward allowing others to come into vital contact with who we really are. Psychotherapy is about relationship (i.e., community). Psychotherapists are skilled at understanding the level of relationship clients are initially capable of, entering into this level in the role of an accepting parent, and promoting clients' growth into more mutual levels of relationship.

While the CD model promotes a way of life in which honesty, experiencing feelings, and entering into community are activated throughout one's day, the PT model promotes a confined experience in which clients are called upon to activate these forces in the here and now. Both are valuable.

THE AFFIRMATIVE RELATIONSHIP
BETWEEN CHEMICAL DEPENDENCE
AND PSYCHOTHERAPY APPROACHES
TO HEALING

I have taken some risk in drawing distinctions between counseling and psychotherapy. This calls for two caveats.

First, these distinctions are not meant to apply to professional titles. Many licensed "counselors" practice psychotherapy, while many licensed "psychotherapists" work within the counseling framework. I could have termed the two treatment frameworks "supportive" versus "dynamic" psychotherapy. In general, it's best to avoid letting labels obscure concepts.

Second, since the healing process is essentially the same for all human beings, treatment within each of the two modalities works by activating the same healing forces. There is no incompatibility between healing which occurs through counseling and that which occurs through psychotherapy, although it may not be possible for the same therapist to work within both modalities simultaneously. Ideally, counseling within the CD framework and psychotherapy can work synergistically.

An example of how PT principles might benefit CD counselors involves treatment of the distorted relationship to willpower and control seen in chemical dependence (and co-dependence). The CD field describes this "distorted relationship" as a dysfunctional belief system, but this explanation is not encompassing enough. Belief systems can be discarded and replaced. But, unless the underlying character structure changes, any new beliefs will quickly be subverted.

The identity of the believer must also be considered. When a client says, "I should be able to control . . . ," who is the "I" that is talking? It is this "I" which must change, and not simply the belief system the "I" is following. And, until that "I" does change, it is the only "I" which therapists can deal with.

Psychotherapeutic principles teach therapists to assess the limitations of the character structure before them, and to be aware of the distortions this will create in the therapeutic relationship. Meeting a client where he is at the moment means not only honoring his belief systems, but interacting with his very sense of identity, without losing sight of your own.

On the other side of the coin, there are many tools learned in the process of recovery which can be of great benefit to the psychotherapist who understands them. Simply understanding the language of Twelve Step programs can be a useful shortcut with some clients. I recently had a client who was paving the way to have an affair by convincing herself that her husband would not be hurt if he discovered it. When I mentioned that she might do a fourth step on her sexuality with her sponsor, she immediately understood the process of systematically reviewing her strengths and weaknesses in regard to her sexual activity, and discussing them honestly with another human. By the time she returned to therapy the next week, she was out of denial about how her husband would react and much more willing to look at the possibility that the affair she thought she wanted was a substitute for the lack of sexual relationship she had with her husband.

The Twelve Step program of recovery is an excellent preparation for clients' entering psychotherapy. It has taught them the value of rigorous honesty, thereby decreasing their self-censorship of thoughts and feelings during therapy sessions. It has taught them the pain that comes from grandiose efforts to control, which prepares them to accept their own echoistic needs to be dependent. It has taught them to face the unknown with the faith that they will be given the strength needed. Above all, it has taught them the reality of paradox.

Seemingly contradictory notions can sometimes be true (notwithstanding our common sense). In the case of recovery, acknowledging one's inability to control the effects of alcohol once it is ingested leads to freedom from its devastation. Victory comes through admitting defeat. From deflation comes a more solid sense of self. Rigorous honesty creates greater security than secrecy. Allowing people to know who you really are leads to closer friendships than managing their impressions of you. All of this seems ridiculous to anyone who has built her identity around a grandiose sense of control. During the recovery process, clients become comfortable with the reality of paradox, and develop the faith to abandon common sense in favor of the unknown.

The maturation of character structure requires the same two elements of paradox and faith. Clients must often act in ways which are contrary to the painful lessons their experience has taught them. Abandoned or betrayed during childhood, they are called upon by psychotherapy to reenter, on a symbolic level, the kind of relationship which earlier brought such disappointment and pain into their lives. People learn by experience, and when your experience has taught you that being in a vulnerable and dependent position with an authority figure is dangerous, it takes a leap of faith to proceed.

Once the leap of faith is taken, clients are transported back to stages of development where they are called upon to integrate seemingly contradictory impulses. Narcissistic needs to be the center of relationships and echoistic needs to build relationships around the strength of others, seemingly at terminal odds with each other, mature and meet in the rapprochement crisis. An identity—a sense of self—built predominantly on one need or the other will forever be unable to integrate the two.

What is required is an expanded identity, capable of incorporating both needs. By abandoning the sense of self that is more protective of one need or the other, a deeper, more solid sense of self can be born. Neither need is abandoned, as the two are matured and transformed by an identity which, paradoxically, can integrate them both. The recovery process is excellent preparation for accomplishing the work of psychotherapy.

2

TREATING STRESS-RELATED
CHARACTERISTICS
IN ACAs

There are four primary symptoms which result from experiencing traumatic levels of stress during childhood: reexperiencing the trauma, psychic numbing, increased arousal, and survivor guilt. The first two are of greatest importance in the development of treatment plans.

Clients who continue to be overwhelmed by reactions to the original trauma, or who are emotionally shut down, may be harmed by inappropriate treatment approaches, and are rarely good candidates for dealing with transference in psychotherapy. Just as active chemical dependence must be addressed before treatment can be effective, the effects of early trauma must often be addressed first as well.

A distinction must be made between *traumatic events* and the *defenses* which clients developed to cope with them. While the former must eventually be explored in realistic detail, this is rarely advisable, or even tolerable to clients, before the therapeutic alliance is firmly established. On the other hand, defenses which arose during traumatic events can, and often must, be addressed at the very outset of treatment. These defenses serve as a pervasive grid through which all the client's experience is filtered. And since this filtering is present in the therapeutic setting as well, it must be treated before the client can be open to new experiences. The first step in treatment is often to dismantle a client's barriers to fully experiencing his immediate reality. For traumatized ACAs, this usually means treating their tendency to reexperience the trauma and/or their psychic numbing.

This chapter outlines the treatment of reexperiencing the trauma, psychic numbing, increased arousal, and survivor guilt. For didactic purposes, it is best to begin with psychic numbing.

PSYCHIC NUMBING

Clinical experience with psychic numbing in Vietnam veterans is directly relevant to the ACA field. The approach first taken to these veterans contained a serious mistake which has permeated psychotherapy for generations. Specifically, therapists confused catharsis with treatment. In line with the medical metaphor of an abscess, they believed that healing depended on lancing the wound and releasing the "emotional pus." Theoretically, once forgotten memories were remembered and repressed feelings were released, veterans would no longer need to remain detached from their experience.[1]

Early treatment focused on helping veterans remember their traumatic experiences and "get in touch with their feelings." Different therapists used different techniques—hypnosis, verbal analysis of defenses, guided imagery, gestalt work, neurolinguistic programming, psychodrama, etc. A "good" session often meant that previously repressed memories and feelings had been retrieved after weeks, or even months, of creative work on the therapist's part. The usual response to a client's regaining access to these memories and feelings was for the therapist to push forward energetically. Until the emotional pus was expelled, it was assumed that the psychic numbing would continue. However, it was quickly noted that "good" sessions were frequently followed by missed appointments and premature terminations of treatment. Clearly there was something wrong with "lancing emotional boils" in Vietnam veterans with psychic numbing.

The stress-response cycle, described in Chapter 3 of Volume One: *Evaluation*, gives us important insights into how these veterans should have been treated. To briefly summarize, a stressful event may trigger immediate *denial*, which protects us against being overwhelmed by grief, anger, or pain. Over time, memories and images of the event begin to *intrude* into our awareness. We work through major stresses by swinging back and forth on an internal pendulum between denial and intrusiveness, "biting off" and dealing with the stress in small, manageable chunks. If nothing interferes with this process—if nothing stops the pendulum's swing—we eventually reach resolution.

In psychic numbing, the pendulum is stuck in denial. In reexperiencing the trauma, it is stuck in intrusiveness. Treatment for both symptoms is the same: restoring the pendulum's ability to swing freely.

In other words, it is the pendulum, not the emotional boil, which needs attending to. When therapists pushed Vietnam veterans to emote more fully just as they were first beginning to retrieve memories, the veterans' worst fears were realized. The reason their internal pendulum was stuck in denial was their fear of being overwhelmed if they allowed even a small portion of their feeling into the light of day. When they finally responded to the therapists' efforts, it was as though the therapist had forcibly grabbed the pendulum and physically thrust it over into intrusiveness.

The therapists' drive toward catharsis had several negative effects. It made the treatment setting more dangerous. It underestimated the intensity of emotion, and even the degree of trauma, locked inside the client. And it did nothing to build up the client's faith that the lid could be put back on once it had been taken off. The veterans learned to replace the lid by not coming to the next session, or dropping out of treatment altogether.

Effective treatment of psychic numbing is a lot less dramatic than catharsis. It entails many of the same techniques used to open a client to the point where catharsis is a possibility, but it does not attempt to drain emotional pus. Rather, it ministers to the pendulum. When the pendulum is stuck in denial, it must be unstuck. When it begins to swing wildly toward intrusiveness, it must be stopped and returned toward denial. The sensitive therapist recognizes that a client who has been firmly stuck in psychic numbing for years is likely to feel threatened by even the slightest swing of the pendulum toward intrusiveness. Sometimes, before any real progress can be made, the therapist must start by exploring the client's fears about the pendulum swinging.

The lesson from Vietnam veterans is that catharsis is only one aspect of healing. As therapists, we have the responsibility to understand when catharsis is therapeutic, and when it simply reinforces a client's conviction that burying feelings is the only way to avoid being overwhelmed. Healing from psychic numbing starts with strengthening a client's ability to modulate feelings enough to tolerate them. This applies to the three primary forms of psychic numbing among ACAs: loss of memory for childhood events, compartmentalization of feelings, and dissociation.

Loss of Memory for
Childhood Events

An astonishingly profound amnesia for childhood events exists in many ACAs. Clients have reported total absence of memories for extended periods of time, a decade or more. The only "memories" from such amnesiac periods are facts and stories which have been told to the client by someone else.

More commonly, amnesia is selective. ACAs may remember nothing of home life while demonstrating good recall of school events. There may be memories of daily family life but none of traumatic episodes. Or there may be loss of memory for one parent only. Such memory losses are so common that it is a rare ACA who does not have fewer childhood memories than can be accounted for simply by the passage of time.

A few difficult distinctions must be made here. When is a lack of memory for traumatic events the result of repression, the product of denial, or the effect of dissociation/depersonalization during the traumatic event? While there may be no easy way to answer this question with a particular client, it's important to recognize that all three possibilities exist, alone and in combination. The best way to treat loss of memory depends on your own best guess as to its cause. It's always prudent to be flexible and willing to abandon a chosen approach on the basis of a client's response.

Denial and repression are related, but they are not one and the same process. While the two defenses both work to defend one against unwanted memories and feelings, they occupy different positions in the psyche. Denial is more easily produced and disrupted by conscious forces; repression lies deeper in the unconscious. At its most conscious levels, denial is indistinguishable from what is called "suppression"—the deliberate inattention to needs, feelings, and thoughts. In a sense, denial is a tool used in the service of one's personality, while repression is an integral aspect of the personality itself.

Education and confrontation can chip away at the cognitive underpinnings of denial. Denial can often be dismantled through supportive counseling techniques and is more susceptible to influences by social systems. Dysfunctional families instill denial, and recovering communities can nurture an individual's discarding of it. Repression, in contrast, is more related to primitive mechanisms of fight and flight, being activated by the excitement of traumatic events or overwhelming impulses. The fundamental building blocks for repression invariably reach far back into early childhood development. Treatment of repression therefore necessarily activates childhood conflicts and taps into developmental issues.

Often the degree of repression present cannot be adequately assessed while denial is still intact. However, once denial is dismantled, clients with underlying repression remain unable to access past memories, or feelings. The most effective setting for clients to stop repressing their experience is when a positive transference is made to the therapist. Only when the therapist takes on the symbolic aura of a "good enough parent" is it safe enough for clients to remember and feel their traumatic experiences. When a client significantly decreases the amount of repression he uses, this invariably signals deep characterological change.

No amount of willingness to experience what has been repressed is effective until the identity of the experiencer begins to shift. Such shifts do not generally occur in response to education, supportive counseling, and participation in a recovering community alone. They require retracing the issues of early childhood development to rework the unconscious "decisions" that created an individual's identity. Submitting to such a process with a therapist is called "working in the transference."

Separate from the mechanisms of repression and denial is the deep dissociation which existed in many ACAs during the time they "experienced" childhood. The quotation marks around "experienced" indicate the special meaning of this word for a person who is profoundly disconnected from her self. Many ACAs stand little chance of retrieving memories which were never vividly recorded. During moments of dissociation, people enter a trance state. Their attention is simultaneously focused and restricted, leaving them no longer fully present to immediate events. In this way, people can survive traumas, simply by paying little attention to them at the moment of occurrence. This is not dissimilar from alcoholic blackouts, although the mechanism for dissociation is psychological, while the mechanism for the blackouts is almost certainly physiological. The point of commonality is that "memories not made cannot be retrieved." It is a lamentable fact that some ACAs will never resolve their loss of memory. This is most likely to be true for clients who continue to demonstrate significant dissociation.

Treatment for Loss of Memory

Treatment for loss of memory among ACAs often begins with referral to community educational programs and Twelve Step meetings. At Genesis Psychotherapy and Training Center, we offer a series of community lectures and workshops, and clients can be referred to family education programs at chemical dependence treatment centers or local chapters of the National Council on Alcoholism and Drug Addiction (NCADA).

Community lectures and Twelve Step meetings are valuable in many ways. Information in and of itself may begin to pierce a client's denial. The experience of sitting in a room with several other ACAs changes many clients' long-held sense of isolation.

Twelve Step meetings allow the stream of personal stories to begin resonating with forgotten feelings. Once the feelings begin to be honored, they start forming affective bridges to forgotten memories and past events.

Continued exposure to Twelve Step meetings is a particularly potent way to invite clients out of denial and promote the reemergence of lost memories. To have their most potent effect, Twelve Step meetings should be attended regularly, and a home meeting should be strongly recommended. Consistency and familiarity generate considerable momentum toward healing.

At Genesis, we have also developed a time-limited, structured group experience and an intensive weekend for ACAs, both of which are useful for retrieving childhood memories. Our 18 Week Program leads ACAs through a logical progression of topics— from feelings about betraying the family secret, to the disease concept of chemical dependence, its effects on the family, and co-dependence—and ends with information about the principles of recovery. Participants do workbook exercises between weekly sessions to prepare for upcoming topics and further integrate information from preceding weeks. Emphasis is placed on the personalization of information; didactic presentations are care-fully woven into group discussion. The goals of the program include providing ACAs with an experience of being less iso-lated, and moving beyond abstract information (e.g., "Alcoholic families keep secrets") to concrete realities (e.g., "The secrets *my* family kept were . . ."). Chapter 6 of this volume describes our 18 Week Program in more detail.

Our Intensive Weekend for ACAs is more experiential and less oriented toward information. It is designed to set a tone of acceptance—for past realities, for one another, for oneself—and to allow participants to experience this acceptance while the feel-ing is progressively deepened. By the end of the weekend, most participants have some sense of release and a vision of what recovery promises. This is all too intense to be fully integrated by the vast majority, however. For the time-limited boost the week-end gives to have a chance of being effectively internalized, I strongly prefer participants to be actively involved in Twelve

Step recovery, if not in therapy itself. Even for those who aren't, the weekend workshop has considerable power to boil up long-forgotten memories. This program is also described in more detail in Chapter 6.

In addition to helping clients increase their access to the past by referring them to educational and experiential presentations, I use four particularly powerful therapeutic techniques to stimulate feelings and memories: affectively bridged associations, multiple sensory modality imaging, family albums, and visits home.

• *Affectively Bridged Associations.* This technique involves focusing on a specific, current feeling which a client tends to resist. It may be a feeling that occurs outside therapy and is reported by the client, or it may be one that occurs in the immediacy of the therapeutic moment. Working with the latter requires a higher tolerance for anxiety and a more firmly established therapeutic alliance, particularly if the feeling is directed toward the therapist.

I ask the client to form a clear image of the feeling, as if he were concentrating on a visual image. I help add greater detail to the feeling image by asking several questions such as: "Is the image more in one part of your body?" "Is it constant, or does it change?" "What would it feel like if it doubled in intensity?" Sometimes it's useful for the client to close his eyes during the imaging process.

When the feeling is recalled in some detail, I encourage the client to allow its intensity to increase. Before the feeling becomes overwhelming, I suddenly ask the client, "Tell me what age you feel at the moment." Most clients immediately report an age. When a client balks, or is unable to take this next step, I pull back and don't force the issue.

When a client does report a specific age, I settle back in my chair and ask him to tell me about life at that age: "Where did you live?" "What was your house like?" "What was happening in your family?" I make my inquiry as broad as possible. The client and I are on a fishing expedition together. I operate under the assumption that the imaged feeling has resonated with an age when this same feeling was prominent. Often the client is thrust back toward the moments when this feeling originally became overwhelming.

If I listen carefully to the information a client gives me about life at this specific age, I usually find new clues about the trauma that still affects him. This technique is more useful with losses of memory due to denial than those due to repression. In cases of amnesia due to deep dissociation, clients may be able to connect an age with the imaged feeling, but remain lost in a haze when trying to report details from their life at that age. There is still value in knowing the age associated with a feeling, since this may provide some indirect information about developmental issues relevant to treatment.

• *Multiple Sensory Modality Imaging.* This technique can either be performed in a formal imaging process (with clients who are open to it) or integrated into conversations.

Memories are often held in a client's mind as disembodied ideas. Multiple sensory modality imaging re-embodies these memories. For example, when a client reports that his parents argued after he went to bed, I may pursue the following line of inquiry: "Can you remember any specific time they argued?" "How loud were their voices?" (These questions evoke auditory images.) "What position were you lying in, in bed?" "Was it warm? cold? breezy? humid?" (Kinesthetic images.) "What could you see in the dark?" (Visual images.) "Were there any smells?" (Olfactory images.) Activating all sensory modalities accesses multiple channels for associations.

This technique is especially useful in the second form of psychic numbing—the compartmentalization of feelings. Occasionally, such imaging may tap into truly repressed feelings, especially if olfactory and kinesthetic associations occur.

• *Family Albums.* Family photo albums are treasure chests for retrieving memories, especially if the therapist remains aware that each photo combines both content and process. Not only is there is an actual image from the past (most importantly, the facial expression of each person pictured); there is also the transaction which took place with each photograph. I may ask questions such as: "Who was holding the camera?" "Did the subjects want to have their picture taken?" "How big a production was it?" On the content level, it is useful to ask in detail the identity of everyone pictured. From this point forward, the therapy will be dealing with specific people, with concrete faces and bodies. The past will be made real.

Continually ask clients for their emotional reactions to different pictures. Encourage them to look at pictures of their own face and to report what they see. What do they spontaneously focus on? Note any pictures that you personally have an emotional reaction to, and ask more detailed questions about them: "Who is this person?" "How did you relate with him or her?" "Were you close?"

It's remarkable to witness how often the family photo album provides a visual record of the age when the client was overtaken by psychic numbing. In pictures from before that age, the child's eyes sparkle; the entire face smiles; a naive confidence seems to be present. After psychic numbing has set in, the eyes seem flatter; the mouth smiles stiffly, while the eyes do not seem to participate in the facial expression; the body is more rigid. The child is producing an appearance. What you see is no longer simply emanating from the child's immediate experience. Spontaneity has been aborted.

It's especially poignant when clients are also able to observe these changes in pictures of themselves. When appropriate, I may suggest that a client choose a favorite picture of herself as a child and display it in her home or office. The goal is to permeate her day with a concrete visual image of her past, gradually making this past increasingly real.

Finally, it is often useful to invoke an awareness that each photograph is an artifact. The very paper on which the photo is printed has existed, and been safeguarded by the family, from the moment the film was developed. It is likely that the client first held this relic from her past within weeks of when the picture was actually taken. In fondling the photo, the client is touching a concrete piece of her history.

• *Visits Home*. At times, the use of family photo albums melds into the next technique—visits home—because many clients must ask their families to dig out and send pictures. This requires a transaction with their family of origin.

Visits home take many forms. They may be imagined. They may occur by written correspondence, or over the phone. Or they may be physical visits, perhaps for a holiday. I have seen clients make visits to grave sites, to houses where their family used to live, and to home towns they have not seen for decades. Because the circumstances vary so greatly, no generalizations about home visits can be made, except for how powerful they are likely to be for most ACAs. And this depends on a variety of factors, including how far into recovery the client is; what his expectations are; whether the family is still together, still drinking, in denial, or in recovery; and so on.

I find it best to leave the idea (and timing) of visits home up to clients themselves. My job as therapist is to explore the feelings and meanings connected to these visits, or conversely, to explore fears about them. An ACA's family is the most powerful trigger in the universe for negative feelings and dysfunctional behavior. And, whether clients are in active contact with their families or not, they *are* still in a relationship with them. Acknowledging the reality of this relationship is part of the therapist's job. Whether visits home occur, or the lack of visits is explored, the inescapable relationship to family is an excellent repository of many lost memories.

• *Children as a Source of Lost Memories*. One more source of lost memories presents itself when clients have young children. This is hardly a therapeutic "technique" in the same sense as the four outlined above. It is, however, a poignant opportunity to penetrate into repressed memories.

The birth of a client's child (particularly the first) presents a rare opportunity to facilitate characterological change *outside* the transference. Successful transition into the parental identity is a developmental task equivalent to those faced in early childhood. The deep empathetic bonding stimulated by one's own child is a powerful force. Just as the onset of puberty forcefully ends one's childhood and begins adolescence, the experience of becoming a parent propels one into a period of rapid flux. Past memories may be mysteriously evoked through the empathic connection to a child. What was repressed has a unique opportunity to be retrieved.

The question facing most new parents is whether their own personalities can meet the challenge of their child's birth. Can their narcissism mature enough that they allow the child to be the center of attention? Can their echoism mature enough that they feel healthy empathy for the child's experience, rather than using the child's existence as the primary source of their own self-esteem? Evolution has made sure that parent-child bonding is a powerful internal maturational stimulus. Therapists have the opportunity to guide this maturation process as clients make the transition to a parental identity. When this transition is successful, characterological growth occurs outside the transference. However, when clients are blocked in the process of developing a parental identity, therapy can help by discovering and exploring issues that do exist within the transference.

Compartmentalization of Feelings

A second form of psychic numbing frequently seen in ACAs is compartmentalization of feelings. This process is usually present when clients are relating detailed information from their past without feelings, or when they are minimizing the effect these events had on their life. Even the most blatantly abusive episodes may be narrated with no more emotion that demographic data.

There is no loss of memory for the *external* details of traumatic events, but there is no memory of the *internal* feeling experience of these events. These feelings have been disconnected and walled off. In most cases, they can be accessed indirectly in the compassion clients feel for other people (especially children) who are having or have had identical experiences. It is through this dynamic that co-dependents come close to their feelings without actually owning that the feelings they are having are for themselves.

For example, Karen reported having had her first experience with marijuana, alcohol, cocaine, and quaaludes at her own mother's hand while still in grade school. When I asked how she felt about this, she could only focus on her mother's motives: "She always wanted to be more of a friend than a parent." When I asked how this had affected her, she was unable to have any feelings about it. She shrugged the memory off and said she had accepted her mother's behavior as normal at the time, and now saw it as ancient history. But when I asked how she would feel if she saw her ten-year-old neighbor being given the same drugs by her mother, Karen was immediately incensed and thought of ways to help the little girl. She was even able to discuss how the events would be likely to impact the child.

Parenthetically, compartmentalization of feelings—the inability to empathize with one's own experience—contributes greatly to development of a co-dependent personality structure, and plays a major role in the gravitation of ACAs into the helping professions. The defense of abused children, the nursing of ill people, the protection of underprivileged peoples' rights, and so on are not merely sublimations of psychic energy, efforts at mastery, or products of repetition compulsion. They are the echoist's displaced attempts to respond to and validate his own deep experience. But because his feelings have been compartmentalized and cut off from the facts of his life, and because he is left to empathize with others of similar fate in an effort to fill his own sense of emptiness, he experiences life as one who is racing along the freeway, unable to get to his home on a parallel frontage road.

Because compartmentalization of feelings is one step toward a more pervasive dissociation, its treatment is described in the section, "Treating Dissociation."

Dissociation

An effective way to avoid being overwhelmed during traumatic events is to dissociate from one's feelings—to disconnect from one's experience. When clients pervasively and automatically practiced dissociation throughout their childhood, few vivid images were registered in the moment, leaving little material to enter into long-term memory. In essence, we can't remember what we never paid attention to.

Treatment for Dissociation

Therapeutic progress is almost impossible as long as a client keeps practicing dissociation. When I notice that clients are refusing to focus attention on the immediate events and feelings of the therapy itself, I invite them to practice what I call the discipline, or Zen, of therapy. This is a process having four steps: 1) choosing the target, 2) focusing attention on the target, 3) self-reporting, and 4) identifying triggers of dissociation. The therapeutic goal is to increase the client's tolerance for immediate experience.

1. Choosing the Target

Therapeutic intervention is preceded by a period of observation, when I carefully note the behaviors which most clearly indicate when the client has dissociated. By intermittently presenting emotionally charged material (either through returning to past memories which the client still fears or focusing briefly on events within our relationship), I observe when the client shuts down and distances herself.

With some clients, there is a smile which does not stem from pleasure, but is a mask. Others divert their eyes. Some pause, go blank, and then return to interacting with me in a slightly different state of mind. Some begin to talk compulsively, or angrily, or intellectually, or defensively. Others simply stop talking and become more rigid.

During this period of observation, I carefully choose a reliable outward sign (such as one of the behaviors listed above) that dissociation is occurring. My choice is guided by these criteria:

The sign must be easy for me to notice, potentially noticeable for the client, and not easily controlled voluntarily. This outward sign becomes the target and will soon take on symbolic importance. It will come to represent all those ways that the client removes herself from actively being alive. It will be transformed into the eye of the needle.

At the same time I am choosing a target, I am also attempting to explore the client's subjective experience of being psychically numb. I ask the client what it's like to be isolated, adrift, and internally empty. As one client so eloquently responded, "I think that I am somehow missing the essence of what it means to be human." I don't analyze or interpret these feelings. My purpose is to develop a vocabulary which the client and I mutually understand—a vocabulary for exploring the many facets of internal, subjective experience.

When clients cannot go beyond saying that they "feel numb inside," or that they "feel nothing," even these responses can be explored further. I may point out that a shot at the dentist's office leaves my mouth numb, but that this feeling can be described in detail. There is the absence of pain, tingling around the edges of the sensation, and a self-conscious feeling that I might be drooling. Numbness is an experience that can be described in some depth. When clients say that they "feel nothing," they can be asked whether this is pleasant or unpleasant, and whatever answer they give can be explored and expanded on.

Armed with the beginnings of a shared vocabulary to describe the experience of psychic numbing, and with a sign of dissociation to use as a target, I move on to the next step.

2. Focusing Attention on the Target

Now, whenever the client dissociates, I begin drawing attention to the target. I point out the smile, or the breaking of eye contact, that occurs when painful feelings are being discussed. Usually the client either dismisses the behavior as meaningless, or becomes embarrassed.

It's important to strike a balance here between being too intrusive and being persistent enough that the client begins to become self-conscious. If I proceed too intrusively, the dissociation deepens, and it becomes increasingly difficult to make contact with the client. The goal is to focus the client's attention on his dissociation until it becomes possible to ask him what it feels like to be in this disconnected state.

For example, I may point out that the client is smiling in response to my having asked how he feels about a parent's drinking. The client may feel "caught" and try to suppress the smile. Frequently, conscious efforts to suppress a target behavior only heighten awareness of its presence. From the therapist's perspective, this process may begin to feel quite insensitive. The social rules of human interaction demand that we not simply leave another person sitting in his self-consciousness. There may be an urge to quiet the client's nervousness or cooperate with passing it off as a meaningless habit.

After the client develops some self-consciousness around the target behavior, I start addressing the dissociation experience itself. I may ask the client, "Where did you go when you smiled?" This question is not always immediately understood. I explain, "I felt more connected with you before you smiled than I did after you started smiling." I ask, "Did you notice any difference in how it felt to be in contact with me before and after?" What I want to establish, using the client's own vocabulary, is that he becomes less "present" during the target behavior. The purpose of this step is for the client to become aware of the dissociation *when it is happening.*

When the client's attention begins to move away from self-consciousness about the target behavior to awareness of the shift in his presence, I begin the transition to the next step.

One note of caution is appropriate here: Therapists should be continuously aware of the opportunity for playing out their own sadistic impulses whenever they are actively provoking uncomfortable self-consciousness in clients. It is prudent to assume that each of us harbors such sadism, probably in greater amounts than most of us realize. We must take great care to focus on the target only when we actively feel empathy for the client's discomfort.

3. Self-Reporting

I start suggesting that the client report to me when the dissociation has begun—that I no longer want the full responsibility for identifying it. I urge the client to take the initiative to tell me that she just "went away," "broke contact," or otherwise exited the immediate experience.

The first time a client successfully self-reports dissociation, a milestone has been reached. She has become aware enough of her subjective states to recognize how present she is in her relationship with me, and when her presence is interrupted.

At this stage, I can begin telling the client how to reestablish contact with me once she notices that she has dissociated. Contrary to the common-sense approach of attempting to reestablish contact with one's immediate experience by trying harder to focus attention in a specific direction (i.e., increasing the use of willpower), the most effective avenue is, paradoxically, to acknowledge to other people that you have temporarily left them. For example, a client might say, "I checked out for the past couple of minutes." Making this subjective experience public is what most effectively reestablishes direct contact. The goal is not to prevent dissociation (which has become a reflex emotional response to threat), but to recognize and return from dissociation with increasing ease.

4. Identifying Triggers of Dissociation

Once a client begins spontaneously identifying for me that he has dissociated (thereby reestablishing contact with me and lessening the dissociation), I start asking him to report the last thing that passed through his mind *before* the dissociation began—for example, "What was the last thing you can remember thinking or feeling before you smiled?" The goal now is to use the dissociation as a meaningful piece of information. The target behavior becomes direct evidence that an emotional charge is present.

At first, I might take the initiative to remind the client of the topic we were discussing at the time he dissociated. Often clients are unable to reorient themselves to what immediately preceded the dissociation, as if the dissociation involves a retrograde amnesia. With practice, clients get better at recalling what triggered the dissociation.

There are times when recalling the trigger is rapidly followed by a return of the dissociation, and these are especially poignant moments to observe. For example, Karen once self-reported that she had "gone behind her wall," and the last thing she remembered before dissociating was my mentioning her mother. Before she could explore the feelings that evoked, Karen shook her head and looked at me in amazement, asking, "What were we talking about?" For the client who has firmly entered into the discipline of therapy, this is further confirmation that the trigger is emotionally charged.

It's exhilarating to watch dedicated clients pursue the specific triggers for their dissociation. By taking it on faith that their dissociation would not be triggered by random events, clients become more willing to discover the feelings they have been avoiding. Like Zen students practicing a discipline designed to focus awareness in the present moment, clients begin to note their dissociation, report the thoughts which triggered it, and explore the subjective experience they had fled from. When this entire discipline has been integrated to where it is motivated from within the client, the process of psychic numbing has been reversed. The gap between a client and his emotions is narrowing. The schism between his self and his experience is starting to heal.

By this point, the client can tolerate immediate experience enough to begin working within the transference, exploring distortions in the client-therapist relationship produced by his early childhood experience. Psychotherapy *per se* has become possible.

This is not to say that transference has not developed and been present before now, in the processes outlined above for treating psychic numbing. The client may well have begun to see the therapist as an expert teacher, a savior guiding the way back to aliveness. As a result, some clients may have already become overly dependent, while others may have begun defending against being overwhelmed by the therapist. It's important for therapists to recognize these transferences and navigate through them. But it won't be until clients are able to tolerate being aware of these transference feelings at the moment they occur that the underlying foundation of a client's personality can be treated.

REEXPERIENCING THE TRAUMA

While the pendulum gets stuck in the denial phase for many ACAs, it gets stuck in the intrusiveness phase for others. For these clients, no part of the traumatic memory, no matter how small, can be bitten off without the entire experience flooding back.

Ellen, whose mother used to strap her into her crib to "keep her safe" when the parents went out drinking, showed an understandable sensitivity to abandonment issues. Whenever a member of our therapy group announced that he or she was leaving, Ellen's feelings quickly escalated into an overwhelming sense of being left alone. She would double over in her chair, rocking and moaning. Engulfed by her feelings, she was transported back in time to the state of mind she used to be in when tied down and left in her crib. She was reexperiencing the trauma.

ACAs with this characteristic are at the mercy of emotional storms which arbitrarily explode and take over their lives. Every feeling is intense and experienced with a mounting pressure to express it as soon as possible. They cannot recall memories, or have feelings, without literally being tossed back into reliving the original, unprocessed experience. This is not to say that reality testing is so compromised that they believe the original traumatic event is recurring (although this is the case during flashbacks). Rather, the parallel (symbolic or actual) between current reality and past trauma is close enough that feelings from the original trauma occur in their original intensity. Since this intensity is again overwhelming, the experience is no better handled than it was in the past. No amount of repeating the experience is valuable as long as it remains overwhelming.

The most common clinical picture involves combinations of psychic numbing and reexperiencing the trauma. Many ACAs remain numb to feelings until this stance can no longer be maintained. The pendulum then swings wildly to the opposite position. Feelings intrude and overwhelm until the numbness can be reestablished. The pendulum has only two, either-or positions.

Picture a dog who is pressed forcefully on the back of the neck to keep it quiet. The dog lies still, but will run about wildly as soon as it is released. The frenetic yelping which follows its release makes it necessary to be forcibly restrained again, which just builds up more pressure on the dog's part to run about the next time it is released. A wildly oscillating cycle has developed. This is the situation some ACAs find themselves in.

Therapy with ACAs who reexperience the trauma often feels like chasing dry leaves across a windblown autumn landscape. No single leaf seems more important than the others. Just when you get your hands firmly on one, the client switches to chasing another.

Each session may be an intense recounting of the emotional storms which have raged during the previous week. Who did what to whom, how the client felt, what he said—all is reported with a sense of pressure. No exploration takes place. Instead, the client seems to demand that you provide answers and techniques for "doing feelings right." What's odd about this somewhat hysterical display is that, while the client's image of himself is that of a person who is exquisitely sensitive to feelings, the reality is that he is being driven to do something—anything—to discharge his feelings as quickly as possible. Rather than expressing feelings for the purpose of communicating them, he is vomiting them out just to be rid of them.

Often I will stop a client like this from reporting a feeling to me, and ask him to sit with the feeling for sixty seconds. We then discuss what it's like to have to tolerate the feeling as opposed to discharging it immediately. As the experience of actually *having* the feeling is explored, it becomes clear that the stakes are extremely high. For ACAs who are reexperiencing a trauma, it's as if their very existence is threatened. Their sense of identity is jeopardized. The drive to discharge the feeling (mistakenly seen to be the goal of "expressing" it) is really the drive to expel it from their experience in order to safeguard their existence.

Treatment for Reexperiencing
the Trauma

The goal of treating dissociation is not to prevent it entirely, but to develop a readily available avenue back from being dissociated. Similarly, the goal of treating reexperiencing the trauma is not to eradicate its presence, but to develop an effective mechanism for reversing its effects. When clients are reexperiencing the trauma, they lose contact with their current experience. They need to be brought back into contact with their immediate surroundings.

In treating such clients, it can be useful to work with more than one sensory modality. This is the approach I took with Ellen, whose abandonment issues were severely triggered whenever a member of our group announced his or her termination. After several such episodes, I could recognize the early stages of the downward spiral Ellen plunged into whenever she became overwhelmed by old feelings. Letting her curl up and rock in her chair seemed to produce nothing of value. In fact, she was terrified even more by continuing to be overwhelmed even in the midst of her therapy group.

We gradually worked to contain her feelings through a series of direct instructions: "Keep your feet on the floor"; "Look into other group members' eyes"; even "Reach out on both sides and touch people's hands." As she gradually tested her ability to tolerate her feelings while following these instructions, Ellen found herself feeling less overwhelmed. She spontaneously added an auditory means of maintaining contact with the group by asking people to speak her name when she began to enter into this downward spiral. All of these stimuli kept her anchored in the present moment.

When therapists fail to recognize ACAs who are reexperiencing the trauma during workshops and experiential exercises, actual retraumatization may occur, albeit inadvertently. What happens is that therapists focus attention on these clients and allow them to flounder in their feelings. Admittedly, such clients make dramatic subjects for psychodrama and gestalt exercises. Other participants in the workshop or exercise who are mired in psychic numbing may actually benefit from the intense feelings that are generated. And the clients themselves may feel a great sense of relief once they are through being emotionally overwhelmed. But is this valuable work for them? The test lies in whether the experience of being overwhelmed by feelings eventually begins to abate. Workshop leaders lack the opportunity to follow such clients over enough time to assess whether their dramatic experiences have led to any change. The bottom line is, emotional catharsis is simply not effective treatment for all clients.

Therapists do no service to clients who are reexperiencing the trauma by allowing them to flounder in their overwhelming feelings. Clients who are reexperiencing the trauma temporarily need some external containment. When treatment plans are being formulated, this intermittent need for containment must be taken into consideration. These clients are not best served by purely transferential or long-term interactional group therapy—not yet. Before either of these modalities can become the treatment of choice, clients must demonstrate an internal ability to contain feelings without denying their existence. The pendulum swinging between denial and intrusiveness must move freely on its own, and no longer depend on external interventions by the therapist.

Clinical Vignette:
The Stoic Gunner

It is nearly axiomatic that honoring a client's defense is the most effective way to open the door to treating it. This is particularly useful when addressing symptoms of post-traumatic stress disorder (PTSD). The following case history demonstrates the back-and-forth, in-and-out flow necessary to manage the anxiety of a

Vietnam veteran with both psychic numbing and reexperiencing the trauma. The process is one of alternately challenging and honoring the client's defenses, continually working to create more freedom in the pendulum's swing between denial and intrusiveness.

The first time I saw Frank, he faced me with a stoic demeanor. He had been interviewed by many therapists since Vietnam, and he knew how to stay in control of himself. My goal was to help him recognize the intensity of feeling that lay beneath his awareness, and to give him an experience of being able to bite off a small portion of this emotion without being overwhelmed by it all.

I began by getting factual information regarding his tour of duty. Frank had been a gunner on a patrol boat, assigned to preventing the enemy from moving arms and ammunition along the coast in village fishing boats. So we could start dealing with concrete incidents rather than generalities, I asked him to tell me about the first combat he encountered.

As soon as he told me that the incident had involved a junk, I stopped him.

"What time of day was it?" I asked.

"Morning. Nine o'clock," he answered.

"Was it cloudy or sunny?"

"Bright sun, deep blue sky."

"Did you feel a breeze?"

"Yes, a cool breeze."

"On your face?"

"Yes."

"Your arms?"

"Yes, my sleeves were rolled up."

"Like they are now?"

He looked at his arms. "Yes."

"How loud was the engine of your ship?"

"Deafening."

"Could you hear sounds of water?"

"No."

"Were there any smells?"

"Vegetation from the shore."

"What colors were the brightest?"

"Blue—water and sky. And green—trees."

"When the junk appeared, how far away was it?"

"A quarter mile."

"What did you first see about it?"

"I saw it first as it rounded a bend."

In this way, the scene was set in elaborate detail, using all the sensory modalities. Frank seemed to sink into a state of reverie during some of his descriptions. His ability to provide crystal-clear verbal pictures hinted that he had probably been more of a witness to the trauma than its victim.

I turned the narrative back over to Frank. He reported that they attacked and sunk the junk. There was no emotion connected to his words. Again, I took control and worked through the episode in exquisite detail.

"Where were you standing?" I asked.

"At the bow gun," he answered.

"What did the gun feel like against your skin?"

"Cool, metal."

"Was it a smooth surface, or gnarled?"

"The stock was gnarled."

"What were you feeling as you watched the junk come closer?"

"They didn't see us at first and kept coming."

"Was it scary? Exciting?"

"A little bit of both."

"What could you see as they got closer?"

"When they spotted us, they were close enough I could see the fear in their eyes."

"How did you react to that?"

"I just thought, `You're dead, mother-----.' And he knew it."

"Who had the authority to give the order to open fire?"

"The captain."

"Where did you fire?"

"First I split the junk in two. Then I hit whoever was swimming in the water."

"How did you know you hit them?"

"They stopped swimming. Some went under."

At this point, the tension in the room was palpable. Frank was struggling against feelings that were boiling toward the surface. I decided to probe one more time, more deeply than before.

"Were you close enough to see blood?"

A sudden sob. "It was bright red, spreading out across the surface."

Frank began to get agitated. He could barely stay seated. It was time to shift the pendulum back in the direction we had come.

I asked, "What company manufactured the gun you were using?" Before Frank could answer, being slightly disoriented by my return to factual, unemotional questions, I asked another one: "How many rounds a minute was it built to fire?"

Frank began answering my questions. His agitation ceased. I had helped him to reestablish his defense. His traumatic experience was contained again.

Throughout the remainder of the session, I continued to weave back and forth between helping Frank mobilize his feelings and giving him a way to contain them. As a result, he went further into his feelings than he had ever gone, without getting overwhelmed. The session was not altogether satisfying to him. After all, most clients, like most therapists, assume that the boil has to be lanced and the emotional pus drained. At the same time, Frank was intrigued by the interview, and willing to continue another day.

Comments

The therapeutic style of the preceding clinical vignette has much in common with counseling alcoholics in early recovery. In both cases, the therapist takes considerable responsibility for modulating the client's anxiety level. This is a much more active role than psychotherapists are used to taking.

If we're going to help our ACA clients who exhibit the PTSD symptoms of psychic numbing and reexperiencing the trauma, we must integrate the treatment of stress-related issues into the psychotherapy framework. It might help to consider that all this really does is to start the client-therapist relationship at an earlier developmental point than we're accustomed to.

The psychoanalytic tradition sees the symbolic "meat" of the client-therapist relationship as lying in the recapitulation of the Oedipal period. Object relations-oriented therapists see it as lying in the recapitulation of the earlier period of bonding, separation, and rapprochement. Treating trauma symptoms simply takes us further back along the chronology of child-parent interactions, to those involving stabilization of the newborn's physiological functions. This is a time when parents must modulate the physical stimulation an infant is subjected to until basic functions (such as eating, digestion, and defecation) become self-regulating and develop their own schedule.

If the relationship between therapist and client begins at this very basic level, and the client is able to assume responsibility for her own regulation gradually, by developing the freedom to swing between states of denial and openness, then the transference which grows out of this phase of the therapeutic relationship is simply that much richer. And the characterological changes available to the client through working in the transference will run that much deeper.

THE ROLE OF VALIDATION

A few comments about the role of validation in treating ACAs are in order here. Much has been written about the need to validate the ACA's perception of early childhood experiences, especially those which were abusive or traumatic. In many cases, the therapist will be the first person in a client's life who reacts to the inappropriateness of his parents' behavior. A therapist who fails to react may perpetuate the trauma by modeling that silence is, indeed, the appropriate response. However, such active validation runs risks which must be acknowledged and understood if they are to be minimized.

The question of how actively therapists should validate clients' perceptions is an integral part of the ongoing debate between trauma and drive theories. (For a discussion of this debate, see *Volume One: Evaluation*, Appendix I.) For example, Alice Miller points out that Freud's discovery of screen memories distracted attention from the fact that many of the cases of hysteria he was treating were, in fact, the result of sexual abuse. In addition, screen memories are often quite accurate in an emotional sense. As Miller notes, "There are other ways of seducing the child, apart from the sexual."[2]

Her awareness of the reality of child abuse, refined until she became sensitive to the pervasiveness of fine and subtle humiliations visited upon children by narcissistically wounded parents, has led Miller to view therapy at times as a form of advocacy. She believes that "a child can only experience his feelings when there is somebody there who accepts him fully, understands and supports him. If that is missing . . . he cannot experience those feelings secretly 'just for himself' but fails to experience them at all."[3] And, in those cases where clients report abusive experiences without experiencing an emotional reaction, Miller urges therapists to react openly, and at times forcefully. To be effective, this reaction must not be judgmental, which requires that therapists explore and integrate their own experience sufficiently to avoid countertransferential reactions.

Herein lies the need for an almost superhumanly delicate balance. On the one hand, in order for clients to regain access to their experience, they sometimes need to be led back into it by the therapist's own recognition and acknowledgment of trauma in the clients' history. On the other hand, how can therapists take such an active role without inevitably, and unconsciously, leading clients toward reactions which are of greater emotional importance to the therapist than to the treatment of that particular client? When therapists do this, inadvertently or not, it may further traumatize clients, because it is a narcissistically motivated action that preys upon the clients' emotions. Clearly, when therapists are themselves ACAs or have a history of their own alcohol or other drug addiction, the possibility of such *counter-transference* increases. In other words, distortions in the relationship between therapist and client are introduced by the *therapist*, as a result of early childhood experiences that unconsciously guide the therapist's perceptions. The more actively a therapist "advocates" for a client's unconscious feelings, the greater the risk that countertransference is at work.

The reason therapists must make the effort to sail between Scylla and Charybdis, rather than take the safer course of remaining impassively neutral, lies in the fact, well-recognized in the child abuse field, that children *do* lose access to their feelings and experiences if they do not see them reflected by others. Unless the ability to recognize and trust one's feelings is developed as a child, its lack may continue into adulthood, and eventually into the therapeutic setting itself. In such cases, validation is the *beginning* of treatment; without it, treatment remains impotent.

Is there an unspoken negative judgment levied against clients who must have their experience validated by another before they can take it seriously themselves? If so, this is tantamount to the same "contempt for those who are smaller and weaker"[4] that constitutes so much of the narcissism of addicted parents. Such contempt is expressed in the exercise of power, blatantly or subtly, over the child by the adult.[5] Clearly, the therapeutic arena provides an opportunity which equals the parent-child relationship in its openness to the expression of such contempt. We are dealing with fire here.

It is equally problematic for therapists too eager to advocate for their clients' feelings to err on the side of expressing contempt for clients' parents. In the end, such contempt will automatically be resisted; the therapeutic relationship will be severely taxed by such contempt, and eventually rupture.

Whatever the risks of countertransference, clinical experience with PTSD teaches that clients suffering from psychic numbing will remain closed to their experience unless they trust that the reality of their trauma will be believed. For this reason, initial treatment of psychic numbing in Vietnam veterans is often most effective within homogeneous groups of other combat veterans.[6] Trust may be granted only to others who have had the same experience. This also helps to explain the value of Twelve Step meetings and therapy groups specifically for ACAs. In such environments, clients feel less shame, more fully and immediately understood, and freer to express feelings. Watching how others react to one's own trauma story normalizes these feelings and allows them to be experienced for the first time. When a client's trauma story is first related in individual therapy, it is important for therapists to register the importance of what they are hearing, even if the client continues to dismiss it.

I am freest to react to clients' trauma stories when I am clearly honoring their perceptions of what has happened to them, including their emotional reactions, and not confirming objective reality. The prudent course is to assume that these symptoms of trauma in ACAs are present for good and sufficient reason, rather than to contribute to the client's sense that there is something wrong with him for overreacting. When a client with evidence of PTSD gives a history of parental alcoholism, or other abuse, it is imperative that therapists make it clear that they are taking this information seriously. They do not have to know yet what the psychological meaning of the information is. But it is important to register its significance not only internally, but externally as well. We must communicate in some fashion to clients that we have heard what they just said, and that we give it weight.

For example, when an ACA reports matter-of-factly that her father used to throw plates against the wall during suppertime arguments, I will usually cock my head and open my eyes a bit wider, at a minimum. Throwing plates is not normal behavior, and many ACAs are used to taking their lead from others in deciding what is normal. My simple reaction gives evidence that I think what my client has just said is important. At times, I may stop clients and say that what they have just told me seems important, but they can come back to it later if they wish.

If the reaction to validation is eventually one of the client's taking his experience more seriously, then the validation has been valuable. If, however, validation throws a client into reexperiencing the trauma, it's clearly not the technique of choice at this point. Therefore, the use of validation should not hinge solely on whether therapists perceive themselves as working predominantly from the trauma or drive model. Clinical experience teaches that clients respond differently to validation, depending on their symptomatology.

Furthermore, the process of validation is not simply a technique used by therapists, but is a transaction between two people. Its presence or absence helps define the relationship. For this reason, it often triggers both negative and positive transferences by clients. For borderline clients, active validation may even feel intrusive, or contribute to their urge to merge with the therapist. Further discussion of working within the transference is found in the next chapter, when the use of the therapeutic relationship itself as an avenue for characterological change is explored.

INCREASED AROUSAL

Exposure to abnormal levels of stress can lead to a permanent state of increased arousal—to constantly being on edge, on the lookout for danger, and wary of the world. Symptoms of increased arousal include hypervigilance and armoring (a characteristic pattern of rigid defenses) on both psychological and physical levels. The nervous system is maintaining a chronic "fight-or-flight" response.

Hypervigilance is a manifestation of basic mistrust. Since humans learn from their experience, those who have random, arbitrary, neglectful, or abusive experiences during the earliest stage of child development learn not to trust. There is no basic sense of the universe's benevolence, or of goodwill within other humans which can be tapped into as needed. If the stance of being "on guard" is required during the first years of life, it may never fade during later years, even if it is no longer appropriate. No amount of contrasting experience mitigates these earliest lessons, unless a person undergoes the extraordinary process of reopening and reworking these earliest stages of development.

Treatment for Increased Arousal

The process of learning to trust in oneself, in human relationships, and in the compatibility of oneself and the universe is often painfully slow, with many layers of the onion needing to be peeled away. The first layers may come with a client's participation in a homogeneous group, listening to other ACAs tell about their experience. For the first time, there's a place where it's safe to reveal one's own history and feelings. Eventually clients come to recognize the discrepancy between how little they trust others, and how much others actually care about them. They begin to see the "insanity" of their fundamental defense against the world. Their continuous sense of incipient catastrophe is not borne out by current reality.

The problem is that many clients are not simply behaviorally hypervigilant in their search for the earliest signs of impending disaster. They have constructed their very *identity* around protecting themselves against the world. Their character is defined by the armor they wear. They cannot abandon this stance without undergoing the existential anxiety of suffering a partial loss of identity. For this reason, the final layers of the onion are best removed in an interactional group, individual therapy, or both.

Individual work provides the opportunity to concentrate session after session on a client's resistance to entering into deeper levels of intimacy with the therapist. Each transition to greater intimacy demands that the client take a risk. While the risk is often surrounded by the same feelings of dread experienced as a child, the outcome differs, so a new learning experience takes place. Positive experiences with therapists will never negate earlier painful experiences, but they may gradually come to balance them out.

One cannot erase the past, but one can acknowledge and mourn it, loosen its power over the present, and regain the capacity to enter into new, healthier relationships, starting with the therapeutic relationship. Voluntarily entering into such a relationship is a leap of faith in the truest sense, considering the experience with authority figures that many clients had as children. Opening up to the world again is what developing basic trust is all about. It requires not only a first leap of faith (the scariest one) but also a second, a third, and so on. In essence, it requires that "leaps of faith" become a way of life. For this to happen, clients must experience a sense of intimacy with the therapist over a considerable length of time, during which trust grows, is practiced, and becomes integrated into a new sense of identity.

Even after clients become psychologically willing to trust, and therefore less hypervigilant, this doesn't mean that their protective armoring on the physical level automatically fades. Chronic intense arousal eventually resets the autonomic nervous system and creates habitual knots of muscular tension. When physical symptoms of arousal (e.g., startle reactions, muscle tension, cardiovascular and digestive hyperactivity) persist, some form of body work may be indicated.

Body Work

So much misunderstanding surrounds body work that I hesitate to even mention it, much less recommend it. My hesitancy is reinforced by the fact that I am no expert on this modality, having had far more personal experience with it (i.e., Reichian therapy) than formal training. Nevertheless, the fact that body work appears to benefit some ACAs suffering from the PTSD symptom of increased arousal behooves me to introduce the topic as best I can.

The underlying assumption of body therapies in the Reichian tradition is that character structure is so pervasive it manifests itself both psychologically and physically, especially in the flexibility and balance which exist between the two portions of the autonomic nervous system—sympathetic and parasympathetic. The sympathetic portion is the foundation for arousal, preparing us for intense physical activity. It is adrenaline-based and springs into action whenever we perceive the need to defend ourselves, either aggressively or through flight. The parasympathetic portion is the foundation for a very different state, one which includes calmer activities such as the digestion and absorption of food.

In Reichian work, subtle indications of which portion of the autonomic nervous system is in the ascendancy, along with observations of tension in specific muscle groups which blocks flexibility and spontaneity, are used to guide the therapist's prescription of exercises designed to dissolve the armoring. These exercises consist of breathing techniques, exertion of specific voluntary muscle groups, and emotionally charged verbalizations.

Misconceptions surrounding Reichian work abound for a variety of reasons, some quite legitimate. Virtually anyone can employ the techniques of body work without regard to even the most basic principles of psychotherapy. The result, often enough, is the release of primitive emotions without their integration—catharsis without growth. Worse yet, the therapist may be insensitive to a traumatized client's perception of intrusiveness. In one case, this led to a therapist's decision to approach a client's newly discovered incest issues through body work performed in the nude on a bed. No wonder the client panicked and reexperienced the original trauma in a totally nontherapeutic way.

The first requirement I look for in a body therapist is that he or she first be a *psychotherapist*, with thorough training in transferential work. This is absolutely essential, since body work involves an intense relationship between therapist and client— a relationship in which the basic character structure is going to be approached. Transference will be evoked and defended against, and those defenses will be explored. The fact that they will be explored on a physical rather than verbal level means that the most elemental passions may be encountered and released, placing great responsibility on the psychotherapist to understand what is taking place.

SURVIVOR GUILT

Unable to cope with feelings of powerlessness, unwilling to recognize that the universe is ultimately out of their control, many ACAs adopt a defensive posture similar to that taken by victims of physical and sexual abuse. They see themselves as being somehow guilty for having survived, as though this dishonors the memory of those who succumbed, or perhaps even contributed to others being hurt.

ACAs often experience survivor guilt for trying to separate themselves from their families and act on their own behalf. They chastise themselves for having "put themselves first" and having "abandoned" their families, when in fact their families have abandoned *them* in their addiction to alcohol or other drugs. Often they blame themselves for their parents' behavior, which adds to their guilt at having survived it. This guilt becomes a straitjacket around their feelings, draining spontaneity from their lives.

Treatment for Survivor Guilt

The treatment of survivor guilt may need to progress through four layers: 1) education and validation to counter the distorted belief in one's responsibility for being abandoned, 2) resolution of traumatic grief, 3) mourning for what has truly been lost, and 4) characterological change through internalization of one's parents, leading to discrimination between loss and abandonment.

Education and Validation

A client's distorted belief that she is responsible for a parent's alcoholism or abusive behavior can be approached on two different levels. On the deeper, identity level, this belief is a symptom of boundary diffusion. When a client cannot separate her identity from that of an addicted parent, she is not seeing the parent as an independent being. She perceives her parent's behavior as a part of herself, and the alcoholism or abuse as something she deserves. Until boundaries can be more clearly maintained (which is a major goal of psychotherapy), mistaken beliefs about what the client is truly responsible for will continue to reappear in an infinite variety of new disguises.

With many clients, profitable work on the cognitive level can often precede, and pave the way for, work on the identity level.

Some of the beliefs stemming from survivor guilt can be put into conflict with the client's reason, and with the combined voices of others who are recovering from similar experiences. Loosening the grip which distorted beliefs about personal responsibility exert over a client's life may make deeper levels of work possible for the first time.

Basic education in the disease concept of alcoholism requires that ACAs take seriously the fact that they did not have direct control over their parents' illness. Although "the disease concept of alcoholism" has become socially sanctioned, this does not guarantee that everyone who accepts this viewpoint understands it or has integrated it on a feeling level. It's important for ACAs to be exposed to basic education until it is both understood and felt. This means that information about alcoholism usually has to be repeated several times throughout recovery. In this way, clients comprehend and accept the facts about alcoholism at progressively deeper levels, until they eventually integrate them into their intellectual frameworks, their belief systems, their emotional reactions, and their very sense of identity.

Twelve Step meetings and the Twelve Steps themselves are excellent tools for loosening a person's grip on the belief that guilt is the reasonable response to tragedy. Even if clients remain emotionally prone to feel guilty, it's useful for them to be immersed in a recovering community which understands the tendency to feel this way, but does not normalize or intensify it. Instead, the Program gently reminds its members that this belief is neither logical nor based in reality. By countering a client's sense of guilt, education and the recovering community facilitate the shift to the grief process, the next step in healing survivor guilt.

Resolution of Traumatic Grief

The process of working through survivor guilt requires effectively grieving for what has been lost. This mourning is continually aborted when clients are faced with *traumatic* grief. Effective grief work requires the ability and willingness to tolerate feelings of loss. Unless this can be done in the immediacy of the present moment, it is not truly being accomplished. When access to one's immediate experience is blocked by the symptoms of trauma, traumatic grief exists, and it is the trauma which must be addressed first. Only after clients are able to acknowledge their losses and tolerate the attendant feelings of sadness, abandonment, pain, and disappointment are they truly able to mourn.

In cases where loss occurred within a context of "intolerable danger, anxiety, and instinctual arousal,"[7] grief may be complicated by the superimposition of other symptoms of trauma. An example would be the sense of loss and abandonment that results when a parent physically abuses a child. The experience of loss is gravely affected by the simultaneous terror that comes from having one's very life threatened. As a result, recollection of loss later in life activates symptoms of trauma as well, and this enhances one's tendencies to enter into psychic numbing or to be overwhelmed by the original experience. The feelings of loss can never be worked through because they are reflexively denied or become too intense to be processed. Before grief work can proceed, the traumatic reactions of psychic numbing and reexperiencing the trauma must be resolved. As a result, survivor guilt is often the last symptom of PTSD which can be treated.

Mourning

So much is lost to the child with an alcoholic parent—safety, emotional contact, innocence, years which were supposed to be devoted to childhood, perhaps even the parent's physical presence (through divorce or death). Alice Miller reaches into the bottom of this experience when she writes that "probably the greatest of narcissistic wounds—not to have been loved just as one truly was—cannot heal without the work of mourning."[8]

Therapy facilitates mourning in two ways. First, there is the dismantling of denial. As this occurs, clients acknowledge the reality of their losses, often for the first time. Included in this reality are their own feelings. There is mourning for the loss itself, as well as for the history of having ignored and even abused one's own feelings about that loss.

Second, with every step taken toward healing, there is greater capacity to comprehend what was lost. This aspect of mourning is in no way unique to COAs. Maturation is the voluntary relinquishment of innocence, an acceptance of the absolute separation which exists at some level between ourselves and all others, and an acknowledgment of our eventual death (among other less important limitations). As therapy proceeds, clients move beyond reacting to the premature loss of illusory union with omnipotent parents, and face the inevitability of this loss. With each step toward healing, a sense of loss is felt.

Therapists facilitate mourning by promoting awareness of the loss, accepting clients' feelings, encouraging clients to experience these feelings, normalizing the process, and projecting confidence that mourning eventually resolves itself. At times, clients are sustained through their mourning only by their faith that the therapist is experienced enough not to allow the process to continue unless it has a realistic chance of achieving resolution. For this reason, it is important for therapists not to encourage clients who are reexperiencing the trauma to continue "trusting the process" *ad infinitum*. Whatever hope therapists tender must be based in reality.

Characterological Change

The final level of treating survivor guilt comes with completing basic developmental tasks needed to achieve a truly separate sense of identity. Only then can loss be differentiated from abandonment, and survival differentiated from callousness.

Not all loss is abandonment, although any loss may be experienced this way. Abandonment seems to have two components. First, there is the intention of the person who is doing the withdrawing. This is more likely to feel like abandonment when parents divorce and leave than when cancer intervenes and takes their life. Second, there is the ability of the one being withdrawn from to internalize the person who is being lost. Any loss is felt as abandonment if there is no ability to internalize the other.

In this context, internalization means the process of identifying aspects of one's own personality which resemble the parent, owning these aspects willingly, and thereby gaining a sense of "carrying a part of one's parent" within oneself, but without becoming fused with the parent and losing one's separate identity. Such healthy internalization is not possible for clients who have yet to traverse successfully the childhood developmental phases of separation, individuation, and rapprochement.

Many ACAs obsess about abandonment. Every current loss reawakens the original sense of being left. In many cases this is due to the stress-related symptom of reexperiencing the trauma. In others it signifies a serious characterological deficit as well. When a child develops the capacity to identify with another person, to recognize those aspects of himself which resonate with the other, to possess these aspects as his own and simultaneously as representations of the other (i.e., to integrate a sense of the other's continuous presence without losing a sense of his own identity), only then has he achieved a level of identity formation which is resistant to being abandoned. Even in instances where another person may callously withdraw, a client with this level of identity formation may experience primarily loss, drawing on memories of the person as he or she was before the abandonment occurred.

On the other hand, clients whose development was arrested before achieving this level of identity formation may be unable to experience anything but abandonment, even in the face of losses where there is no intention to withdraw (e.g., another's death). It is primarily through working within the transference that therapists are able to identify whether a client's continuing sense of abandonment is characterological, and not simply secondary to reexperiencing the trauma. The process of working within the transference is explored at length in the next chapter.

3

TREATING CO-DEPENDENCE
IN ACAs

In treating co-dependence, we must first distinguish between primary, child-onset and secondary, adult-onset forms (see Chapter 4 of Volume One, *Evaluation*). The former may require long-term psychotherapy; the latter can often be effectively treated by psycho-educational and supportive counseling techniques.

In primary co-dependence, disturbances during child development have pervasively affected the process of identity formation. Traits are deeply rooted, rigid, and sufficiently intense to produce personality disorder on their own, without additional outside stressors. The primary co-dependent seems "bound" to enter into a series of dysfunctional relationships and has little or no history of healthy relationships to guide his behavior.

In secondary co-dependence, the individual responds to dysfunction in others by intensifying her own co-dependent traits until they reach the level of disorder. At this point, secondary co-dependence has developed its own momentum and may look indistinguishable from primary forms. However, there is an important difference: Secondary co-dependents have a baseline character structure to return to which lies within the range of normal (i.e., can "return to sanity," in Twelve Step program language), while primary co-dependents must still complete basic developmental tasks before they can lead healthier lives.

Although this chapter contains information on treating secondary co-dependence, its emphasis is mostly on treating primary co-dependence. The rationale for this is that Al-Anon and CD counseling techniques already exist as effective approaches to secondary co-dependence. Understanding these approaches serves as a good foundation for treating primary co-dependence, because therapy often must focus on secondary co-dependence before clients are in a position to enter into the transferential work necessary for changes on the character level—the goal of treatment for primary co-dependence. In other words, treatment for secondary co-dependence is often the first step in treating ACAs, but it is usually only partially effective with primary co-dependents. What is most needed by therapists treating ACAs, whose co-dependence will by and large be child-onset, is a conceptual framework which incorporates principles of the psychotherapy model as well.

I begin by outlining and comparing the principles underlying treatment of secondary and primary co-dependence. This permits specific techniques for treating each to be seen in their proper context.

PRINCIPLES OF TREATING
SECONDARY CO-DEPENDENCE

Treatment for secondary co-dependence has two goals: 1) helping clients regain, and maintain, previous levels of health, and 2) guiding clients toward deeper characterological change, when appropriate. A delicate balance must be struck between these goals—a balance which neither judges clients who do not pursue psychotherapy further, nor creates the impression that counseling a client back from the precipice is the full benefit available from therapy.

I believe that active secondary co-dependence is similar to active alcoholism in one important respect: Behavioral change is often critical early in therapy, both for the sake of the person's immediate health and to increase the ultimate effectiveness of therapy. I promote behavioral change on two levels simultaneously by 1) intervening on the family system as a whole when possible, and 2) helping clients detach from the family system in healthy ways. Actually, these two levels *must* be approached simultaneously and cannot be separated from each other. Any positive shift on the family systems level will enhance the co-dependent's ability to detach from that system, and any detachment on the co-dependent's part must necessarily be reacted to by the rest of the system.

Intervening on the Family System as a Whole

In secondary co-dependence, the individual's co-dependent traits are intensified into a disorder by participation in dysfunctional relationships, usually within a troubled family system. While the co-dependent may be the first family member to seek help, I always explore the possibility of directly affecting the family system as a whole.

This, too, calls for a delicate balancing act. On the one hand, I want to make it clear to the co-dependent that I am present for him alone. On the other hand, I don't want to miss an opportunity to have a wider effect on the family, especially since this might also benefit the co-dependent. There are no ironclad rules for maintaining such a balance.

I assess as quickly as I can whether the co-dependent client has enough ego strength to tolerate my pulling other family members into the evaluation process. Taking a stance that the entire family (or couple) must be evaluated accomplishes several things. In some cases, it plants the seed that helps co-dependents stop taking full blame for their relationship problems. In others, the family's refusal to cooperate in the evaluation highlights the reality that the client is powerless to work on anything beyond her own personal healing.

Some clients must confront their fearful resistance to involving others, which I then explore further before proceeding. Some families participate in the evaluation in a way that makes their dysfunction more public and blatant, again highlighting the realities confronting clients. And some spouses and families take this opportunity to seek help for themselves. More than once, I have asked an ACA's spouse to participate in the initial evaluation and been surprised by the spouse's willingness to seek treatment for his or her own chemical dependence.

If intervening on the system as a whole is possible,[1] this puts the secondary co-dependent in a greatly improved position. While the client must still do personal work to detach from the system's dysfunction and alter behaviors which helped sustain it, toxic forces which intensified the co-dependent's traits into overt disorder have been removed. The family is much less likely to resist the co-dependent's efforts to change herself.

Of course, it isn't always possible to intervene on the system as a whole. The addicted family member may be too deeply in denial for intervention to be successful. There may not be enough support from other family members to make intervention appropriate. The secondary co-dependent may be too frightened to suggest that other family members need help. He may be convinced that he is the only "patient"; conversely, he may be too invested in denying his own dysfunction and pointing to other family members as the ones who need help to be a positive, loving force in any intervention. Or he may simply lack the ego strength needed to tolerate temporary expansion of the therapeutic alliance (i.e., having to share the therapist). In all of these cases, involving other family members in the evaluation process would be premature. Instead, therapy should emphasize detaching the client from the system as a whole.

Detaching the Client from the Family System

While the concept of detachment is anathema to co-dependents, healing depends on their establishing more effective boundaries between themselves and the dysfunctions of others. Education and participation in Twelve Step programs are two proven ways to help clients start doing this. Since both are available as inexpensive adjuncts to therapy, it is usually in clients' best interests to guide them in these directions as quickly as possible.

Education

Secondary co-dependence frequently responds to information on three topics: 1) the disease concept of chemical dependence, 2) the dynamics of dysfunctional families, and 3) the characteristics of co-dependence. A host of books are available on these subjects, and most CD treatment centers and local offices of the National Council on Alcoholism and Drug Addiction (NCADA) provide educational lectures to the public. Referring clients to these lectures has a benefit beyond education: Clients start building a support network rather than focusing all of their efforts on a single therapist.

Twelve Step Programs

Participation in Twelve Step programs offers many specific benefits to co-dependents, both secondary and primary. Practicing the Twelve Steps reinforces realistic boundaries and activates healing forces. Involvement with the recovering community leads to relationships that support and nurture healing. Hearing the stories of others who have "been there" gives hope to clients who are just starting out.

Not all secondary co-dependents will want to participate in Twelve Step recovery. When this is the case, the therapist's role becomes one of helping clients understand their hesitance. This exploration is good preparation for entering into psychotherapy, when and if the time comes for the client to make this choice.

Preparing for Psychotherapy

While some secondary co-dependents undergo true characterological change solely through Twelve Step recovery, many find relief only from the intensification of their echoistic traits. Although the quality of their lives has been greatly enhanced, their susceptibility to co-dependent behavior remains intact. Psychological barriers prevent them from going any further.

This is often the point at which transferential work becomes appropriate. Sometimes the transition to transferential work occurs without conscious effort. At other times, the invitation to enter into psychotherapy can be simple and direct. For example, I might say something like, "The time may have come to make a decision between ending treatment or moving on to another level."

Some clients are aware that parts of their experience have not yet been touched on by the therapy, but are confused by my suggestion that another level of therapy exists. They may want to be led into it or taught about it. When appropriate, I indicate that deepening therapy may involve looking at their relationship to me. Some deny that a relationship exists; some want to keep the relationship just as it is. And some recognize that they are scared of the idea of becoming more vulnerable, dependent, and intimate. Here is where they either decide to participate in looking at the transference, or not. Here is where the therapeutic alliance must form on a deeper level if psychotherapy is to be possible.

Preparing for psychotherapy with secondary co-dependents consists of monitoring the transference throughout treatment, occasionally planting seeds that indicate a relationship exists, and being sure that the invitation to enter into transferential work is offered in a manner consistent with the developmental issues which must be worked on first. For example, clients who are having difficulty moving out of a symbiotic relationship with the therapist may be invited into transferential work most effectively by eliciting their feelings about the lack of intimacy they feel when the therapist refuses to hug them. Movement into deeper levels of therapy means only that more honesty develops in the relationship between client and therapist, not necessarily that more affection is expressed.

Preparing for psychotherapy means continually inviting the client to be more and more present in a relationship with you from the moment treatment begins. Above all, it means that you as the therapist must realize the limitations of cognitive and behavioral changes. No one can be "taught out of" his basic personality structure, and no one can consciously act in ways that are inconsistent with his basic personality structure.

Co-dependents are masters at trying on new ways of thinking and acting, without experiencing changes in their basic sense of identity. Preparing for psychotherapy means holding out the hope of characterological change in those clients for whom it is realistic, without contributing to the client's belief that this can be accomplished by a few changes of psychological clothes.

PRINCIPLES OF TREATING
PRIMARY CO-DEPENDENCE

Since the goal of treating primary co-dependence is deep characterological change, all the basic principles of the psychotherapy model apply. I define psychotherapy as "working transferentially toward the goal of characterological change." Its techniques and structure are designed to reveal and make use of the myriad unconscious assumptions, expectations, projections, distortions, etc., that clients bring into the therapeutic relationship. These assumptions, etc., are the transference. They impact the client's current experience by "transferring" lessons from the past into the present.

Therapists look for patterns in the transference that give clues to clients' developmental histories. Toward this end, psychotherapists often ascribe less significance to *what* a client says than to *how* or *when* it is said. The task of discovering the transference can be aided only indirectly by clients' voluntary cooperation, since even the motivation behind, and style of, this cooperation is more grist for the therapist's mill.

Psychotherapy views transference as residue from unresolved developmental issues and partially completed developmental tasks. Sometimes we are able to learn the specific nature of the forces which stressed and distorted a client's development. More often, however, we can only hypothesize about them from the developmental arrests and distortions which resulted, as if we were observing the lingering smoke from an unheard gunshot.

The assumption is that these effects on a client's development were literally incorporated into his still crystallizing identity, and exist today as facets of his basic character structure. At times, it is less the developmental disturbances themselves, and more the elaborate compensations and defenses against such disturbances, which can be observed in the present day. Character is the workbench upon which clients construct their daily lives, including their behaviors, feelings, attitudes, perceptions, and thoughts. It is the frame upon which they hang the cloak of personality. As such, the elements and structure of a client's character have pervasive and consistent manifestations throughout his current life.

Once a client's specific transferences are identified, the real work of entering into the therapeutic relationship begins. Its "therapeutic" nature stems from the alliance allowing interactions between therapist and client to begin paralleling those between a healthy parent and child. Often, clients are cautious about such a relationship, or don't comprehend and trust it, because of unfortunate lessons from the past. The therapist's skill lies in establishing and maintaining the symbolic equivalent of the relationship which should have existed between parent and child at the developmental stage which was disturbed. This is accomplished primarily through highlighting, and bringing into awareness, those subtle issues between therapist and client which most closely resemble the main issues which are active during the developmental stage in question.

This process cannot be explained to a client before it has been completed. The best we can do is to enlist clients into a therapeutic alliance which mobilizes their rational faculties, their ability to experience the relationship, and their capacity to trust. The client's task is not to understand the process at every moment, but rather to tolerate its ambiguities. The experience of psychotherapy parallels a developing child's alternating between opening up to new experiences and integrating what is learned. For the relationship between therapist and client to be therapeutic, the client must be willing to open up to new experiences, and the therapist aids her integration by tailoring the new experiences to the developmental tasks which need completing.

Psychotherapy not only uses the transference as a clue to which developmental tasks require reworking; it also understands how to invite clients, symbolically, into more and more advanced developmental tasks. For this reason, therapists must have a firm grasp of child development and the process of identity formation. They must also understand the "bootstrapping" dynamic between interpersonal relationships and the developing sense of self.

It is only through interactions with others that our own sense of identity develops. It is only through interactions with our parents that we come to know who we are, which allows us to interact with our parents on a new level, which permits us to learn a bit more about who we are, and so on. As client and therapist work together to recapitulate this cyclic process, it gradually becomes less symbolic. Eventually clients develop a firm enough grasp of themselves that they are able to enter fully into the actual relationship which exists between themselves and the therapist. It is at this point that successful termination becomes most possible.

While the psychotherapist is not alone in the room, he is alone in many of his thoughts. Just as parents cannot expect their children to comprehend the adult experience (the most that can be achieved on the child's part is empathy for the fact that a parent's experience is different), so, too, must psychotherapists refrain from requiring their clients to have any experience but their own. And, since the structure of psychotherapy tends to throw clients back into reworking their childhood experience, it violates this dynamic to require the client's permission for how the therapy is conducted.

While this description of the relationship between therapist and client may sound horribly hierarchical, it is precisely the mutual acceptance of this inequality which gives that relationship legitimacy and power. The fact that such a potentially dangerous relationship can be carried out successfully between two adults is proof in itself that the world is significantly different than how the client experienced it as a child.

It is the relationship between client and therapist which is the vehicle of healing in psychotherapy. But this is not to say that the therapist's love cures the client. Rather, it is the presence, the regard, and the competence of the therapist which creates a relationship capable of facilitating the client's own efforts to forge a new identity.

Experiencing the Transference

How do psychotherapists become aware of the transference? Is it seen, or heard? Discovered analytically? Intuited? Felt?

The answer is . . . all of these. Transference enters the therapist's awareness because it is experienced. It is a pervasive element of the client-therapist relationship which you, the therapist, recognize is not of your own making—such as an aura of danger in the room which comes from a client's hidden caution. Sometimes the transference is as blatant as when a client misinterprets a simple question as a criticism. Other times it comes from a sense that you are being unclear with a client, when in fact the client is unwilling to listen to you, and secretly blames you for being "unclear."

Transference is what you see when you squint your eyes, or what you hear when you "squint" your ears. It is what you intuit as lying between the lines of what the client is saying. Or it is the lines on which the client's words are written. It can be found in feelings you are having toward the client which you wouldn't expect to be having. For example, you may find yourself suddenly and uncharacteristically reluctant to confront a client. When this reluctance is in response to a client's unexpressed view of you as a sadistic person, you are experiencing transference. On the other hand, if the reluctance is based on activation of your own needs to "take care" of certain kinds of people—e.g., "fragile" women or "hurt" men—you may be dealing with your own transference, which is called countertransference (explored in Chapter 8).

Transference is one subtle facet of your own experience with each particular client. Unless you are open to being aware of your own experience, *whatever* that may be, you are likely to miss the most important information you need to help your client. Getting this information is your responsibility. There is no way to ask the client what the transference is, for it is woven so thoroughly into everything she does and is that she has no awareness of it, like breathing while one sleeps.

Projections and Projective Identification

Much of a therapist's experience of transference involves the dynamic of projective identification.[2] When relationships are affected by projective identification, a complex loop is created between the sending (i.e., projecting) and the receiving (i.e., identifying) members of the interaction. The projecting client "sees" the therapist in ways that distort who the therapist truly is and what she is actually doing. What is "seen" may be aspects of himself which the client cannot tolerate, and therefore disowns, or it may be the result of expectations which stem from real experiences the client has had with significant figures in his past. If the therapist inadvertently identifies with these projections and begins embodying them, the dynamic of projective identification comes into existence.

For example, if a client is afraid of his own anger, or expects authority figures to be angry because he was raised by a rageful alcoholic parent, he may incorrectly interpret much of what the therapist says as expressions of anger. He will treat the therapist as an angry person. If the therapist ends up being angered by this, the client's distortions are verified. This does two things. It makes it extremely difficult for the client to gain perspective on his own role in the dynamics of the client-therapist relationship. And it provides an extremely strong glue for their interactions. The past has been recreated—not symbolically, but actually.

Therapists inevitably experience a pull to identify with clients' projections. In George Vaillant's words, such projection induces "a breakdown of clear knowledge of what is mine and what is thine."[3] The person receiving the projection feels a vague but powerful pressure to behave in ways that are consistent with the client's expectations. This results in therapists' experiencing clients as striving to induce, seduce, or bludgeon them into changing their behavior to conform with the projections. In truth, this "pull" should be seen as a projection on the therapist's own part.

In response to the therapist's *not* identifying with a projection, clients often have difficulty understanding the relationship. Their experience doesn't jibe with their past experience of relationships. They may come to distrust the therapist, seeing her as manipulative, aloof, uncaring, capricious, enigmatic, playing games, rigidly following technique, or simply being unavailable. While it is possible to blame these client reactions for putting greater pressure on the therapist to conform with expectations, the truth is that it is the therapist's own anxiety which pushes her into behaving as the client "sees" her.

In projective identifications, the identifier takes this role to satisfy her own needs. The way to shirk responsibility for identifying with a client's projection is to project the blame outward, "seeing" the projecting client as "pulling" on the therapist to behave in specific ways. When this happens, the therapy is in jeopardy unless some common ground can be found for the therapeutic relationship to stand on.

In essence, psychotherapy involves the therapist's empathic resistance to the client's projections, the development of a common ground (through engaging the client in as much direct human contact as possible) where the client can learn to tolerate frustration of these projections, and the eventual transformation of the client's sense of self to the point at which the client stops making the projections. Working in the transference can be simplistically described as a process of refusing to connect with clients through projective identifications, and doing this in such a way that the client is optimally frustrated, and thereby encouraged to complete unresolved developmental tasks.

Projective Identification:
Two Examples

An example of projective identification can be seen in Sally's behavior and Bill's response during an interactive therapy group for ACAs.

Sally came to the group straight from work, unaware of the anger she was feeling toward how her boss had treated her that day. She immediately saw Bill, another group member, as being very angry. Bill had come to the group feeling comfortable with his day and couldn't understand why he started feeling angry within the first ten minutes of the meeting. He began to accuse the group of "bringing him down" and criticized Sally for "never contributing much" emotionally.

It was only after Bill stopped and questioned why he was getting angry that he began to suspect he had become the vessel for someone else's feelings. When he pulled back, Sally became so intensely angry at him that she had to look more closely at where the force of her feeling was really coming from. Eventually she was able to see that Bill had started treating her like her boss, who had originally activated her anger. Because she felt that it wasn't possible to express this anger at work, she had pushed it out of her awareness. Bill became the target of her projection because he looked like her boss and had a history of quickly identifying with other people's projections.

An example of projections which were not identified with occurred between Rob, a client, and his wife, Sue, when they were preparing a dinner party for several friends. As Sue asked Rob to help her decide which glasses or linen should be used, Rob became increasingly irritated at what he perceived as her anxiety over a trivial event. "We'll be among friends tonight, so there's no reason for you to be anxious," he insisted.

Rob began to resent the way Sue "always ruins" such events by becoming overly sensitive to others' opinions. He finally sat her down and tried to deal with her anxiety, only partially hiding his negative judgments about her "immature behavior." Since Sue had not identified with Rob's projected anxiety, she was genuinely confused by his serious talk about her need to settle down. When she simply stated that she wasn't anxious and asked Rob if he was, this stopped Rob in his tracks. He had to acknowledge that he was a bit anxious, but quickly dismissed his anxiety as ridiculous. Then he attempted to blame his anxiety on his fear that Sue would ruin the event by her anxiety, but this made little sense to either of them as soon as he said it. Rob was forced to begin re-owning his own feelings.

Avoiding Identification with Projections

In the real world, most episodes of projective identification are mutual. Each member of the relationship is both a sender and a receiver.

Consider again the co-dependent client who projects her own narcissism onto someone else. If the person receiving the projection is also in the habit of disowning his own echoism through projection, there is a perfect match. The two members of the dyad are changed in opposite but complementary directions. Each becomes a bit of a caricature of himself or herself. The co-dependent becomes more thoroughly co-dependent by finding a partner to accept her disowned narcissistic needs, and accepting the echoistic needs which are projected back at her. The narcissist becomes more thoroughly narcissistic by finding a partner to accept his disowned echoistic needs, and by accepting the narcissistic needs which are projected back at him.

This is how members of a couple rid themselves of their own intrapsychic conflicts, at the price of polarizing their relationship. The intrapsychic conflicts end up being played out between the two members of the relationship. The therapist's role, in contrast, is to enter into relationship with a client without entering into the dynamics of projective identification.

Some projections are relatively easy to avoid identifying with. They may be so out of sync with the therapist's personality that the relationship with the client has a "what's-wrong-with-this-picture?" quality. Or the client's perceptions may be so inaccurate as to be almost delusional. The client may misinterpret the therapist's comments as rejection and criticism, when the therapist is actually feeling genuine acceptance for and admiration of the client. Something is wildly out of joint. At times, the first experience of such transference may simply be a vague sense of disorientation. I sometimes start to feel light-headed when a client and I are responding to vastly different realities.

Other projections are less obvious and more difficult to avoid identifying with. This is particularly true when there is a kernel of truth in a client's projection. For example, the client may assume that a therapist is self-assured for reasons that have more to do with the client's transference than with any real knowledge she has of the therapist. In those cases where the therapist is indeed self-assured, it will be difficult to tease out the portion of a client's perceptions which are the result of the transference.

The most difficult situations arise when a client's transference taps into the therapist's countertransference. For example, female clients with a history of sexual abuse may only be able to seek nurturing from men (while simultaneously fearing them). Male therapists who see women as needing to be "saved" by men (perhaps as a result of their own over-involvement with their mothers) are likely to act on the projections of these clients and inadvertently confirm them. When this happens, client and therapist have entered into mutual projective identifications. While this is inevitable to some degree in all therapeutic relationships, it must be noticed and resolved as quickly as possible. The best way for a therapist to deal with his own unique susceptibilities to mutual projective identifications is through an extended period of close supervision with a senior therapist to discover his countertransference, and personal therapy to resolve these issues.

The projections a therapist is most likely to notice and deem significant are tightly related to her perspective on child development. For example, because the original Freudian psychoanalysts tended to see the Oedipal period (ages 3-5) as the most critical stage of child development, they were particularly sensitive to projections of power and sexuality (e.g., who is dominant, and who is submissive?). With the development of schools of Object Relations (or Human Relations) and Self Psychology, the emphasis has shifted to developmental stages at earlier ages. Therapists working within this framework are sensitive to projections that have to do with autonomy, dependence, and abandonment (e.g., where are the boundaries between you and me, and do I exist if I am separate?).

Before going any further, it will be useful to review the critical developmental issues and tasks which are disrupted in the development of primary co-dependence. This will help to clarify transference issues which will most often be encountered in the treatment of ACAs.

Developmental Issues Leading to Primary Co-Dependence

My work with ACAs has led me to a perspective on child development which integrates four compatible theoretical threads:

1. *Margaret Mahler's framework for Separation/Individuation.*[4] All children begin life symbiotically fused to the mother (or the primary caregiver), with little or no individual identity apart from her. As children gradually become autonomous (both by separating enough to be independent, and individuating enough to be different), they must begin to find peace with the human condition of being simultaneously independent and dependent, separate but related. To come into relationship with their parents, without denying their own autonomy (i.e., to achieve rapprochement), children need the active participation of an empathic parent in the original parent-child bond.

2. *Daniel Stern's concept of Affect Attunement.*[5] All children enter into interpersonal relationships and begin developing a sense of self from the earliest neonatal period. Mirroring is the currency of exchange between parent and child which provides the interpersonal experiences used to construct progressively fuller identities.

3. *Object Relations Theory.* All children are ultimately motivated not only to satisfy bodily needs, but also to establish meaningful human relationships. The desire for relatedness is as much a motivating force as hunger and sex.[6] From this perspective, pre-Oedipal events become more significant for personality development than Oedipal ones.

4. *Self Psychology.* All children develop two antithetical interpersonal needs at the time their symbiotic union with
mother ends. Heinz Kohut's description[7] of the needs to be
perfectly mirrored ("the grandiose self") and to be fully
dependent ("the idealized parent") can be seen, respectively,
as normal narcissistic and echoistic needs, which must
mature and be integrated into a coherent sense of self. The
development of a sense of self which encompasses maturing forms of both these needs occurs with rapprochement.

Integration of these four threads, with an eye to comprehend-
ing the transference seen in primary co-dependents, produces
the following framework for child development:

Step 1: The sense of self and sense of other are inextricably intertwined.
Interpersonal interactions and development of the self constitute
a system. Neither exists without the other; they are complementary and contemporaneous. Developmental advances in one
"bootstrap" progressions in the other.

This perspective translates the maxim that "humans are social
animals" into its most literal implications: Without interpersonal
interactions to serve as a blueprint and the raw materials for
intrapsychic development, infants will not become fully human.
The most severe early neglect leaves people lacking both the
capacity to enter fully into human relationships, and clear enough
boundaries to have a well-formed, coherent sense of self. Both
the interpersonal and intrapsychic worlds are fragmented and
impoverished. Again, humans are social animals, irrevocably and
inextricably.

Step 2: The development of these senses begins at birth. There is minimal, if any, evidence that human infants enter extra-uterine life
with a concept of others (and therefore, of self). However, there
is evidence that little or no lag time elapses before they begin
participating in interpersonal events.[8]

Presuming that some learning always exists before behavioral manifestations are present further emphasizes that, while infants may experience themselves as symbiotically fused to their parents most of the time, they are also capable of at least rudimentary interpersonal interactions from the very earliest age. It is during these brief forays into the land of relationship that significant seeds of development are planted. There are no compelling reasons to doubt that such seeds can be planted during the hyper-alert state babies achieve during the birth process itself.

Step 3: Symbiosis ends with the development of dyadic awareness. A time comes when the infant's consciousness of some separation and differentiation between self and other has been sustained long enough to develop its own momentum. This consciousness becomes knowledge which cannot be ignored at will—much as Adam and Eve's knowledge of good and evil was an irrevocable event. Once it is learned, it cannot be unlearned.

For the infant, dyadic awareness does not have to be continuously present in order to be irrevocable. The seed has sprouted and taken root. There is nothing left but to ride along with the process and be prepared to harvest whatever crop develops.

Step 4: With dyadic awareness come two antithetical interpersonal needs—narcissism and echoism. Awareness of the separation between self and other ends the security of symbiosis. Both narcissistic relationships (being perfectly mirrored by one's parent) and echoistic relationships (becoming the perfect mirror and depending on one's parent) can temporarily recreate the stability and security experienced during earlier symbiosis, except for two things:

- Neither of these two interpersonal needs exists in isolation, unless the other is pathologically disowned. The two naturally butt up against each other from their inception.
- Both needs run afoul of reality, particularly the reality of parental limitations, as long as they remain in their primitive, immature form.

In other words, no parent can mirror a child as much as the child wants. Nor can any parent provide perfect security.

Step 5: The process of separation-individuation requires optimal frustration of both narcissistic and echoistic needs. "Optimal frustration" is a process, leading up to and through the rapprochement crisis, whereby the child's narcissistic and echoistic needs are initially met as thoroughly as possible, then gradually frustrated in doses the child can tolerate. The more frustration a child tolerates, the more he is capable of tolerating. In effect, he is being progressively introduced to the realities and limitations of human relationships.

When frustrations are experienced in an optimal way, they lead to growth of a sense of self at an ever quickening pace. For example, a child may initially need her every action validated to experience her parents as nurturing. When she continues to feel her needs for validation are being met even after her parents start ignoring less desirable behaviors, this is evidence that her narcissistic needs have begun to mature.

Step 6: Rapprochement occurs when narcissistic and echoistic needs have matured sufficiently to be experienced simultaneously. The maturation of narcissistic and echoistic needs moves the two from being mutually exclusive to being merely paradoxical. At the same time, the child's sense of self has expanded to the point that incompatible feelings can now be simultaneously entertained.

This new capacity to tolerate paradox is manifested externally in the child's ability to resolve the rapprochement crisis: How can relationship occur in a meaningful way once the separation between self and others is accepted as being absolute and irrevocable? The answer lies in a combination of events:

- realization that the limitations on relationships are universally present, and are not the result of one's parents' whims or personal inadequacies;
- acceptance of these limitations; and
- maintenance of an empathic connection by one's parents throughout the child's struggle.

It is the child's willingness to base the relationship with his parents on this empathic connection, rather than on the magical ability of parents to gratify archaic needs, that permits life as an individual to proceed without plunging into the darkness of isolation from others. It is at this point that the terrible tantrums of two-year-olds melt away into the pleasing cooperativeness of three-year-olds, and blatant magical thinking begins to become a thing of the past.

Step 7: The Oedipal period marks further expansion of interpersonal interactions, from dyadic to triadic relationships. While issues of separation, abandonment, dependence, and individuality permeate the pre-Oedipal period, issues of power and control now come to the fore.

Until the Oedipal period, children perceive themselves as having dyadic relationships with both mother and father. With the dawn of the Oedipal period, they realize that Mom and Dad have their own dyadic relationship, which is out of the child's purview, and often takes precedence over the parent-child relationship. As this new interpersonal level develops, children experience parallel internal changes. A sense of values, rules, ideas, guilt, and conscience (the superego) emerges.

It is largely through borrowing a parent's values and weaving them into the very fabric of the self that children come to peace with the world of triadic relationships. Another cycle of having to tolerate the increased anxiety of separation long enough to grow into a more mature relationship with others has occurred. It is at this point that children derive more comfort from knowing they can be like a parent, and therefore require less direct mirroring of their immediate experience.

This second level of rapprochement is complete by the fifth or sixth year of life—which emphasizes the critical need for parents to remain emotionally available to their children from birth through the preschool years. The chronic use of alcohol diminishes a parent's ability to fulfill this critical role in a child's life. It is prudent to assume that the abuse of alcohol inevitably has a direct, negative impact on a child's developing sense of self and capacity for healthy relationships.

Comments

A child's experience with these developmental steps occupies a special place in her history and often reverberates throughout her life. However, wide paths are created only when people walk them again and again. Character disorders become ingrained only when developmental distortions are reenacted over and over, on a thousand subtle levels, within the family system.

For example, as powerful as the initial rejection of a child's normal narcissistic needs might be in producing co-dependence, the child will probably not totally disown these needs unless they are systematically and consistently rejected throughout her childhood. Early lessons are reinforced when later lessons confirm them.

The business of psychotherapy is to provide new interpersonal experiences. These interpersonal experiences must be tailored for each individual client, on the basis of transference issues which develop during therapy. The point is not to eradicate but to balance earlier childhood learning.

Transference in
Primary Co-Dependence

The primary co-dependent enters therapy with a predictable and recognizable transference. He assumes that you are thoroughly narcissistic while simultaneously having an archaic echoistic need for you to occupy the role of perfect parent. Each of these factors affects your relationship.

Since the co-dependent (in an effort to get you to like him) has disowned his narcissistic needs and projected them onto you, he assumes that he must mirror you in order for there to be a relationship. He sees you as needing to feel special and incapable of empathizing with any tendency he has to disagree with or be disappointed in you. He fears that you will lose interest unless he continuously pleases you. In my own clinical work, the majority of my co-dependent clients eventually reveal that they don't feel they are "interesting enough" to hold my attention over the long run. (As would be expected, this is the opposite of the attitude seen in most narcissistic clients.)

There are many ways a co-dependent client might react to "seeing" a therapist as needing to feel special, ranging from acquiescence to rebellion, with awareness and expression of the more hostile reactions truncated by the co-dependent's fear of being abandoned. The client's desire for a perfect parent she can depend on absolutely for sustenance and self-esteem fits hand-in-glove with the projection that the therapist expects the relationship to revolve around himself. The assumption is, "If only this great person can be made to love me enough, all of my problems will disappear!" The client believes that the way to win your love is to be what you want: a perfect client who mirrors your perfection. Whenever this dynamic is frustrated (for example, by your refusal to hug the client, or your failure to reflect a feeling accurately), she plummets through feelings of abandonment into self-hatred and despair—then seeks a different way to please you.

There is a wrinkle in this otherwise predictable process: Co-dependents are often so exquisitely sensitive to the unspoken desires of others that they accurately perceive when you don't want perfect compliance. When this happens, they may try to appear independent. But even though they disguise their behavior in sophisticated ways, the underlying dynamic of relying on others for one's self-esteem remains intact.

The goal of psychotherapy—characterological change—is more reliably measured by shifts in motivation and attitude than by shifts in behavior, although these are not mutually exclusive. For example, it is moments when a co-dependent client places her needs before yours (perhaps by asking to reschedule an appointment to free up an afternoon for tennis) that signal the onset of characterological change and let you know that she is starting to re-own her normal narcissistic needs. The same behavior (asking to switch appointment times) does not have the same significance, however, if the client has read in this book that such behavior constitutes progress, and undertakes it to look like she is improving.

Psychotherapy consists of recognizing the transference and using it to discover the developmental tasks which are available to be symbolically reworked. The co-dependent client imports pre-Oedipal, separation-individuation issues into the therapeutic setting. Therapy helps the client re-own his narcissistic needs, mature his primitive echoistic needs through optimal frustration, and expand his sense of self until these two needs can coexist. Much of this work is done through eventually allowing the client to experience your inability (and unwillingness) to gratify every echoistic need, showing empathic interest in the client's sense of abandonment in the face of this frustration, and remaining in non-judgmental contact with the client as he struggles through the ambiguity of his relationship with you and re-owns his narcissistic needs.

Therapists facilitate this process by being sensitive to the most subtle and attenuated expression of narcissistic needs, validating them, and meeting them when appropriate. For example, when the client who wanted to change her appointment time hesitantly asked me (apologizing profusely and giving me every opportunity to say no), I granted the request after checking my schedule and indicating that I could make an adjustment to accommodate her. Then I stayed in close empathic contact as she experienced the gratification of her narcissistic need.

It's important to do this, because most clients' past experience is that such gratification has a price, most often abandonment. Therapists must not be threatened by maintaining empathic contact at times like these and allowing clients to be the center of attention. If anything, they should be pleased when their clients' narcissistic needs are met, and they should permit clients to see this pleasure in their own facial expressions. Otherwise therapists risk reopening clients' original wound of being rejected by a narcissistic parent.

On the other hand, as clients do start re-owning their narcissistic needs, this can lead to uncomfortable confrontations. Clients may demand that therapists "do their job better" and "care more" about the client. They may begin feeling more righteous in their anger when echoistic needs are frustrated. They may even threaten to terminate therapy. Such confrontations should be met with an empathic connection to the disappointment clients are experiencing.

Clinical Vignette:
The Dependent Student

Sarah was a young college student who had been raised by a drug-addicted mother. Her parents had encouraged her to seek therapy and were paying the fee. I had been seeing her for six months when she was unable to pay her bill for a few weeks because her check from home had not arrived. When we first faced the fact that I would not continue to see her unless she brought her bill up to date, Sarah immediately accepted my financial needs as being important and primary. Because she had not re-owned her narcissistic needs, she felt no entitlement to treatment.

After another year, Sarah's parents decided to discontinue paying for her therapy, and Sarah had no practical means of earning the money herself. During termination, it became apparent that Sarah had begun to re-own some of her own narcissism when she castigated me for being callous and uncaring because I wouldn't keep seeing her for no compensation. She nearly ended therapy a few weeks earlier than necessary as a way of rejecting me first.

I saw this as evidence that she was finally re-owning narcissistic needs which had been disowned at a very early age. Because these needs were still in their archaic form, they appeared as a stark sense of entitlement. My basic therapeutic strategy was to validate these needs, archaic as they were, rather than to give her the sense that I was challenging them by trying to get her to explore their meaning. I then began to optimally frustrate her narcissism, primarily by empathizing with the pain and sadness that come from having one's sense of entitlement unanswered by others.

Although this case had an unsatisfactory ending because of Sarah's having to terminate prematurely, I felt that she had taken some important first steps. Her anger at having the therapy taken away from her was a healthy re-owning of her sense of entitle-ment. By expressing the anger at me, rather than at her parents, she had a safer place to experience that she could be angry with-out being abandoned. I listened to the anger and continued to empathize. When we did have to part, her echoistic needs had matured enough that she was able to understand my need to stop seeing her as a financial decision (which I allowed her not to like), not as a personal rejection or proof that I no longer cared about what happened to her.

Clinical Vignette:
The Militant Seeker of Reparenting

Some clients hold on to their basic co-dependence even after letting go of the fantasy that they will be "loved" back into health. A client named Simon illustrates this point.

Simon assumed that my job as therapist was to love and vali-date all the parts of him which his alcoholic parents had ignored. Armed with the latest literature on the subject of reparenting clients, he had specific ideas for how this process should work. A series of struggles ensued around trying to have social contact with me, the fact that I didn't express enough affection for him, and my refusal to end our sessions with a hug. I was seen as withholding, inadequate, the negative side of his narcissistic par-ents. I saw his anger as secretly being motivated by a belief that he could shame me into giving him the form of "reparenting" he thought he needed. This belief tumbled away when he attended one of my public lectures and was treated like everyone else in the audience. Simon suddenly realized that he wasn't going to get the love from me that he had come for.

This was followed by another difficult period. Simon nearly left therapy before reaching the intellectual understanding that no amount of love from me, or anyone else, could save him. He stopped seeing me as inadequate and withholding, and accepted the reality that he had been deluded about the value uncondi-tional acceptance actually has. But his co-dependence continued to flourish. My having "taught" him this lesson, and having remained empathically connected to him during his painful struggles to bludgeon me into loving him, only served to complete my coronation as the perfect therapist. Simon set out to heal himself by studying me so he could turn his life into an imitation of my own. He redoubled his willful efforts to become the perfect mirror. If he couldn't make me love him, he would bask more fully in my reflected glory.

Of course, this tactic got Simon nowhere closer to himself. It did, however, further disappoint his echoistic expectations. Simon began to be optimally frustrated. He told me that he hadn't gotten his parents to love him enough as a child to feel good about himself. He had tried to get his wife to love him enough, but this hadn't worked either. "After all," he said, "I ended up choosing someone who was just like my mother!" He had no choice about his parents, and his wife was a "bad choice," influenced by his experience in his family of origin. Armed with new insights into ACA issues and healing (many of which were garnered from my own writing), he saw me as his first fully informed and healthy choice. Again, he was disappointed. When he learned that my love couldn't cure him, and that patterning himself after me wouldn't help, what possible reason could there be to continue therapy with me?

The answer to this question was simple but hard to get to. Simon began to realize that throughout our struggles, I had never disparaged him, never rejected him, never judged his desire to be loved by a perfect therapist or his demands that I treat him as unique and special. I had simply been there, staying in contact with him at a human level. He began allowing the possibility that I liked something about him, and took the risk of saying what he liked about me. His expectations for what I could do for him were certainly very reduced, and he grieved about this.

Meanwhile, something else important was happening. Throughout our tumultuous relationship, the quality of Simon's life outside therapy had quietly improved as the lessons learned in treatment were generalized to his other intimate relationships. Although he remained unable to identify the direct connections between what had transpired in therapy with the improvements in his life, he was convinced at a deep level that our work had played an important role.

Comments

It's the terrible truth that parents (and, by proxy, therapists) cannot live their children's lives for them, cannot directly give them self-esteem, and cannot guarantee their success or happiness, no matter how hard they try. A child's acceptance of this truth, and development of the willingness to remain in relationship with parents anyway, form the crux of interpersonal development. Likewise, a client's acceptance that the therapist cannot provide the wished-for cradle of love that will make life "right," and development of the willingness to remain in the therapeutic relationship anyway, form the interpersonal crux of psychotherapy.

The art of psychotherapy is to usher clients into these realizations through their *experience* with the relationship, rather than presume that such growth can be "taught." The latter approach only confirms to clients that therapists have secrets to reveal and wisdom to dispense, which reinforces clients' co-dependence instead of helping to heal it.

Focusing on Compulsions

People develop many defenses to avoid the sense of abandonment which comes with having their lives controlled by archaic echoistic needs. Until these defenses are dismantled, it may be impossible to directly affect the underlying co-dependent personality structure.

Two such defenses frequently found in ACAs are compulsions and the distorted relationship to willpower typical of alcoholics. The CD model for focusing on compulsions, used widely in the treatment of secondary co-dependence, has great value in dealing with these defenses in primary co-dependence as well, especially when integrated into a psychotherapeutic approach.

Compulsions are valuable windows into clients' subjective experience and unconscious, provided that therapists are practiced in helping clients peer through them. I often focus on a compulsion not because its resolution is integral to the therapy, but as an avenue toward characterological change.

Consider, for example, the co-dependent client who smokes tobacco and expresses a desire to quit. The first step in facilitating change is to take her seriously, which eventually pushes her into exploring her basic relationship to willpower. The sooner she learns that her best efforts to "make" herself stop wanting cigarettes are doomed, the closer she comes to relinquishing one of the most important forces maintaining her co-dependence.

The realization that one *cannot* abolish the urge to smoke by sheer power of the will has a cascading effect within a client. As her primary strategy for achieving self-esteem is stripped away, a period of despair and helplessness ensues. As the bankruptcy of this strategy gradually sinks into her consciousness, more and more areas of her life where the strategy still holds sway are called into question. Without any alternative strategy to replace it, denial about its bankruptcy may return. As this denial becomes transparent, the client starts distrusting much of what her mind tells her about willpower. A panicky depression may set in. There seems to be nothing left to sustain the client as she struggles to overcome life's problems.

Once reliance on willpower has been relinquished, the CD model points clients toward reliance on others. This would be the natural direction for co-dependents to turn ("Here, I can't do it; I need you to help me"), but usually is done in a subtle, last-ditch effort to assert control ("If I ask for help, surely that will make my urge to smoke go away!"). From a therapeutic standpoint, asking for help for whatever reason is an opportunity for clients to become more realistic about what others can and can't do for them. Therapists can guide clients toward a healthier, more realistic dependence, one in which they openly acknowledge and share the reality of their powerlessness—not because this accomplishes anything, but simply because it's true. When clients accept for the moment that relationships can be based on the truth about who they are, they have taken a leap of faith, a sign of characterological change.

Focusing on compulsions in treating ACAs has another benefit. It provides a potential empathic connection with the client's chemically dependent parents. This is a win/win situation. The client will either arrive at a more realistic relationship to willpower, or find out first-hand how difficult this transition can be. And the harder it is for the co-dependent ACA to abstain from his own compulsion, the harder it is to judge someone else. This provides valuable material for introspection on the fate of one's parents. Eventually the co-dependent may realize that much of a parent's behavior was the result of internal compulsions, and not due to anything the client did as a child.

In the end, parental chemical dependence, and the effects this had on the family, are nothing personal. By experiencing these same dynamics within himself, whether or not they are successfully resolved, the ACA learns something about his parents which he could not comprehend during childhood. The result, frequently, is a decrease in the blame felt toward one's parents, and occasionally the beginning of forgiveness.

THERAPEUTIC MODALITIES FOR
TREATING CO-DEPENDENCE

Now that the basic principles for treating primary and secondary co-dependence have been outlined, we can turn our attention to specific treatment modalities and techniques.

I organize this information in the following way: First, I present general guidelines for determining whether an individual client should be referred to individual and/or group therapy. Next, I outline individual and group techniques for treating secondary co-dependence. Finally, I present individual and group techniques for primary co-dependence.

INDICATIONS FOR INDIVIDUAL
AND GROUP THERAPY

There is a bias toward group therapy within the co-dependence field, and probably for good reason. Co-dependents often prefer to remain in a less vulnerable, more controlled one-on-one setting, where their sensitivity to the unconscious needs and desires of others can be fully focused on the therapist. Subtle collusions between client and therapist are difficult to avoid and can lead to an appearance that clients are doing good work, when in fact they are simply complying with the therapist's unspoken expectations.

Group therapy prohibits such collusions. Clients can't monitor the reactions of everyone in the group simultaneously without being paralyzed by the effort, or forced to see how their compliance is dominating their behavior, if not their very sense of identity. The power of group therapy is that it jams co-dependents' attempts to control everyone's perceptions. This compels them to deal more honestly with others, but in a less emotionally charged context than individual therapy, where the client-therapist relationship is the only one available to be observed and worked on. The power of group is further enhanced by the increased validation that comes from the group itself. Many voices raised in support are mightier than one, especially if there is any sense that individual therapists are "paid" to be supportive.

But group therapy is not universally valuable, and there are at least two reasons why. First, many different styles of group exist, with some being more appropriate for secondary co-dependents and others being better for primary co-dependents. These distinctions will be outlined later in this chapter. Second, a variety of factors may make individual therapy preferable, without regard to whether the client has secondary or primary co-dependence. The bottom line is that referrals must always be made on a case-by-case basis.

In general, individual psychotherapy provides more focused attention and greater opportunity for exploring childhood events while provoking issues inherent in hierarchical relationships. Group, on the other hand, provides less focused attention (thus requiring the development of clients' negotiation skills) and greater opportunity for exploring a range of present-day events while provoking issues inherent in peer relationships.

With these guidelines in mind, at Genesis we recommend individual psychotherapy in the following cases:

• *Clients in crisis.* When clients seek therapy because of crisis (most often precipitated by abandonment issues), what they need most is unconditional attention. This is not the time for them to explore how best to negotiate with others for a piece of the group's time and attention. Individual therapy lets clients know that their crisis is being taken seriously and their request for help deserves full attention.

The recommendation for individual therapy also protects ongoing groups from having to suspend their current work in order to attend to a new member's crisis. While the group's excessive willingness to put someone else's needs first (and a stranger's, at that) could be useful for the group to explore, this is usually already an issue in co-dependence groups without having to import it.

• *Clinical depression.* Groups don't work well for depressed clients, especially if the depression has begun to deactivate their coping skills. Issues of deep depression, such as the possible need for medication (especially to disrupt the physiological contributions to the depression), suicidal thoughts, pathologic mourning, and traumatic grief, are all best dealt with in individual psychotherapy.

Whenever possible, ACA groups should be protected from having to contend with seriously suicidal members, as this is nearly impossible for co-dependents to avoid turning their full attention toward.

• *Intense anxiety.* Many clients will experience extreme anxiety at the prospect of being vulnerable within a group setting. Their level of trust in others is so compromised that they could not tolerate the anxiety of group work. Individual work provides a better opportunity for helping clients modulate this anxiety.

• *Dual diagnosis/internal disorganization.* Dual diagnosis in and of itself is not a reason to recommend individual over group work. But it often leads to levels of internal disorganization which are more easily dealt with in individual psychotherapy. Clients who cannot track questions well, who are unable to structure their thinking sufficiently to provide a coherent family history, and/or who are tangential, delusional, or actively hallucinating are not good group candidates.

At Genesis, we treat borderline clients in individual therapy until there is sufficient evidence that they can tolerate interactional group. Whenever the issue of containment is present (i.e., whenever clients are unable to avoid being overwhelmed by their impulses and feelings without the active help of a therapist), individual work provides maximum control over the therapeutic process.

• *Post-traumatic stress disorder.* Clients with untreated symptoms of PTSD, especially reexperiencing the trauma and psychic numbing, usually benefit from an initial course of individual work before it can be determined whether their co-dependence would best be treated in group or individual therapy.

• *Clients who vacillate between co-dependence and narcissism.* Clients who respond to fulfillment of their echoistic needs with narcissistic pride, but tumble back into co-dependence whenever their narcissistic needs are frustrated, are best treated in individual psychotherapy. This gives therapists the flexibility needed to meet such clients at whichever end of the continuum they swing to.

The therapeutic alliance with narcissistic and co-dependent clients rests on different empathic connections, as discussed more fully later in this chapter. When clients alternate between the extremes of co-dependence and narcissism, this may be too confusing for members of a group to deal with therapeutically.

• *Clients who resist group.* A certain percentage of clients are simply unwilling to value group therapy as much as individual therapy. They may believe this to be an objective assessment, but it is more often motivated by fear of being in the group. However, experience has taught me that "going with the resistance" is usually the most effective initial approach. When such clients can effectively enter into individual psychotherapy, referral to group can come later, if warranted.

• *Clients with problematic hierarchical relationships.* Human relationships fall into two categories, hierarchical and peer. Hierarchical relationships begin with our parents and persist throughout our lives. They involve our children, our bosses and employees, the authorities, God, the heads of organizations (from boards of directors to neighborhood associations), elected officials, etc. Peer relationships exist among equals, such as between brothers and sisters, spouses, neighbors, co-workers, etc.

While clients' problems always involve a mixture of hierarchical and peer relationships, it is sometimes possible to identify one category as causing the most intense or pervasive difficulties. Individual psychotherapy is the most effective forum for working with co-dependents who have problematic hierarchical relationships, since the client-therapist relationship is itself hierarchical. On the other hand, group therapy may be most effective for co-dependents with problematic peer relationships, since the group provides several peer relationships to work on.

TECHNIQUES FOR TREATING
SECONDARY CO-DEPENDENCE

By definition, secondary co-dependence means that the client has a baseline character structure which lies within the range of normal, but has fallen into increasing dysfunction in response to an unhealthy living situation. The goal of treating secondary co-dependence is to help clients return to previous levels of health. This is achieved through a combination of intervening on the system in which they are living, and supporting their detachment from the unhealthy aspects of that system. The CD/counseling model serves as the most effective framework for treatment.

Individual Therapy

There are no indications for individual therapy which stem directly from the diagnosis of secondary co-dependence, beyond the supervening factors, listed above, which make clients unwilling or unable to enter group therapy. In particular, secondary co-dependents in crisis, immobilized by depression and/or anxiety, suffering internal disorganization, or with dual diagnoses (especially PTSD, borderline, and narcissism), are often helped by entering into supportive individual counseling. Those who avoid group out of fear (conscious or unconscious) that it will confront them with their issues too effectively can also be taken into individual therapy, but not without thoroughly exploring this fear early in their treatment.

Perhaps the strongest therapeutic force in the treatment of secondary co-dependence stems from a therapist's effective modeling of non-co-dependent behavior. By not taking responsibility for solving the client's problems, not responding to the drama of crises, and not staking one's worth as a therapist on being able to love the client out of her depression or calm her out of her anxiety, therapists begin to involve the client in a healthier relationship than any the client has at home. Even if the client attempts to become the mirror image of the therapist (a very co-dependent trait), this will have positive effects, as it will bring the client back into touch with the healthier aspects of herself that became less available as she regressed into active co-dependence.

In addition to modeling, therapists have three other treatment avenues to choose from when providing individual therapy to secondary co-dependents: 1) traditional counseling techniques, 2) the tools of recovery, and 3) facilitating the use of outside sources of support.

Traditional Counseling Techniques

Several traditional counseling techniques are useful for bringing secondary co-dependents into greater conscious awareness of their feelings, motives, behaviors, and choices. Simple reflective listening and the use of clarifications can give clients a badly needed sounding board. Direct validation of their feelings may lead to helpful catharsis. Cognitive exploration of alternative responses to family problems expands their choices. Continual attention to their perspective reinforces the importance of their perceptions and begins to remove the focus from the behavior of other family members. Throughout the treatment, therapists can actively manage the anxiety clients are experiencing, facilitate needed grief work, refer those clients with major depressions for drug therapy when appropriate, and begin the process of helping those with PTSD learn to tolerate their immediate experience.

Education is a major component in the supportive counseling of secondary co-dependence. Clients frequently need information about chemical dependence, the dynamics of family dysfunctions, the characteristics of co-dependence, ACA characteristics, recovery, and the community supports available to co-dependents. When clients are not yet willing to seek education outside the therapy setting, it is important to provide it directly.

The process underlying such supportive counseling is designed to communicate faith in the client's inherent capacity to be healthy. The narcissistic need to be the focus of attention is unquestioningly satisfied by the mere fact of being taken into therapy, which makes the experience of therapy very different from home life. The therapist's assumption is not that the client must develop the *capacity* for self-worth, but that the self-worth the client has felt in the past simply needs to be reaffirmed. Echoistic needs are met from the beginning within their realistic limits, since the assumption is that secondary co-dependents have already experienced the maturation of their echoism through optimal frustration. By continually encouraging clients to tap into outside sources of support, therapists reaffirm that they cannot personally provide everything that the client desires. This models precisely what clients must put into effect in their personal lives.

Client-centered techniques such as reflective listening, empathy, and clarification of feelings place clients at the center of attention, supporting and validating all their emotions nonjudgmentally. Two pitfalls await the therapist during this stage of treatment. First, there is often a shared delusion regarding the power of love to heal. The client's co-dependent character structure may lead him to believe that salvation comes through getting a special person to love him completely.

Therapists can unwittingly contribute to clients' misconceptions about the power of love to heal. Unconditional positive regard, and perhaps even love itself, is an essential foundation for effective therapy, but it is not the whole essence of therapy. Many therapists overestimate the value of wrapping clients in a cocoon of supportive validation, as though some positive force emanates from the therapist, travels toward and into the client, and results in greater self-worth and a firmer sense of identity. The dynamics of co-dependence suggest that such therapeutic grandiosity is, in part, the result of projective identification. Clients' primitive echoistic needs for a perfect parent to merge with, combined with the disowning and projection of their narcissism, sets the stage for therapists' own narcissism to resonate with and be reinforced by clients' projections.

The second pitfall of supportive validation involves the issue of self-revelation by therapists. For co-dependent clients who are struggling to shift attention from other peoples' problems to their own, undergoing bouts of despair and hopelessness along the way, self-revelation by a therapist can be of tremendous value. Imagine the alcoholic, struggling to come to terms with the shame of acknowledging his disease, who learns that his therapist (someone he admires greatly) is also a recovering alcoholic! This revelation can trigger massive transformation in a client's perspective. Similarly, many clients can accept information about co-dependence only when they trust that the therapist is not "talking down" to them, but has "experienced" these facts from the inside out. The therapist's present health becomes a testimonial of hope at a time when hope feels unrealistic and risky.

But the value of self-revelation must be tempered by two considerations. First, if the therapist "leads" clients too much with such revelations, this turns clients into mirrors and reinforces their co-dependence. For revelation to be most effective, it must often occur as a reflection of the client. For example, if a therapist reveals that she, too, had to struggle with a sense of shame when acknowledging her own alcoholism, she reflects what the client is already feeling, normalizes this feeling, and keeps the client at the center of attention. But if she reveals at their first meeting that she is recovering, without making any connection to an experience the client is having, none of this happens. Instead, it proves to the client that the therapist is perfect, someone to be mirrored.

Second, while a therapist's self-revelation may be an effective counseling technique, it creates substantial barriers to eventually entering psychotherapy. Self-revelation may color or even abort the transference. Self-revelations can never be taken back, and few clients can tolerate a shift in the therapeutic relationship away from a therapist's willingness to reveal himself. To draw an analogy, consider the parent who has a peer relationship with a child for a period of time, then suddenly tries to reassert an authoritative parental role. It's as if the parent (or therapist) is saying, "Forget that we used to be equals; forget all the secrets I shared with you; I'm in charge now." Transferential psychotherapy is difficult enough without these added complications.

There are two ways around the problematic nature of self-revelation. First, many therapists confine their use of self-revelation to encapsulated treatment settings where counseling techniques are wholly appropriate: educational lectures at treatment centers, workshops, and time-limited, structured counseling groups for co-dependents. Second, clients' active participation in Twelve Step meetings frequently accomplishes the same goals as self-revelation by the therapist—i.e., normalizing clients' feelings and instilling hopefulness. If clients can be successfully encouraged to get these needs met outside the therapy setting, self-revelation can be minimized and its effectiveness enhanced.

Tools of Recovery

Tools of recovery fall into two categories: remedial skills, and translation of the Twelve Step program. By remedial skills, I am referring to assertiveness training, communication exercises, parent effectiveness training, and so on. Many of these skills wither when an individual slides into increasingly dysfunctional relationships. Introducing clients to such training, directly or by referral, allows them to start taking concrete steps for health. This enhances their self-esteem in and of itself.

Some clients initially resist attending Twelve Step meetings.

But when therapists consistently translate the essential features of the program—when they put them into language palatable to each client—their hesitance often dissolves. For example, one of my clients enthusiastically related how she had taken an evening to write down all her weaknesses and strengths as honestly as she could. I affirmed that such an exercise is very useful, told her that many others had discovered the same thing she had, and explained that this had been institutionalized in Twelve Step programs under the guise of taking a "Moral Inventory" of oneself. When such translating is done in a non-patronizing way, clients often begin to feel an affinity with the wisdom of Twelve Step programs.

Perhaps the three most important translations of the program involve willpower/surrender, detachment, and a Higher Power. Therapists should explore in minuscule detail clients' efforts to force specific solutions to work on specific problems. For example, how do they "keep themselves from getting angry?" How do they think they accomplish this? When clients begin to understand the ways they have tried to control the uncontrollable in their lives (i.e., a distorted relationship to willpower), therapists can refer to how the program understands the level of fear that comes with any thought of abandoning habitual uses of willpower (i.e., surrender). The purpose is to continually expose clients to the fact that a massive community of people has been grappling with the very problems currently stumping them, and that these people have discovered some effective solutions.

Few concepts are more difficult for some clients than detachment. Co-dependents who have not yet changed their relationship to willpower rarely understand it properly. For them, detachment is a way of forcing their feelings out of awareness. Typically, clients may say, "Well, I can't do anything about my husband's drinking, so I just won't let it bother me anymore." Therapists can help by explaining that detachment has nothing to do with controlling feelings. In fact, it embodies the opposite approach. Detachment means no longer attempting to influence whether you have feelings, what feelings you might have, or how deep they might be. It means simply allowing feelings to be what they will be.

Openness to one's spirituality may be the most powerful of all recovery tools, but it is also one that is very contaminated for many people. Early religious experiences that were too rigid often leave people with a fear of being controlled and losing their sense of integrity if they take spirituality seriously. Therapists can translate the Twelve Step approach to spirituality by emphasizing that it is intended to honor the very impulses which brought the client into therapy: There is legitimate reason to be hopeful; you do not have to rely only on yourself; you are wise to open yourself to the possibility that there are forces in the universe which mean you well.

Facilitating the Use of
Outside Sources of Support

Counseling secondary co-dependents is a process of continually affirming the level of autonomy they possess in their baseline character structure. This differs greatly from the psychotherapeutic approach to primary co-dependence, which encourages clients to acknowledge their primitive echoistic needs to depend on the therapist so that these needs can ultimately achieve greater maturation than the client has ever experienced. Such characterological change is not the focus with secondary co-dependents. Rather, the goal is to help them regain access to the health which lies dormant within them, after which it can be decided whether deeper characterological change is needed or desired.

For this reason, therapists should encourage clients to tap into a wide variety of outside supports, including Twelve Step programs, churches, chemical dependence treatment center programs for family members, literature, workshops, etc. When clients do not use these supports, the therapist's role should be to explore this resistance. Is it motivated by fear, misunderstanding, the inability to mobilize oneself because of deeper levels of depression than were originally thought to exist, or a persistent, magical belief that contact with a therapist is all that is necessary for one to be taken care of?

For clients who have never attended a Twelve Step meeting, I use these meetings as "Rorschach inkblots." As they tell me all the reasons why they don't want to, or can't, attend, I am learning about their unconscious fears. In other words, clients must contend with Twelve Step meetings whether they attend them or not. I may ask them to drive by a meeting while it is in progress in order to observe their feelings and fantasies. I may ask them to park the car one week and walk by the meeting, for the same purpose. This sets up a win/win situation. Either clients are faced more and more directly with their fears, or they act out and attend the meeting. Either result is valuable.

Group Therapy

Whether a client's co-dependence is secondary or primary, it invariably has a major impact on interpersonal relationships. Group settings maximize the opportunity to observe this impact and address it directly.

Therapy groups vary along a continuum from counseling to psychotherapy. The success of any group rests on how clear therapists are about the group's goals (e.g., education, support, experiential awareness, characterological change), whether their treatment techniques are compatible with these goals, and how carefully they select clients to participate in the groups.

Groups toward the counseling end of the treatment continuum are designed to promote greater access to healthy attitudes and behaviors which already lie within the co-dependent's grasp. Through education, awareness, and support, they help people extract themselves from situations, attitudes, and behaviors which intensify their co-dependent traits. This process closely parallels the alcoholic's use of abstinence to begin recovery; in fact, the underlying assumption of most counseling groups is that the co-dependent's current involvement in dysfunctional relationships and behaviors is a "toxin," similar to alcohol for the alcoholic. Counseling groups are valuable both for secondary co-dependents and as an initial phase of treating primary co-dependents.

For secondary co-dependents, such groups may be all the treatment they need to return to previous levels of health. While this does not change the tendency for "encounters with Narcissus" to activate and intensify co-dependent traits, the tools of recovery learned in group do diminish the likelihood of returning to a full co-dependent disorder. This is especially true for clients who actively participate in Twelve Step work. For this reason, most counseling groups are specifically designed as adjuncts to Twelve Step recovery. To the extent that counseling diminishes resistance to self-help meetings, clients may not require further treatment to live satisfying lives.

Counseling groups can serve most directly as an adjunct to Twelve Step work by quite literally guiding clients through working the steps. This is in the tradition of many inpatient alcohol treatment units, which often see their primary roles as integrating clients into AA. A less direct method of integrating treatment and Twelve Step work is to focus on the intertwining goals of detachment and concrete behavioral change. Neither of these is achieved without substantial emotional upheaval. Counseling groups help clients deal with the emotions they experience as they strive toward these goals, primarily through education, supportive validation, and experiential work.

Education

Education may come in many guises, from open didactics to basic reality testing, but it is a part of all therapy. Irvin Yalom expressed this when he described the dual nature of the therapeutic process as "an emotional and a corrective experience. We must experience something strongly, but we must also, through our faculty of reason, understand the implications of that emotional experience."[9]

For active co-dependents, education is invaluable. It is largely through understanding the existence and nature of co-dependent traits within oneself that denial is dismantled. The label "co-dependent" provides a fulcrum for reworking perceptions of one's entire world. Understanding co-dependent characteristics guides awareness inwardly instead of allowing it to dissipate into externalizing defenses. Simply being able to name many of the factors that create pain in one's life gives them enhanced reality. When properly used, an accurate cognitive framework helps create the container needed to validate and permit all the feelings which arise in early recovery.

The initial information needed by co-dependents can be summarized briefly as follows:

1. *Definition of Co-dependence:* Co-dependence is a pattern of painful dependence on compulsive behaviors and on approval from others in an attempt to find safety, self-worth, and identity.[10]
2. *Internal Nature of Co-dependence:* Co-dependence exists within you yourself; it isn't the "fault" of someone else.
3. *Hope:* Recovery is possible. A willingness to concentrate on your own contribution to the misery in your life is the most effective road to healing.
4. *The Characteristics of Co-dependence:* Co-dependence has five characteristics. They are:
   - changing who you are and what you are feeling to please others;
   - feeling responsible for meeting other people's needs at the expense of your own;
   - low self-esteem;
   - being driven by compulsions; and
   - denial and a distorted relationship to willpower.
5. *Co-dependence and the Family:* Co-dependence arises within dysfunctional families and can create family dysfunction.
6. *The Nature of Chemical Dependence:* When co-dependence exists in relationship to a chemical dependent, the nature of addictive disease must also be understood.

In Their Own Words:
How Clients Experience the
Five Characteristics of Co-dependence

It is extremely useful to teach the five characteristics of co-dependence in terms which match co-dependents' experience. The following quotations from the Johnson Institute video, "Co-dependence: The Joy of Recovery," provide examples of language and metaphors which the general public can relate to.

Changing who you are and what you are feeling to please others.

"We co-dependents are split between two worlds. One world is the facade which we show other people—the false version of ourselves. The other world is how chaotic, and fearful, and empty our life feels underneath. Someone once described being co-dependent as like being a lifeguard on a crowded beach, and being the only one who knows that you don't know how to swim.

"All of us co-dependents know what it feels like to put on a brave front, while we are crying, or dying, inside. We do this to protect ourselves from our fear that things will only get worse if we let people know how we really feel, or who we really are.

"We also do this because we co-dependents sacrifice our own identities in order to feel close to others. One co-dependent told me of struggling for years to become a professional actor, only because this was what his wife wanted him to be. Every time he began to doubt that this work was right for him, he bargained with his feelings until he could find some way of trying to be happy with this profession. He was afraid that, if he ever disappointed his wife, she would leave him. And so, for years, he tried to be something which he really wasn't. Like most co-dependents, he was terrified of being rejected and abandoned.

"We co-dependents have a tendency to change who we are in order to please other people. And, in the process, who we really are becomes more and more of a stranger even to ourselves. As co-dependents, many of us no longer know who we are, or what we want, unless we are in a relationship, and can take our cues from another person."

Feeling responsible for meeting other people's needs at the expense of your own.

"We co-dependents have our antennae up and working all the time, scouting the environment, watching everyone's face and listening to their tone of voice, always searching for signs of their disapproval or looking for ways to fix *their* problems. We actually get more upset if others are disappointed or hurt than if our *own* problems go unsolved.

"Most of us co-dependents believe we act like this because we're so generous. But real generosity stems from love that seeks no return. The truth is that we co-dependents are so afraid of rejection that we'll do anything to keep other people happy, including sacrificing our own needs in order to keep them from leaving us.

"How many of us at the end of a day have felt like we've been pulled in a hundred directions by other peoples' demands and needs, and wished we could have just ten minutes to do what *we* want to do? How many of us do not know how to say 'No' when we should?"

Low self-esteem.

"Most chemically dependent people feel ashamed of themselves. Despite their defensiveness and anger toward others, most are inwardly very critical of themselves. So perhaps it isn't strange that we family members also begin to feel badly about ourselves.

"As co-dependents, our low self-esteem comes from two main places: It comes from having very little *sense* of self to esteem. By always pleasing others, by always giving our power away, we turn our whole identity over to them, until we don't even know who we are any more. It's hard to respect people who seem afraid to exist, even when it's yourself!

"Low self-esteem also comes from believing that we truly *are* responsible for someone else's disease, for someone's alcohol/drug use. Once we believe this, we'll always feel inadequate when we can't control the chemical dependent's behavior. This mistaken sense of what *should* be under our control is at the very core of both co-dependence, and chemical dependence . . .

"Once low self-esteem is accepted as what we deserve to feel, it reinforces our belief that we need to please other people—because we have no faith that anyone would tolerate being with us unless we're serving them."

Being driven by compulsions.

"Most of us know what it's like to feel our life is being *driven*, that we don't have any real choices about what is happening to us. Instead, almost everything we do feels like it's a demand on us. The compulsions we co-dependents feel are endless: to keep the family together, to stop the drinking or other drug use, to save ourselves and the family from shame, to work, to eat or diet, to take physical risks, to spend or gamble, to have affairs, to be religious, to keep the house clean, and on and on. . . .

"The driven quality that compulsions bring into our lives accomplishes two things: First, it creates excitement and drama. As we battle our compulsions, the adrenaline begins to flow, and simple decisions, such as what to eat or how much to work, are turned into life-and-death struggles. This drama temporarily gives us a feeling of being more fully alive.

"Second, compulsions occupy a lot of time and block us from our deeper feelings. We co-dependents often get locked into our own compulsive behaviors in order to avoid more painful feelings of fear, sadness, anger, and abandonment caused by someone's chemical dependence.

"Compulsions can eventually affect our physical health as well."

Denial and a distorted relationship to willpower.

"And this brings us to the core of co-dependence. This final characteristic is the most critical. During our recovery, dealing with it becomes the eye of the needle through which we *must* pass if we're ever going to find the freedom, joy and self-esteem we long for.

"Denial, and an unwillingness to accept human limitations, are the two most destructive parts of the 'ism' of alcoholism. In our own way, we co-dependent family members fall into the same distorted relationship to reality and willpower. Just like the alcoholic, we deny reality and think we can change anything if we use enough willpower.

"We often refuse to see that a family member is chemically dependent, or we refuse to acknowledge that our children are being hurt. Our shame, and our desire to keep things under control, cause us to underestimate the problem, to excuse it in order to avoid having to admit that someone in our family has a disease. We hide the problem from others who might be able to help. We hide our feelings from ourselves. And we deny our own compulsive behavior. . . .

"As co-dependents, we are driven by the firm belief that our strategies fail because of personal inadequacy. When we can't control the drinking or other drug use of someone we love, we blame ourselves for not trying hard enough, or for not trying the right way. There's nothing wrong with trying to figure out how to help someone who is chemically dependent, as long as we realize that we're not the cause of it, that we can't control or cure it. But, when our own overbearing sense of responsibility and self-esteem begin blinding us to the fact that we don't have direct power to stop another person's chemical dependence, we actually become part of the problem.

"The ability of our willpower to change the world is far more limited than most of us want to believe. We co-dependents are stubborn about looking realistically at the limits of our willpower, especially the limits of our willpower to control other people, or our own emotions."

Supportive Validation

The facts about co-dependence can be condensed into a few formal lectures, but internalizing these facts and applying them to one's own life may take considerable time and effort. This is the period of treatment when supportive validation of clients' feelings becomes increasingly important.

The single most powerful approach to supporting a secondary co-dependent's struggle back to health lies in the validation that comes from his peers. The majority of groups run for co-dependents fall into this valuable category. The primary technique employed in such groups is the shared story. Group members empathize with each others' failures, understand the depth of pain that comes from feeling abandoned, and normalize, even celebrate, steps each makes toward health.

Therapists are free to help clients explore some of their individual blocks to feelings, or to connect with the group. Each member of the group is challenged to stay out of every other member's story, and therapists are charged with modeling this as well as possible. When group members attempt to fix someone's problems with willpower, this can be pointed out. When the group shies away from someone's feelings, this can be pointed out. When co-dependent interactions begin to develop in the group—for example, when one member takes responsibility for another member's feelings, this can be pointed out.

The overall effect of such counseling groups is to generate a supportive enough atmosphere that members can begin to explore what the characteristics of co-dependence actually look like in their own lives. Some therapists work best with a topic-oriented structure. Others start with check-ins and develop the group from material presented at the beginning of each week's meeting. Still others stimulate interactions with designed exercises. In all cases, the goal is the same: to bring into awareness behaviors and feelings which stem from group members' co-dependence. Denial and ignorance melt in the solvent of support and validation.

Experiential Work

Experiential work in counseling groups is popular with many clients and therapists. Perhaps this popularity stems largely from the message implied in therapists' initiating experiential exercises: "Your feelings are so valid and legitimate that I will search for them." This invitation to experience feelings is very powerful, as are the techniques of guided imagery, psychodrama, family sculptures, trance induction, etc. It is this very power which makes me cautious, and therefore a less than objective commentator on the subject. While experiential work is undoubtedly useful with some clients, enabling them to retrieve lost memories and rediscover previously rejected emotions, it is not without dangers.

Experiential work is valuable only to the extent that clients are able to integrate their evoked experiences. Powerful experiential techniques often present clients with more psychic material than they can integrate at the moment. These techniques are too frequently used in settings (workshops, lectures, time-limited programs) which don't permit follow-up of the continuing effects of opening clients to deep emotions. The danger of overwhelming clients increases when elements of PTSD are also present. In general, the most powerful work should only be attempted with clients who have been thoroughly screened, and in groups which provide the time and guidance for clients to integrate the experience. The most prudent approach is to restrict experiential work to clients who are already in ongoing therapy.

The very nature of co-dependence creates additional dangers with experiential techniques. Because co-dependents are such perfect mirrors, it is always difficult to distinguish which experiences have truly been reawakened within them, and which have merely been taken on due to clients' excessive suggestibility. The leading, trance-inviting techniques inherent in experiential work should be expected to have special power with clients who take their identities from others. It is not uncommon for clients to view therapy as a process of having something dramatic done *to* them. Such a perspective is clearly consistent with a co-dependent personality structure, and may be reinforced by experiential work.

Finally, the pull on therapists to work their magic exerts compelling force toward the creation of gurus. The willingness to occupy such a role is not outside the realm of possibility for any therapist with unmet narcissistic needs. Perhaps it is recognition of this tendency within myself which makes me cautious with experiential work. On the other hand, perhaps medical training, with its caveat to "First, do no harm," has also had its effect.

TECHNIQUES FOR TREATING
PRIMARY CO-DEPENDENCE

By definition, primary co-dependence means that the client's baseline character structure has been co-dependent since childhood. The goal of treating primary co-dependence is to help clients re-own their narcissistic needs, mature their echoistic needs, and achieve a sense of identity which is capable of moving through rapprochement. These characterological changes are achieved through using the transference to rework childhood developmental tasks. The psychotherapy model serves as the most effective framework for treatment.

Individual Therapy

The criteria for determining whether an individual client with primary co-dependence should be referred to individual or group therapy are essentially the same as for secondary co-dependence: crisis, depression, anxiety, internal disorganization/dual diagnosis, PTSD, vacillating between co-dependent and narcissistic character structure, resistance to group, and problematic hierarchical relationships, or simply a preference for individual work (when this does not conflict with the client's best interests).

Individual psychotherapy for primary co-dependence follows essentially the same course used in the treatment of most personality disorders. It proceeds through four stages:[11] 1) engagement, 2) identifying distortions in the client-therapist relationship, 3) replacing these distortions with reality, and 4) termination.

Stage 1:
Engagement

Most individuals who enter psychotherapy have little or no concept of what they are getting into. Indeed, most clients lack the *capacity* to comprehend what they are about to experience. In a sense, this is the reason they enter therapy in the first place. Although this state of affairs is frequently hidden behind a wall of knowledge about the concepts of therapy, it is the *identity* of the person who has this knowledge which psychotherapy aims to affect. The current identity cannot grasp what the *experience* of an expanded identity will be.

Engagement begins when the therapist's affect attunements to the client are received—for example, when the co-dependent shares her fear of being abandoned by the therapist and allows the therapist to respond to this fear. A direct human connection has been made—an emotional link. There is now a basis for trust.

Establishing an emotional link doesn't mean that you have to intuit a client's feelings or have the same feelings. It does mean that you must be present and focused enough to recognize when the client is having feelings and respond appropriately.

Unlike narcissistic clients, who make it extremely difficult to form emotional links, co-dependents actively seek empathic connection with others. The fact that they make it so easy can obscure several important points. First, the emotional link is often lopsided, with co-dependent clients more linked to the therapist than they can tolerate the therapist being linked to them. Second, co-dependents often restrict the empathic connection to feelings they have about events *outside* the therapy setting. The therapist is used as confirmation that other people are treating them badly, and that they have a right to feel hurt and angry.

It's much harder for co-dependents to tolerate an empathetic connection to feelings about events *inside* the therapy setting, since this creates an immediacy to the relationship which is hard to control, and therefore anxiety-provoking. That is why, in many cases, it takes considerable time to engage co-dependents on the level beneath their public facade. Until this happens, there can be no direct work on the transference level. The client cannot tolerate interpretations of the transference.

An indirect way to approach engagement is through detailed discussion of childhood and family-of-origin issues. Focusing on the relationship that exists between a client and his parents provides historical information about any projections the client is making, opens the world of hierarchical relationships to discussion, and allows enough experience to accumulate between the two of you for the client to develop enough trust to permit engagement in the here-and-now.

It is useful to explore the different approaches necessary to engage narcissistic and co-dependent personalities, since the two are complementary to each other. (For a detailed discussion of the development of these two personality disorders and their relationship, see Chapter 4 of Volume One, *Evaluation*.) The basic principle of treating narcissistic personality disorder is to forge an empathic connection with the client's vulnerability, which his grandiosity is designed to protect against.[12] In other words, getting the narcissist to share his pain and disappointment at being limited, and his fear of being inadequate and dependent, is the gateway to forming a potentially therapeutic relationship. The more he shares with you, the more willing he becomes to depend on your empathy. This differs from simply listening to the narcissist's recitation of resentments, which points the finger externally. An empathic connection exists only when the focus is turned inward.

The basic principle of treating co-dependent personality disorder is to forge an empathic connection with the client's fear of separation and autonomy. In other words, getting the co-dependent to share his desire for, and fear of, autonomy is the gateway to forming a potentially therapeutic relationship. The more he shares with you, the less isolated he feels, despite your willingness to acknowledge the inevitability of that separation. This differs from simply listening to the co-dependent's descriptions of being abandoned, which point the finger externally. The reality of this abandonment, perceived or actual, must be respected. But abandonment can be survived if autonomy develops. An empathic connection with the co-dependent's fear of this autonomy exists only when the focus turns inward.

Stage 2:
Identifying Distortions in the
Client-Therapist Relationship

A client's initial stance toward you will be governed by her unconscious effort to get you to be the parent she never had. In a sense, "parenting" is what you will do during therapy, but not the kind of parenting your client thinks she needs. Because she developed her image of the "perfect parent" in the midst of developmental arrests, her idea of parenting and the benefits it will bring is presumably more infantile than yours. Your task, in the midst of all this, is to identify three facets of transference which distort the client-therapist relationship: 1) expectations based on how the client experienced her parents, 2) projections based on feelings she is disowning, and 3) distortions born of archaic needs surviving into adulthood.

1. Experience. Human beings learn from their experience. Since the therapeutic relationship is a symbolic recreation of the hierarchical relationship that existed between a client and her parents during childhood, your client is likely to expect the same behavior from you that she saw from her parents. For example, if her parents were untrustworthy, it's going to be difficult for her to trust you immediately. Expecting her to feel otherwise is expecting her to be freed from her past.

It's only logical that the defenses raised in response to parental behaviors will be imported into the therapeutic relationship from the beginning. If these defenses are met with anything resembling a frontal attack, this will simply confirm the need for them. The transference of old defenses into the therapeutic relationship creates a filter through which all the client's current perceptions are sifted. This leads her to imbue you with the same emotional importance her parents had. Because of her biased perceptions, she continues to see her defenses justified in the here-and-now events occurring in your relationship.

2. Projections. Projections stem from those aspects of ourselves we attempt to disown, such as anger or aggressive impulses. Co-dependents invariably project their normal narcissistic needs onto others, especially those who assume a parental role. As a result, your client will likely see you as more self-possessed, confident, and self-centered than you may really be.

When you are present empathetically, this will be assumed to be just another therapeutic technique. The client believes that if she weren't paying you and providing you with interesting material, there would be no emotional connection. She projects her own disowned narcissistic sense of entitlement onto you.

3. Distortions. Distortions are reflections of the client's own archaic co-dependent needs, which lead her to see you as perfect and as an appropriate source of her self-esteem and security. Unmatured echoistic needs require a perfect parent to serve as the object of total dependence and the source of total love (including self-love).

These needs rarely appear in their naked form in adults. Rather, they are cloaked in layers of civility and adult rationality until their manifestations are greatly modified. Still, the basic needs are unchanged, and they continue to produce unrealistic expectations for how relationships can substitute for individual growth. Your client expects your special training to enable you to produce self-esteem in others, namely her. Your inability to do this is interpreted as unwillingness. She responds by becoming more ingratiating, trying harder to get you to care enough to work your magic.

After engagement, psychotherapy with the co-dependent client involves detailed observation of the distortions being imported into the therapeutic relationship. As noted earlier, much of the information you collect will stem from your own internal experience while in direct human contact with the client. The therapeutic process can advance only after these distortions are placed in a coherent developmental context.

Stage 3:
Replacing Distortions with Reality

The goals of this stage include 1) frustrating your client's unrealistic and archaic echoistic needs in such a way that they begin to mature, rather than being rejected and disowned; 2) promoting the re-owning of projected material, and 3) disconnecting transference of past experience from the present reality.

Maturation of echoistic needs means accepting the limitations that reality imposes on their gratification. One way to help your client's echoistic needs mature is by allowing her to experience your human limitations, then empathizing with her disappointment at your inability to "fix" things for her.

Promoting the re-owning of projected material, especially the client's normal narcissistic needs, means giving her room to express them and responding appropriately. For example, when she asks to reschedule an appointment to free that time for something else she wants to do, agreeing to reschedule helps her to re-own needs she may have disowned since childhood.

When you disconnect past experience from the present, you

enable the past to become the past. Transference sinks back into being feelings about past realities. This goal can only be achieved when the client is capable of acknowledging the full force of feelings connected to past events (i.e., connecting the emotional intensity with its original source), and focusing on the here-and-now realities of the therapeutic relationship enough that healthy experiences of intimacy can start balancing past, less healthy experiences.

The primary tools you will use during this stage include 1) a firm sense of your own boundaries, 2) comprehension of the transference, and 3) empathic responses to the client's frustration with this process.

The boundaries therapists use in treating clients are difficult to define. They are not physical realities, but neither are they merely concepts. In a way, they are like our skin, separating us from the rest of the world. Our minds possess a similar separateness from the surrounding world, although infants lack any sense of this separateness during their earliest symbiotic experiences.

The process of separation involves not only recognizing our separateness as a fact, but also exploring its nature. If you and I are not one and the same person, then where do I leave off and you begin? Which emotions are mine, and which are yours? Having personal boundaries means understanding and accepting those parts of the world you can be responsible for, those parts other people can be responsible for, and those parts which are out of everyone's control.

Therapists don't achieve a firm sense of their own personal boundaries from lectures and books. Instead, they achieve it through experiencing healthy relationships, whether in their own families of origin, or through undertaking their own psychotherapy, prolonged supervision, and/or disciplined practice of a program of recovery. Boundaries are not intellectual constructs. They are sensed as palpable psychological realities. When they are challenged, something akin to a physical sensory experience occurs. It should come as no surprise that individuals with their own co-dependent issues are at particular risk of losing a sense of their own boundaries by becoming therapists who treat ACAs, co-dependents, chemical dependents, borderline clients, and those with narcissistic personality disorders.

Comprehension of the transference means recognizing when clients import distortions into the therapeutic relationship (a process which is possible only when your own boundaries are clear), and placing these distortions into their proper developmental context. Placing here-and-now issues (such as a client's frustration at not having archaic echoistic needs gratified) into their developmental context informs you about their underlying significance and suggests specific therapeutic directions to take.

For example, when a client named Gwen asked me to hug her at the end of a session, I responded by exploring her request. She told me that a friend of hers was seeing a therapist who was "much warmer" than I—the two of them exchanged hugs at the beginning *and* end of each session. Gwen felt that her therapy depended upon whether she could get me to become equally warm and demonstrative.

When I refused, Gwen was hurt and frustrated. But instead of empathizing with her frustration, I made the mistake of explaining in very rational ways that she was trying to "make" my love heal her, that she was substituting a physical show of intimacy for the real thing . . . I may even have offered a lame comment about how physical contact could confuse the transference. Meanwhile Gwen got the message that she wasn't supposed to be frustrated by my refusing to hug her. My explanations were pulling her out of symbolically replaying her childhood issues and into her adult experience, which she was supposed to understand and not feel. It was not until I changed course and began empathizing with how difficult it was to be frustrated by my refusal, rather than why it was important for me to refuse, that we were able to get back on track. This allowed Gwen to have a new experience with someone in a hierarchical relationship who was simply confronting her with an uncomfortable facet of reality.

In cases like this one, the client's echoistic need is not rejected. By being optimally frustrated, it is actually affirmed, even as it is not being met in the way the client wants. Therapists must rest quietly in the knowledge that empathy is the appropriate response to expressions of the universal echoistic need which cannot be satisfied directly. As clients' echoistic needs begin to mature, they will find that these needs are increasingly being met.

Remember that the work co-dependents must do within the transference is twofold: While they are maturing archaic echoistic needs, they must also re-own normal narcissistic needs. For the co-dependent ACA, becoming more realistic about the disease of chemical dependence and how it affected his parent can remove a major obstacle to re-owning his projected narcissism. Otherwise the parent continues to serve as a very convenient receptacle for the client's disowned narcissism ("convenient," because it is usually true that the addicted parent was functionally narcissistic—but this doesn't alter the fact that the client is using this parent to rid himself of his own narcissistic impulses). Interestingly, one reason some ACAs resist the disease concept of alcoholism is because it disrupts the projective process. The parent's role as "whipping boy" begins to be undermined by a reassessment of reality. As the parent's image is rehabilitated, it becomes more difficult to spill one's own narcissism into the same vessel.

Some moments in therapy provide unique opportunities for helping clients re-own their narcissistic needs. A particularly valuable one is when clients cannot tolerate praise or appreciation. Being the center of such intense attention feels uncomfortable and dangerous to them. They may humbly demur while simultaneously feeling great anxiety.

The reality is that permitting oneself to be seen as praiseworthy requires re-owning one's narcissistic needs. You can facilitate this process by refusing to be deflected by a client's false humility or anxiety. Seize the moment by confronting him directly with your praise, exploring how this feels to him, and encouraging him to tolerate, if not enjoy, the experience. There's a big difference between trying to heal clients through praise (which is what co-dependents think they want) and what I am describing here: *using* praise to help clients confront their disowning of normal narcissistic needs.

The ultimate goal of this third stage in the process of individual therapy for primary co-dependents is a *relational shift* between client and therapist. As Sheldon Cashdan describes it, "patients begin to realize that their maladaptive ways of relating to the therapist are no longer viable. Their behavior takes on a less driven quality and they begin to interact with the therapist somewhat differently. . . . A series of difficult interchanges has been enacted and the participants have come through much together. There are still some important occurrences that loom ahead, not the least of which is termination, but the character of the therapy has definitely changed."[13]

"The Militant Seeker of Reparenting" vignette presented earlier in this chapter illustrates a relational shift. When Simon fell into despair after trying everything he could imagine to get me to love him enough to make him healthy, he seriously considered leaving therapy, convinced that he was never going to get what he came to therapy for. The shift came for him when he realized that he had gotten *some* of what he wanted from me. I had held him in high regard from the moment we had met. While this did not solve his problem of low self-esteem, it was too valuable an experience to lose by leaving therapy. He revised his reasons for being in therapy. In a sense, he decided to settle for less than what he had originally wanted. But his reason for settling was a healthy one. He saw that what I was giving him was all that a therapist could give him. When he began relating to me from this perspective, a relational shift had occurred.

I interpret this relational shift as evidence that characterological change has begun. The client has made it through a symbolic reenactment of the rapprochement crisis. He has come to more realistic terms with the therapist through the processes of maturing echoistic needs, re-owning narcissistic needs, and expanding his sense of self enough to experience both of these needs simultaneously. He can even experience paradoxical needs, such as the need to be autonomous and the need to be dependent. As a result, he can now have relationships which contain elements of paradox, such as an acknowledgment of the separation between two individuals who nonetheless strive for whatever human contact is possible.

Only *after* a client has come out on the other side of this relational shift can he begin to understand the transference. To tell a client that he is treating you in a particular way because of unresolved feelings toward a parent (i.e., to make a transference interpretation) is pointless as long as his transference is causing him to perceive you as being no different than that parent. He will see no reason why he shouldn't react to you in the same way he reacted to the parent.

Only *after* a client has personally experienced that you're different from the parent can he begin to see the truth of transference interpretations. From this point on, interpretations will provide him with one more perspective (usually a new cognitive framework) for understanding, and thereby integrating, the changes which have occurred in the course of therapy.

In general, I use transference interpretations less to promote the therapeutic process than to facilitate the integration of change which has already begun. As a result, I use interpretation more toward the final stages of therapy.

Stage 4:
Termination

Termination with co-dependent clients is no different than termination with any other successfully treated personality disorder: The process is a bittersweet affair during which most issues of loss, abandonment, and dependence are revisited one last time, often over a period of several months.

I usually have two goals for termination. First, I like to measure a client's readiness for termination by how she responds to my efforts to explore her motives and feelings about ending therapy. Does she resist exploring all of her potential feelings? Do defenses reappear, and is she willing to acknowledge and explore them? Does she remain emotionally present during those moments when sadness and loss coexist with pleasure and celebration?

Second, I maintain a steady focus on the here-and-now, even when old issues are being retraced. Clients often resist confronting their here-and-now feelings about termination by focusing on past events which are being recapitulated. This can be a way to avoid dealing with the real relationship between client and therapist, which is ending. By concentrating their attention on the real losses occurring in the present, clients can significantly deepen the work they have done to resolve the rapprochement crisis. Termination is the first event which puts this new resolution to the test—not hypothetically, but in concrete and emotionally charged terms.

When clients have developed enough faith in themselves (a function of matured narcissism) to trust that they can tolerate separation without perceiving it as abandonment (a function of matured echoism), individual therapy has reached its most glorious, and truly bittersweet, conclusion.

Group Therapy

For primary co-dependents, groups at the counseling end of the treatment continuum (described earlier in this chapter, in "Techniques for Treating Secondary Co-Dependence—Group Therapy"), may prove absolutely critical as preparatory treatment for transferential work. Although these groups are not designed to promote the characterological change necessary to permanently alter the baseline level of co-dependence, they can keep clients sufficiently out of a crisis mode, or sufficiently detached from dysfunctional relationships and behaviors, to make them available for transferential work. Facilitating clients' participation in Twelve Step groups as well is especially valuable, since the ongoing support they provide smooths the difficult transition to transferential psychotherapy. Transference dynamics are less diluted and confused when this support comes from an anonymous program rather than a counseling group.

The goal of psychotherapy, as I have defined it, is to promote basic characterological change through working with clients' transference. While pursuit of this goal is optional for secondary co-dependents, it is essential for primary co-dependents. Rationale for the use of group psychotherapy stems from the object relations belief that significant aspects of mental illness emanate from disturbed interpersonal relationships. Freely interactive groups develop into social microcosms in which the members inevitably recreate the same interpersonal dysfunctions which characterize their lives outside the group.[14] Group therapists thereby have the unique opportunity to see a client's co-dependent behavior manifested in a variety of interpersonal relationships with other group members, as well as in the events which trigger it.

Clients have a strong and immediate tendency to see their group as a symbolic family.[15] This tendency is enhanced whenever a group is homogeneously composed of adults from dysfunctional families of origin. This "family transference"[16] leads clients to recreate the same roles for themselves and others, adopt the same defensive postures, and experience the same feelings as they did in their original families. Because primary co-dependence is intrinsically interpersonal in nature, resulting from distortions and arrests in the development of autonomy, interactive group therapy can be an extraordinarily powerful treatment modality *for those clients with sufficient ego strength to work effectively in an unstructured setting.*

However, our experience at Genesis with psychotherapy groups explicitly organized for co-dependents (i.e., members meet diagnostic criteria for co-dependence, and are currently, or have recently been, in a dysfunctional relationship) has been that they often have difficulty moving beyond the initial, cautious stages of interaction into effective group work. (This difficulty is present, but less so, when groups are explicitly organized for ACAs.) The intrinsic tendency of co-dependents to exist through reflecting others creates a polite atmosphere in which confrontation is almost phobically avoided. Left to their own devices, homogeneous groups of co-dependents may slip into frictionless states of stable equilibrium. The predominant transference is that other group members, including (and especially) the therapist, are controlled by narcissistic needs. There is fear that voicing dissatisfaction with the group will be seen as being critical of others, which puts the speaker at risk of being abandoned. At the same time, voicing dissatisfaction also implies accepting one's own personal needs—a trait which is largely absent in co-dependents.

Despite difficulties in pulling co-dependents into effective group work, the basic techniques and dynamics of interactive group psychotherapy with co-dependents (described in Chapter 6 of this volume) do not differ from other populations. For the moment, it is important only to stress the delicacy of interactive group work. Creating an atmosphere in which clients act with maximum spontaneity is essential to the effectiveness of such groups, but spontaneity is a precarious quality. The conditions that foster it must be carefully and jealously guarded, for they can be contaminated by a therapist's most innocent actions and subtle influences. Whenever a therapist becomes overly active, this gives clients reason to believe that their own behavior in group has been induced or provoked by the therapist's actions. Unless clients feel they are acting spontaneously, they are unlikely to see their own responsibility for problems that arise in the group.

There is an infinite number of ways in which therapists can inadvertently intrude on the interactive group process. Many of these intrusions are countertransferential in nature—e.g., an inability to tolerate silence; a narcissistic need to remain the focus of attention; emotional blind spots resulting from personally unresolved issues. On the other hand, many of these intrusions come from lack of clarity regarding the nature of interactive group therapy. Groups are optimally effective only if they are set up as interactive from the start, and only if therapists consistently restrict their interventions to exploring the relationships which spontaneously develop, or fail to develop, in the group.

This means that techniques such as guided imagery, formal group check-ins, meditations, homework assignments, experiential exercises, etc., are *strictly contraindicated*. While they have their legitimate place in other settings with other therapeutic goals, they disrupt the interactive group process. They set a tone which is symbolically equivalent to the therapist saying, "If you group members don't spontaneously generate anything important on your own, I'll take over and make something happen!" A message like this doesn't have to be given very often to have a pervasive effect on the life of the group.

Metaphorically, the difference is between giving fish to a man or teaching him, through an apprenticeship, how to fish for himself. If the message is that clients are going to learn how to fish, but the therapist sneaks a fish into their basket whenever clients aren't learning their lessons and are getting a little hungry, the meaning of the entire endeavor is transformed. Ultimately, clients learn that the therapist lacks faith in their ability to take care of themselves in trying times.

When a therapist's self-esteem and identity are tied up in the ability of an interactive group to produce intense, dramatic interpersonal events, or simply to "work" continuously, clients are exposed to a restricted vision of what therapy can offer. And when the group members are co-dependents, they have little ability to separate from the therapist's limited vision. Any dissatisfaction a client has with the results of therapy are likely to be taken personally by the client and attributed to her own failings ("I didn't try hard enough"). She is not likely to voice her displeasure, out of concern for the therapist and fear of abandonment.

Therapists steeped in training for individual therapy often have difficulty changing their perspective to a systems focus. By "systems focus," I mean more than an acknowledgment that each member of the group, or "system," is affected by the actions of all other members, and that intrapsychic dynamics are influenced by processes occurring on the systems level. Interactive group therapists maintain a systems focus by being pervasively aware that every single member of the group participates in every single event in the group. The recurrent patterns of this participation begin to define roles for the members, and every single member has a perception of the roles all other members are playing. It is the experience of interpersonal events, and the subtle influences the group brings to bear to suppress or encourage the expression of these experiences, which is the raw material out of which interactive group work is fashioned.

Because interactional therapists focus attention primarily on group dynamics, they must have considerable tolerance for projections group members make upon them. Effective group work requires enough patience to give the group time to react to the distortions one of its members is making in her perceptions of the therapist. The therapist is then able to explore how these distortions are affecting relationships within the group, including how the individual member is responding to being confronted with the group's different perceptions, and what it feels like for the group to initiate feedback to one of its members.

While the theory and practice of interactive group therapy do not have to be modified to respond adequately to properly screened co-dependent clients, a homogeneous group may be expected to produce particularly intense pressures on the therapist to be a "guiding light." When in the midst of massively frustrating a group's call to be the ideal parent with whom everyone can merge, it's hard to resist the temptation to *teach* clients that gratifying this need would not be in their best interests. The goal of interactive group therapy with co-dependents is to accept their echoistic need as normal and legitimate, even as clients experience its frustration. To "teach" them out of this need is to reject it on a subtle level, while inadvertently subverting the group process by confirming that the therapist does in fact have the wisdom group members have come for.

RESIDENTIAL TREATMENT
FOR CO-DEPENDENCE,
PRIMARY AND SECONDARY

A variety of residential treatment programs for co-dependence have arisen, usually in conjunction with established chemical dependence treatment units. These programs generally range from five days to four weeks in length. They are usually based on Twelve Step approaches that parallel inpatient CD programs. Treatment consists of a mixture of educational lectures, experiential exercises (e.g., psychodrama and gestalt), videos, group meetings, individual counseling, journal writing, homework exercises, meditation, physical and nutritional therapy, Twelve Step study, and recreation. Aftercare is based on the same premises as aftercare for chemical dependence—namely, a less intense continuation of what has occurred during the inpatient phase. Shorter programs tend to move clients through their program in phase, while longer programs are designed to permit clients to enter the treatment at any point in the program's cycle.

Residential programs differ in many ways, including how they define co-dependence (and the clarity of their definition), how much pre-admission evaluation occurs, the sophistication of their treatment outcome studies, and their diligence in arranging adequate follow-up treatment. In some cases, treatment enthusiasm has outstripped treatment competence, a state of affairs motivated by sensitivity to the historical lack of treatment for co-dependence, ignorance of the complexities of psychotherapy for characterological issues, and monetary pressures.

The framework I have developed for co-dependence as a set of personality traits complementary to narcissism does not in and of itself suggest a major role for residential treatment. However, there are two sets of circumstances in which residential treatment represents an attractive choice for some clients.

First, co-dependents do sometimes reach crises of life-threatening proportions, whether through depression, suicidal thoughts and behavior, or potentially catastrophic stress-related medical complications. Cases like these clearly warrant hospitalization during the crisis, and treatment of the life-threatening symptoms will benefit from directly addressing co-dependence issues as well.

Second, recovery is often difficult for co-dependents who remain enmeshed in dysfunctional relationships, or whose energies are depleted by the problems of daily living. In such cases, residential programs permit a period of detoxification from forces which keep a client's co-dependent traits activated, and provide a safe enough treatment milieu that intense experiential techniques can be used to push a client through material that would otherwise remain unavailable and unresolved.

Of these two sets of circumstances, the first—life-threatening crises—represents compelling medical necessity, and can occur with either primary or secondary co-dependence. For the second set—dysfunctional relationships, problems with daily living—residential treatment is potentially useful (versus medically necessary) for clients' recovery, and must be considered elective rather than essential.

In any event, the benefit of such experiences, for all their intensity, may be short-lived unless they are part of an ongoing commitment to the discipline of recovery and, in many cases of primary co-dependence, long-term psychotherapy. The danger of residential treatment lies in the implied "quick fix." The benefit lies in providing validation and structure to the client's decision to devote maximum effort to addressing his or her co-dependence.

TWELVE STEP PROGRAMS
AND CO-DEPENDENCE

Although Twelve Step recovery groups are *not* "therapy," they can be powerful promoters of healing. Therapists wishing to maximize their effectiveness with co-dependent clients must be intimately familiar with the steps and traditions guiding these fellowships, as well as with the content and dynamics of meetings. This knowledge increases your ability to refer clients to self-help programs and to keep therapy consistent with, and building upon, a client's recovery experience. It also ensures that what you offer your clients goes beyond what is available in working the Twelve Steps. Because of the critical importance of Twelve Step work for many, if not most, clients, a description of their relevance to co-dependence is in order here.[17]

As AA began drawing alcoholics into recovery in the late 1930s, many close relatives realized that their own personal problems could be solved by applying the same principles to themselves. During the early 1940s, wives of AA members began holding their own AA meetings for the specific purpose of focusing on their own common problems. By 1948, these family groups were being sought by so many that they applied to the AA General Service Office for official listing.

The decision was made that AA is for alcoholics; and so, at the suggestion of Bill W., several of the AA wives began their own Clearing House Committee in 1951 to coordinate the close to 90 family groups already in existence. These groups soon evolved into a separate fellowship, which contracted the first few letters of Alcoholics Anonymous into "Al-Anon Family Groups," formally adopted the Twelve Steps of AA almost verbatim, and later added the Twelve Traditions.

Today there are over 28,000 weekly Al-Anon Family Groups worldwide, including Alateen (begun in 1957), and the total continues to rise each year. Over 1,000 of these meetings focus attention on adults with one or more alcoholic parents (Al-Anon Adult Children of Alcoholics meetings). With each Al-Anon meeting averaging 12-15 members, an estimated 336,000-420,000 visits to meetings occur each week. Using data from an Al-Anon survey regarding the average number of meetings attended per week, it can be estimated that a quarter of a million people visit an Al-Anon meeting each week.

Two more fellowships have recently arisen: Adult Children of Alcoholics (ACA) and CODA (Co-dependents Anonymous). Both of these are proving to be new avenues for co-dependents to work essentially the same program of recovery first described by AA.

Since the Twelve Steps and Twelve Traditions guiding self-help programs based on the AA framework were explained in some detail in Chapter 7 of Volume One, *Evaluation*, they will not be repeated here. For those readers who do not have access to Volume One, a discussion of the critical role the steps and traditions play in recovery is repeated in Appendix I of this volume.

4

TREATING UNDERLEARNING
IN ACAs

The treatment of underlearning in ACAs takes place on two levels. The first level consists of providing basic information every ACA should be exposed to as early in treatment as possible. At Genesis, we address the primarily cognitive aspects of this level with a yearly Community Lecture Series, and the affective aspects with a Weekend Intensive Workshop for ACAs. A time-limited group, the Genesis 18 Week Program, weaves informational and emotional elements together to help clients relate what they are learning to their own personal lives. This program is discussed in Chapter 6.

The second level consists of identifying and addressing the random gaps in experience each ACA has as a result of having grown up in an alcoholic family. These gaps are unique to each individual. We address this level by attempting to distinguish resistance from underlearning, and to correct underlearning directly, when appropriate.

BASIC UNDERLEARNING

Alcoholic families can be remarkably unaware. Their children can directly experience a parent's alcoholism without learning a thing about the disease itself. They can live through the disruption of family life by parental alcoholism without developing any cognizance of what has been disrupted or how. And they can design their lives to be the direct opposite of their parents' without having a clue that this keeps their parents in a central role.

Because of their family background, many ACAs enter therapy needing a considerable amount of basic information about the disease of alcoholism, normal family dynamics, how alcoholism disrupts these dynamics, abuse, neglect, child development, co-dependence, and recovery. The Genesis Community Lecture Series provides this information in four weekly two-hour lectures titled "The Family," "Growing Up in Fear," "The Struggle with Intimacy," and "A Time to Heal." The lectures are delivered in a supportive atmosphere designed to dissolve the sense of isolation most ACAs still feel when they are new to recovery.

Although the role of lecturer differs substantially from that of therapist, the human emotions being dealt with are the same. The early development of an empathic connection is as critical to successful communication in the lecture hall as it is in the therapy setting. It isn't essential for lecturers to be ACAs. And if they are, it isn't necessary to tell the audience about their personal history. But the willingness of speakers who are ACAs to disclose this information forges an important link with the audience, immediately creating trust and hopefulness.

While the therapist in the speaker recognizes that the basis for this trust involves a great deal of projection and wish fulfillment on the audience's part, the speaker in the therapist is more interested in using these feelings than exploring them. The goal is to give people information, to make the information relevant and palatable, and to motivate listeners to do something with the information they receive. Developing an empathic connection with the audience facilitates each of these goals.

We preface all public lectures by acknowledging that the topic may unleash deep and powerful emotions. We give audiences permission to experience their feelings as fully as they wish, and to use the tools all ACAs have to keep from being overwhelmed by their feelings: daydreaming, intellectualizing, physically leaving the room, note-taking, etc. By respecting both the power of peoples' feelings and the usefulness of their defenses, we gently remind the audience that we cannot tailor the presentation to every individual's particular needs and tolerances. Each member of the audience must remain responsible for monitoring his own feelings.

We begin many of the lectures with music. Songs such as "The Greatest Love" (George Benson or Whitney Houston), "The Rose" (Bette Midler), "The Living Years" (Mike and the Mechanics), and "Fast Car" (Tracy Chapman) are a few of our choices— songs about personal dignity, the need to be loved, blame and guilt, chemical dependence, and other topics with which listeners will feel a personal connection. Music cuts through many layers of defense against feelings and orients the audience to the emotional significance of what is about to be said. At the same time, it permits the speaker to remain somewhat apart from the trigger for these emotions, which establishes her as the source of safety— as the container rather than the releaser.

Lecture 1: "The Family"

When I give this lecture, I start with a bit of personal history describing my own experience with an alcoholic father. This introduces the idea that many ACAs have little experience with healthy families, which leads naturally into a description of the characteristics of healthy, functional families. (These are described in detail in Volume One, Chapter 2.)

Characteristics of Healthy Families

Healthy families share the following characteristics: 1) safety, 2) open communication, 3) self-care, 4) individualized roles, 5) continuity, 6) respect for privacy, and 7) focused attention. These characteristics exist with relative consistency rather than absolute constancy, a fact I emphasize when discussing them.

• *Safety* issues include the basic needs for food, clothing, and shelter; restraints and limitations to prevent accidental injury;

provision of adequate health care; protection from the parents own hostile and aggressive impulses; and sufficient emotional availability on the parents' part.

• *Open communication* is attained by a balance between encouraging all family members to express their needs and concerns honestly, and respecting the age-appropriate abilities of each family member to comprehend the world. In other words, the value of open communication is balanced against children's need for safety.

• *Self-care* encourages each family member to take responsibility for getting his own needs met. The assumption is that the family as a whole will function better if members are supported in reaching their own individual goals.

• *Individualized roles* are chosen by each family member. Discussing this characteristic gives speakers an opportunity to introduce the "traditional" roles found within alcoholic families, and to move people beyond concrete thinking about these roles.

Sharon Wegscheider-Cruse's descriptions of the Hero, Scapegoat, Lost Child, and Mascot roles[1] in alcoholic families have become such an integral part of the "folk wisdom" about ACAs that it's important to include them here. Many ACAs gain their first insight into the patterns of their own lives through hearing about these roles.

I talk about the *symptoms* of these roles (overachievement for the Hero, delinquency for the Scapegoat, solitariness for the Lost Child, and clowning/hyperactivity for the Mascot) and the underlying *feelings* of each (inadequacy/guilt for the Hero, hurt for the Scapegoat, loneliness for the Lost Child, and fear for the Mascot). I emphasize that each role arises out of the needs of the alcoholic family and are arbitrarily and rigidly imposed upon children. Then I compare this to healthy families, where children are helped to discover the unique and flexible roles which arise from their own needs.

• *Continuity* of the family provides us all with the counterpoint for a wildly changing world. Family rituals (such as birthday and holiday celebrations) and routines (such as dinner time practices)[2] maintain this sense of continuity and connect our nuclear families to extended relatives and ancestors, giving each of us a place in history.

• *Respect for privacy* overlaps with safety and self-care. Healthy families recognize the need of every member to dwell alone in her internal world from time to time, as well as the need we all have for modesty (physical and emotional). Respect for each individual's private world is a concrete manifestation of the boundaries which exist in healthy families.

• *Focused attention* has two facets: *schedule* and *quality*. Children don't need continuous attention, but they do need their parents' attention to be wholly focused on them from time to time. Healthy families focus this attention primarily according to the children's needs (schedule), not the parents'. The quality of this attention is measured by the range of emotional responsiveness the parent brings into the interaction with the child.

At this point in the lecture, I describe the two normal but incompatible needs experienced by little children: the need to be seen as important, and the need to be dependent. I point out that parents must respond to both of these needs in their children, and not focus primarily on one to the exclusion of the other. This plants the seed for later descriptions of co-dependence.

More Perspectives on Families

After introducing the characteristics of healthy families, I offer two additional perspectives for thinking about families: 1) the Family Life Cycle,[3] and 2) the phenomenon of Wet and Dry Cycles observed in alcoholic families.[4]

• *The Family Life Cycle.* Adults must grow into their role as parents in order for families to successfully navigate three tasks:

1) clarifying membership in the new family, 2) developing the major themes which characterize their particular family, and eventually 3) passing its legacy on to new families it has spawned.

Descriptions of the Family Life Cycle set the stage for understanding how arrests in a parent's gradual maturation (such as those that occur due to alcoholism) invariably stress the family environment and affect developing children.

• *The Wet and Dry Cycles.* While people are often aware of the personality changes which occur in alcoholics when they drink, they are less aware of the simultaneous changes which occur in family relationships. Not only does every member of the family have to relate differently to the alcoholic, depending on whether she is intoxicated or not, but non-drinking family members often relate to each other differently during wet and dry cycles. For example, levels of honesty which exist between siblings when the alcoholic parent is intoxicated may be stifled when the alcoholic is dry, in an effort to keep from rocking the boat and provoking another wet cycle.

Peter Steinglass' description of the cycles families go through in response to a member's intermittent alcoholism serves two purposes here. First, it captures the interest of audience members whose parents were binge drinkers by emphasizing the additional stress of never knowing when another binge was going to begin. It also serves as a transition to discussing alcoholism itself.

I end this part of the "Family" lecture with Steinglass' definition of the alcoholic family: one in which chronic alcoholism has become "a central organizing principle around which family life is structured . . . an inseparable component of the fabric of family life."[5] Alcoholism has inserted itself into virtually every aspect of family life and affected every family member.

The Disease of Alcoholism

Now the lecture shifts to a discussion of the disease of alcoholism, for ACAs must understand the nature of this unwelcome visitor before they can understand how it affects the family. There are two reasons why I stress the importance of studying alcoholism: 1) because every COA runs the genetic risk of being susceptible to the disease, and 2) few ACAs were taught the objective facts about alcoholism by their families. Direct experience with an alcoholic parent frequently leaves ACAs with childhood impressions of the facade an alcoholic parent presents to the world, but little understanding of the disease hidden behind that facade.

Our preference at Genesis is to have information about alcoholism presented by a staff member who is an ACA recovering from chemical dependence. This creates a special bond with the audience which would not exist if the speaker were identified only as a recovering alcoholic. The fact that the speaker can describe alcoholism from both an objective and subjective perspective further enriches the audience's experience.

We use three questions—"How did I get alcoholism?" "Why can't I control it?" and "Why do I continue to drink even when I know it hurts?"—as a framework for discussing 1) the disease continuum of alcoholism, 2) the disease concept of alcoholism, 3) the genetics of alcoholism, and 4) the role of denial and willpower.

1. The Disease Continuum. The effects of alcoholism range from a subtle stunting of emotional growth to overt physical dependence. These effects also change over time, with a gradual progression of symptoms as the disease worsens.

We encourage audience members to resist asking the black-and-white, yes-or-no question of whether one's parent was or wasn't alcoholic, and instead to explore whatever effects alcohol consumption might have had on a parent's personality. The symptoms of alcoholism are so numerous and varied that no individual can demonstrate them all. Because of this, every alcoholic can point to some symptoms he doesn't have, thereby disproving the diagnosis in his own case.

It's important to validate the fact that the majority of people who are harmfully involved with alcohol also appear to be socially respectable. The National Council on Alcoholism and Drug Addiction states that as many as 70 percent of alcoholics remain employed and part of a family. I call these the "polite" alcoholics, and stress that they greatly outnumber the stereotypical "skid row" alcoholic.

2. *The Disease Concept.* The target organ for alcohol is the brain—precisely the organ needed to understand that one is alcoholic. The effects of alcohol on the brain, which we describe in our lecture, include memory loss, blackouts, impairment of thinking skills, emotional constriction and distortion, impaired judgment, personality changes, and blurred boundaries. We place special emphasis on the fact that these impairments continue *beyond* the period of direct intoxication.

A few comments are made about the pervasive effects alcohol has on the rest of the body, especially the liver, stomach, muscles, endocrine system, and heart. I also note the probability that several members of the audience have lost their parents prematurely to alcoholism.

3. *The Genetics of Alcoholism.* To call attention to the elevated risk of chemical dependence that ACAs (and their children) face, we present the latest evidence for the genetic transmission of alcoholism. (Chapter 2 of Volume One, *Evaluation,* explores this topic in some detail.)

There are many ACAs who are not themselves chemically dependent. But the genetics of alcoholism still has serious implications for their children. Genes don't disappear just because they haven't been expressed. This is something all ACAs need to know.

Information about the genetics of alcoholism is also valuable to those ACAs whose parents were themselves COAs.

4. *The Role of Denial and Willpower.* Denial and willpower may be the most difficult aspects of alcoholism for ACAs to comprehend. Yet it is vital that they *do* comprehend them.

Within each ACA, there is still a child's voice, imploring the parent to understand the pain his drinking is causing the child.

The parent's failure to heed this voice is interpreted in the only way that seems logical to the child: as a personal rejection and proof that the child is not important to the parent. This voice is the reason ACAs attend lectures on alcoholism. It is also a major impediment to their understanding the real dynamics propelling their parents' alcoholism: denial and a distorted relationship to willpower.

I describe denial initially in fairly simple terms—as a normal human reaction to unpleasantness—and relate it to the difficulty all ACAs have acknowledging their parents' alcoholism. Denial is integral to alcoholism for many reasons: the impaired judgment which results from the direct effects of alcohol on the brain, the social stigma of being alcoholic, and the deep personal shame which most alcoholics feel as a result of their drinking. I illustrate the baffling nature of denial by telling the story of a therapist who "diagnosed" her sister as an ACA three months before realizing that she was one, too.

At this point, I don't try to explain the alcoholic's problems with willpower in any great depth. That comes later, in the discussion of co-dependence that is the topic of our third lecture, "The Struggle with Intimacy." For the time being, I describe the doomed efforts of the alcoholic to "prove" that he isn't alcoholic by controlling his drinking. While his efforts may seem praiseworthy, they are really part of his denial. I tell the audience that we will return to these ideas in the weeks ahead.

Conclusion

The "Family" lecture ends with a review of how the characteristics of healthy families are affected by the presence of an alcoholic parent. Emotionally evocative clinical examples are used to illustrate each point.

For instance, when discussing how *safety* may be destroyed on every level, either through neglect or abuse, I tell about the alcoholic physician who was responsible for watching his five-year-old in the swimming pool. He sat down to watch Saturday afternoon baseball on television and drank until he dozed off. *Open communication* becomes dangerous as those who speak directly about the alcoholism and how they feel about it are labeled "troublemakers."

Individual family members' efforts at *self-care*, such as attending Alateen meetings, are seen as "attacks" on the rest of the family. Children are pressured to take specific roles the family system needs for its survival, rather than being helped to discover their *individualized roles*. Family *continuity* is destroyed by the personality changes occurring in alcoholic parents, the random and arbitrary disruptions that take place whenever a family member gets drunk, and the invasion of family routines and rituals by the alcoholism.

Respect for privacy is trampled by intoxicated parents who continually ignore boundaries—like the father who bursts into the bathroom to urinate while his 13-year-old daughter is in the tub. *Focused attention* is given when the alcoholic needs closeness, which may happen in the middle of the night, and not according to the child's *schedule*. And the *quality* of this attention is gravely attenuated, leading to parents who may be less likely to recognize when a child's cut needs stitches because alcohol has made them biochemically unable to feel anxious.

It is important to place this first lecture in a wider context, since it tends to stir up people's pain without much talk about recovery. To counteract feelings of hopelessness, I preview for the audience what will be discussed in the following three weeks, emphasizing that the only justification for removing the scab which has covered childhood wounds for so many years is the promise of more effective, deeper healing.

Lecture 2:
"Growing Up in Fear"

We begin by briefly reviewing the "Family" lecture from the previous week, reminding the audience that alcoholism is a chronic disease which disrupts a family's normal functions (safety, open communication, etc.). Then we introduce the topic for this week's lecture: trauma.

Trauma

We describe trauma as the effects abuse and neglect have on children and tell how they may linger into adult life, ending with comments about what it's like when the drinking is not just a part of the past, but continues into the present day.

I find it helpful to introduce ACA characteristics by telling the story of Huckleberry Finn (see Appendix II). Huck has several qualities that many ACAs may see in themselves. For example, he gets bored when his life lacks drama. He is vulnerable to feeling intense guilt and depression. He escapes by faking his own death (a good metaphor for how many COAs minimize their own emotions and needs). He has a chameleon-like quality, allowing others to see in him whatever they need to, and a tendency to avoid conflict. He shows little reaction to news of his father's death, and he is unable to stop running away even when it's no longer necessary.

Mark Twain's story also contains some vivid scenes of Huck being held hostage by his intoxicated, hallucinating, and abusive father. Despite his many problems, Huck is a likable character. Because he is likable, audience members are willing to begin identifying some of these same characteristics within themselves.

Child Abuse

The topic of child abuse is highly charged for ACAs. Many are struggling with powerful feelings which threaten to explode whenever they come close to acknowledging the physical, sexual, or emotional abuse they experienced as youngsters. A sense of betraying the parent may conflict with their efforts to admit the truth. A deep sense of being "bad"—of "deserving" to be punished and abused—may arise as memories of abuse start entering their awareness. Other ACAs may have no specific memories of being abused, yet respond to information about abuse as though it had personal relevance.

We address this topic directly and give audience members a framework for thinking about it. Specifically, we talk about the five forms of psychological abuse identified by James Garbarino,

Edna Guttman, and Janis Wilson Seeley: 1) rejecting the child, 2) isolating the child, 3) terrorizing the child, 4) ignoring the child, and 5) corrupting the child.[6]

Next, we focus on the direct effects of the trauma of such abuse, using the framework of Post-traumatic Stress Disorder. We discuss the symptoms of PTSD—reexperiencing the trauma, psychic numbing, increased arousal/hypervigilance, and survivor guilt/depression. (The five forms of psychological abuse and symptoms of PTSD are described in detail in Volume One, Chapter 3.) We make it clear that these symptoms of being subjected to abnormal levels of stress are not the same as co-dependence, which we will look at more closely in the following lecture.

We end the first part of "Growing Up in Fear" by describing the normal defenses children develop in the face of trauma. In their black-and-white world, children begin to see themselves as "Sinners" in a world of "Saints," a view that offers a ray of hope, however illusory. (Again, for more on this, see Chapter 3 of Volume One.)

Characteristics of ACAs

The final part of this lecture is a review of the characteristics commonly seen in ACAs. Rather than present these in a confusing "laundry list" or in a highly structured clinical framework, we try to personalize them.

For example, I talk about how I, an ACA, went about preparing this talk, and what it's like to be giving it. I humorously own each of the following characteristics, making each more human and permitting audience members to identify with them through their empathy for me: fear of losing control, fear of feelings, fear of conflict, an overdeveloped sense of responsibility, guilt feelings, the inability to relax and have fun, harsh self-criticism, denial, difficulties with intimate relationships, feeling like a victim, compulsive behavior, a tendency to confuse love and pity, fear of abandonment, black-and-white thinking (especially when under pressure), somaticizing (experiencing emotions as physical problems), suffering from a backlog of delayed grief, being a reactor rather than an actor, and finally, being a survivor.[7] All of these characteristics are consistent with Claudia Black's three rules of survival for COAs: "Don't Talk. Don't Trust. Don't Feel."[8] Nearly every ACA with any awareness of recovery has encountered and recognizes these rules.

Detachment and Intervention

After describing the characteristics of ACAs, one of us relates our personal story of a parent who is currently drinking. At this point, the light-hearted tone of the lecture gradually gives way to the seriousness of dealing with a parent who is self-destructing. It becomes apparent that ACA characteristics are ineffective tools for coping with such a situation, and actually contribute to the pain, inadequacy, and hopelessness the ACA is experiencing.

The point of this story is to introduce the concept of detachment. The parent is still drinking, but the ACA has found ways to say what he needs to say, and has found release from the belief that there ought to be something he can do to make a parent stop drinking. We go on to explain that detachment is developed through two channels: by participating in Twelve Step Programs such as Al-Anon and ACA, and/or by seeking professional consultation about a potential intervention.

Intervention is a formal procedure for presenting reality in a receivable way to someone in denial.[9] Most ACAs have not explored the possibility of intervening in their parents' drinking. Encouraging them to seek professional consultation gives them permission to rely on someone else's perspective on the problem. The ACA is not expected to have sufficient objectivity to assess whether there is enough support among relatives, friends, and co-workers to do an intervention. By turning this decision over to a professional, the ACA is relieved of having to take personal responsibility for it. If the professional determines that an intervention is not possible, two things become clear to the ACA: she has done her best, and it's not her inadequacy that is preventing her from stopping her parent's drinking. The facts are simply that not enough of the family is willing or able to support the intervention, or else the alcoholic has divorced himself from the family enough to render their opinions impotent.

The value of exploring intervention is that it lets ACAs know they are not responsible for "making" a parent be different. If, in the process, the ACA is able to express her concerns, frustrations, and caring to a parent, her own recovery will grow, even if the rest of her family stays the same. This is the real message of recovery: that what needs to be done to achieve self-esteem is under our control, even though we have no control over the rest of the world.

This point is used to preview the next two lectures. We explain that the third lecture looks closely at co-dependence, including its mysterious facet, willpower. The fourth and final lecture outlines the steps which bring recovering ACAs closer to detachment.

Lecture 3:
"The Struggle with Intimacy"

We begin the third lecture with a bit of history on the concept of co-dependence, including these quotations from the AA "Big Book" and Vernon Johnson's *I'll Quit Tomorrow*:

- "Cessation of drinking is but the first step away from a highly strained, abnormal condition . . . [in which the] entire family is, to some extent sick."[10]
- "For every harmfully dependent person, most often there are two, three, or even more people immediately around him who are just as surely victims of the disease. They too need help and should be included in any thoroughgoing model of therapy. . . . The only difference between the alcoholic and the spouse [and children], in instances where the latter does not drink, is that one is physically affected by alcohol; otherwise both have the same symptoms."[11]

We then give several definitions of co-dependence to help the audience understand that important aspects of their own experience are being dealt with here. For example: "A co-dependent is someone who has another person's life pass before his eyes when he dies." The audience's reaction to this definition is significant—

some people groan, others giggle, others burst out laughing—since it indicates that several people in this room actually understand the strange idea this definition communicates. The speaker uses the laughter of self-recognition to begin breaking the isolation that keeps most co-dependents from sharing their experience. The point is made that co-dependence is a common human condition.

The Myth of Narcissus and Echo

The Greek myth of Narcissus and Echo is an effective metaphor for introducing co-dependence to the general public and professionals alike. (This myth is presented in Chapter 4 of Volume One.)

Co-dependents are very sensitive to Echo's fate. They identify intuitively with her experience, for it is theirs as well. In our lecture, we paraphrase Freud by saying that self-centered people are particularly attractive to those of us who have disowned our own need to be focused on as a way of making ourselves lovable. Subjugating oneself to someone else's narcissism is something most co-dependents can certainly understand.

We explain the origins of co-dependence in COAs by describing the child's incompatible needs to be important and to be dependent. Narcissistic parents are incapable of recognizing the child's need to be important, and encourage the need to be dependent. This naturally leads to a child's disowning her need to be focused on, while preventing her need to be dependent from maturing. The child becomes a co-dependent adult.

Characteristics of Co-Dependents

After exploring the myth of Narcissus and Echo, we go on to discuss the five characteristics most co-dependents share.

1. *Co-dependents change who they are, and what they are feeling, to please others.* This characteristic can be described as "impression management."[12] We illustrate it with many examples, including such mundane situations as being asked "What do you want to

do tonight?" and responding, "I don't care; whatever you'd like," or pretending to enjoy the same flavor of ice-cream as another person in an effort to make him like you.

2. Co-dependents feel responsible for meeting other people's needs at the expense of their own. Most co-dependents can relate to descriptions of going through an entire day without ever feeling they are doing anything *they* want to do, but are only responding to what others demand of them. They have no sense of choice. At the end of the day, they desperately need at least 10 minutes to do what they want, but even this is sacrificed to make sure that some final chore gets done.

3. Co-dependents have low self-esteem. If one's self-esteem is based on the ability to bring uncontrollable parts of the world under control, then one is doomed to fail. This idea has particular relevance to anyone who bases his own sense of self-worth on whether a family member stays sober.

We make the point that co-dependents have very little sense of "self" to esteem. In connection with low self-esteem, we introduce the concept of shame.

4. Co-dependents are driven by a variety of compulsions. As noted above, co-dependents can relate to descriptions of being tugged on from every direction all day long until they collapse into a chair late at night, pleading for just a few moments for themselves. The lack of the sense of choice they experience at times like these is also at the core of being driven by compulsions—of feeling that everything you do *has to be done.*

This lack of a sense of choice can be attached to a wide range of compulsive behaviors, from rescuing others to eating, cleaning, working, gambling, praying, sexual behavior, spending, etc. We explain that such compulsions serve several purposes: They organize one's time. They add drama to one's life. And they push other, more negative feelings into the background.

5. Co-dependents use the same denial and distorted relationship to will-power seen in alcoholics. This final characteristic is one that half of the audience will already understand, and the other half will be relatively impervious to. Comprehension doesn't rest on understanding specific facts as much as it depends on awareness of how willpower creates many of the problems in one's own life that it attempts to solve.

I approach the topic of willpower by describing it as the "eye of the needle" through which ACAs must pass before recovery can repair the fabric of their lives. Threading the eye of this needle begins with viewing willpower as a tool.

Like all tools, I explain, willpower is designed to perform certain tasks. Just as a hammer is great for pounding nails but useless for sawing boards, willpower has its limits, too. It can't affect the weather or reverse gravity. It can't make me grow taller. It can't directly dictate someone else's emotions, nor can it really dictate my own. For example, even if I decide to wake up in ecstasy tomorrow morning, that doesn't mean it will happen. What willpower *can* do, within broad limits, is to direct my attention and my muscles. Sheer determination *does* affect whether I stay in denial or become more aware of my feelings. Willpower may not be able to stop my impulse to drink, but it can force my legs to walk into an AA meeting in response to this impulse, rather than into a bar.

I conclude by arguing that ACAs have learned much of what they think they know about willpower at the knee of an alcoholic parent, who was gravely confused about the proper use of willpower. Recovery from co-dependence is similar to recovery from chemical dependence: Each requires extensive exploration of the realistic role willpower can play in human affairs.

Shame

Because shame deeply affects many ACAs, we insert a special section on it into this part of the lecture. Our goal is to validate and normalize many of the feelings audience members are having. Our message about shame covers these three points:

1. Shame is not shameful. Shame is a universal and important emotion in human development. As social animals, we are programmed to feel shame whenever our behavior deviates from that of the group. To be shameless is to not know how to behave, and to lack all modesty.

2. *Shame can become toxic.* When shame is used to take away a child's sense of worth, or when a parent's shame is unconsciously handed down to the next generation, it becomes destructive. Shame can be used to indoctrinate children into dysfunctional families and contribute to youngsters' hiding their true feelings behind a facade. When a child's shame does not evoke a parent's empathy, it becomes associated with feelings of abandonment.

3. *Recovery involves an acceptance of imperfection.* By expressing our real selves within healthy, recovering communities, we can discover what is appropriately private, versus what is shamefully hidden. By breaking the "don't talk" rule about our toxic shame, we can stop carrying the extra burden of inherited shame and our false selves. This leaves us better able to endure the human condition of imperfection—in ourselves, in others, and in our relationships.

Love and Sex

It is in "the struggle with intimacy" that co-dependence raises its head and becomes most destructive. Nowhere is this more true than in those relationships that combine love and sex, so we end this lecture by addressing this topic directly.

Love frequently begins with a gloriously romantic experience of being "swept off one's feet" and out of oneself. The euphoria of feeling complete often hides a dangerous loss of autonomy. During the first hot blasts of romance, few humans are capable of immediately distinguishing the difference between true attraction to another person and the compulsion to be with them. Co-dependents are handicapped in their ability to make this distinction for three reasons: 1) they confuse love and pity; 2) they fall in love with the drama of falling in love—and when the drama fades, they compulsively and repeatedly seek it elsewhere;

and 3) the mutual projective identifications between Narcissus and Echo are powerful glue. The immediate "chemistry" of such relationships can fuse people together into a tight relationship that actually has little to do with love.

Sex for co-dependents is frequently disappointing, compulsive, and/or terrifying. Disappointment is inevitable when actual sexual behavior is measured against the fantasies of ideal love. Sex can become compulsive when the co-dependent either 1) takes responsibility for the disappointment and feels compelled to fix it, or 2) substitutes the fleeting experience of acceptance that orgasm brings for the more solid sense of acceptance that comes from building a relationship based on mutual respect.

Sex coalesces, concretizes, and focuses virtually every core ACA issue, not just co-dependence. This is especially true if there is any hint of sexual abuse or impropriety in an ACA's history. To help audience members empathize with themselves if they are uncomfortable with their own sexuality, we describe the following five reasons why sexuality may scare them:

1. *Sensuality.* The capacity to be sensual (whether this is sexual or not) suffers when you armor yourself against feelings, have the tendency to be other-focused or to dissociate, and have a core sense of shame about your body.

2. *Vulnerability.* Few activities expose one to potential rejection, shame, and actual physical danger as concretely as does opening one's legs to be penetrated or allowing another person to fondle one's genitalia freely.

3. *Trust.* If you can't trust that others have your interests at heart and will not abandon you, it may be difficult to tolerate their using your body in pursuit of their own sexual pleasure, or passing off into sleep after orgasm.

4. *Personal needs.* There are few occasions when personal desires must be expressed in a more concrete form than during sexual

behavior. When this isn't possible, and especially when fulfillment of the other person's needs takes precedence, personal satisfaction becomes unlikely.

5. *Loss of Control.* Since loss of control is emotionally charged, moments of intense orgasm can be problematic. ACAs who cannot relinquish control will be terrified by orgasm, or unable to achieve it. On the other hand, compulsive sexuality can result if the circumscribed and contained nature of orgasmic loss of control becomes the only acceptable avenue away from an overly controlled life.

We end the third lecture by foreshadowing next week's topic— the hopefulness of recovery.

Lecture 4:
"A Time to Heal"

We approach recovery as a process of healing, characterized by a developmental sequence of steps which can be aided by both Twelve Step Programs and therapy. This approach divides the lecture into three natural components: 1) stages of recovery, 2) using Twelve Step programs, and 3) the role of psychotherapy.

Stages of Recovery

Originally, when telling ACAs about the changes that occur in recovery, we focused on four stages: 1) Survival, 2) Reidentification, 3) Core Issues, and 4) Integration. (These stages are discussed in detail in Chapter 7 of Volume One.) We soon learned that not all ACAs benefit from knowing about these stages. Some use them to denigrate their own lack of progress; others view them as mileposts to be raced through or trophies to be earned. Currently we still make mention of these stages, but we have developed two additional approaches to the topic.

First, we use narrative to teach about recovery. We tell a true story about the changes seen in an actual ACA's life as a result of recovery. In other words, we describe the features of the four stages but de-emphasize the labels. In fact, there is no clear division between the stages, and individuals tend to cycle back and forth between them, progressing by fits and starts as they work to deepen their recovery. Telling a story humanizes recovery and avoids giving ACAs a way to grade themselves.

Second, we present a framework for understanding recovery that is more cumulative than linear. We talk about the natural "healing forces" that exist within each of us, then describe three activities that seem to promote these healing forces: 1) honesty, 2) experiencing feelings, and 3) entering into community. (These activities are discussed in Chapter 1 of this volume.) ACAs can evaluate their lives in terms of these three activities—for example, by looking at the degree of honesty they are pursuing, the freedom with feelings they have achieved, and their willingness to enter into community with other recovering people.

It is only when all three activities are being fully engaged in that recovery can fully blossom. These activities comprise the discipline of recovery. They must be practiced daily, even moment-by-moment, to unleash the natural forces that heal psychic wounds. In this sense, discipline and faith are intimately related, for it is an act of faith to practice the discipline of recovery even during times when the fruits of recovery seem impossibly distant.

Using Twelve Step Programs

At this point in the lecture, we introduce and describe two aspects of Twelve Step programs: meetings and the Steps themselves. Describing what happens at meetings can take the mystery out of them for people who have yet to attend one. For those audience members who already do attend meetings, this part of the lecture can be made interesting by talking about how being in fellowship helps to free up the natural healing forces.

We discuss the Twelve Steps and the Twelve Traditions with an eye toward dissolving the more blatant resistances—for example, by stressing that the Twelve Steps are a spiritual, not a religious, program—and piquing people's curiosity about the benefits of attending meetings. (For more about the Steps and the Traditions, see Chapter 7 of Volume One or Appendix I of this volume.)

Few people will be moved simply by hearing that the Twelve Steps are intellectually stimulating, emotionally challenging, and genuinely substantive. They must somehow experience this stimulation, challenge, and substance in the speaker's authentic and coherent manner of communicating. On the other hand, testimonials praising the program are not all that's needed either. It's perfectly appropriate, even preferable, for the speaker to also express doubts and confusion about the Steps and meetings. These can be reassuring to people who fear being swept away into a "cult" experience.

The Role of Psychotherapy

Not all ACAs choose to enter psychotherapy; not all need to. But all should know something about when to seek therapy, how to find a therapist, and what being "in therapy" means. We try to provide at least some of this information in our final lecture.

In *A Time to Heal*, I suggest that ACAs ask themselves the following questions to help them decide whether to consider therapy:[13]

- Is your life threatened or your health in jeopardy?
- Are you in a self-abusive relationship with alcohol or other drugs?
- Are intimate relationships a problem for you?
- Do you find yourself unwilling to attend Twelve Step meetings?
- Do you have difficulty enjoying the quality of life you have achieved?

Today I include two more questions:

- Are you being physically, sexually or emotionally abused?
- Do you feel compulsive and out of control?

Many people, once they decide to enter therapy (or at least to explore the possibility), don't know where to start looking for a therapist. While the best way to begin is usually by obtaining recommendations from friends and other advisers, the final choice must be made by the individual. I suggest that therapists be chosen on the basis of their training (encouraging clients to inquire directly about this), their personal health (encouraging clients to trust their own instincts here), and the level of trust they inspire (encouraging clients to look for therapists who pursue honesty more than comfort).[14]

Finally, there is the question of which is "best," individual or group therapy. To help audience members start thinking about this, I offer a brief description of each. I say that group therapy is a powerful way to look at repetitive and dysfunctional patterns of relating to others, and individual therapy is a powerful tool for dealing with intense anxiety or depression, psychic numbing, crises that demand concentrated help, severely disorganized thinking, and excessive intellectualization, and for exploring the unfinished business that remains between a client and his or her parents.[15]

Although the preceding information is clearly presented in the form of guidelines, it can create problems that fall into the category of "a little knowledge is a dangerous thing." The sophistication of some ACAs, who have read about "healing the child within" and even "using the transference to symbolically rework developmental tasks of childhood," can feed a resistance to therapy just as much as it can help the process. The central issue here is that a therapist's understanding of therapy can never be adequately communicated to anyone who has not experienced it. Discussing transference with potential clients is comparable to describing the Mona Lisa to someone who has been blind from birth. The frames of reference of the speaker and listener are simply too far apart.

Similarly, it's reasonable to expect that many ACAs' concept of the therapist's "unconditional positive regard" does not include the optimal frustration necessary to mature the relationship beyond a child's conceptualization of parent/child inter-actions. In short, any meaningful discussion of therapy requires the development of a shared frame of reference, and that can ultimately be accomplished only through therapy itself.

Whether to give potential clients information about therapy, what kind of information to give, and how to ascertain whether they understand what you're saying is, admittedly, a dilemma. I take comfort from assuming that early analysts were equally bedeviled when they first encountered clients who were sophis-ticated enough to enter therapy "because they were neurotic."

In an effort to avoid fueling this dilemma, I impose the follow-ing guidelines on myself when discussing psychotherapy in the lecture setting:

A. I clearly state that I am stepping out of my role as a thera-pist for the moment.

B. I emphasize, above all else, that "getting into therapy" is the trick, and that this is a different process for each individ-ual. Seeing a therapist on a regular basis is not necessarily evidence that a client is "in therapy," which implies the client's willingness to enter into a therapeutic alliance for the purposes of facilitating introspection. All descriptions of what happens in therapy are understood differently, depending on whether a person is "in therapy" or not.

C. I explain that this difference is due to the fact that therapy is an *experience* which cannot be fully captured in intellec-tual concepts. A mystery is left lying at the core of this therapeutic experience.

D. I then proceed to provide all the information I have tradi-tionally given, contenting myself with knowing that, as a therapist, I cannot control the public's concept of therapy, and each individual client's preconceptions are just more grist for the mill.

Final Comments

The final lecture of our Community Lecture Series ends with an acknowledgment that the audience and speakers have been through a great deal in their eight hours together. We express our sense of privilege at being able to speak out on topics of such importance to each of them, and our hope that the information we provided has been useful.

At this point, we briefly describe the Genesis 18 Week Program (described in Chapter 6), explaining that it is designed to help people personalize and integrate all the information they have just been exposed to. We encourage people to explore Twelve Step meetings. We end by playing a song which celebrates recovery (such as "Together" by Hal Atkinson) and saying the Serenity Prayer: "God, grant me the serenity to accept the things I can not change, courage to change the things I can, and wisdom to know the difference."

IDIOSYNCRATIC UNDERLEARNING

During the course of either group or individual therapy, it's quite common for therapists to encounter ACA clients who profess ignorance of what constitutes normal human behavior. This ignorance may take a variety of forms. Intrapsychically, a client may be wondering how the "average person" reacts to a specific event, and with how much emotional intensity. Interpersonally, a client may question how the average person asks her boss for a raise, or informs his spouse of his anger. Within the therapeutic relationship, a client may ask for guidance regarding what she can appropriately expect from the therapist.

In all of these cases, the uncertainty a client is expressing represents a transaction between client and therapist. When the motivation for this transaction is resistance, rather than the result of idiosyncratic underlearning, the client is attempting to dissuade the therapist from applying any pressure toward action or change. Professing ignorance is intended to serve as a rationale for why the client should not be expected to act differently. It is a plea to be allowed to maintain the current level of pathology, usually to avoid deeper levels of anxiety that would result if real change started taking place. It is important to understand the sources of this fear before trying to remove a client's defenses.

On the other hand, when professing ignorance is motivated by a desire to receive guidance from the therapist to make action and change more possible, it would be a disservice to interpret such a request as resistance.

The traditional approach to resistance is to flush it out into the open, raise it into conscious awareness, explore it, and support a client during the process of change. The assumption is that resistant clients possess all the "knowledge" they need to make changes, but are blocked from action for one of two reasons: Either they are unconscious of their fears and therefore remain focused on "reasons" why change is not possible, or they are conscious of their fears and believe that their defenses will be overwhelmed if they enter the unknown territory of any new behavior.

The defense of rationalizing throws up one reason after another to explain the impossibility of change until it is exhausted, at which point it degenerates into a final, last-ditch effort—confusion and "not knowing." ACAs often speak of "feeling confused," as though this were a primary emotion. I do not consider confusion to be a feeling. It is the product of a rational mind at the end of its rope. Believable rationalizations have been tried and discarded, and all that is left is a murky cloud of debris, the disjointed bits and pieces of discredited "reasons." While we all react emotionally to being in such a state of confusion, the confusion itself is not a feeling.

Once clients accept that their confusion is not an emotion, they are often more willing to explore the fears and fantasies which lie on the other side of their resistance. By no longer censoring their thoughts during this exploration, clients allow subtle material from the unconscious to bubble up into awareness. It is often in the uncensored fears and fantasies about what might lie on the other side of change that a deeper level of resistance is discovered. Faith in this process stems from a belief that the closer clients come to dealing directly with the real source of their resistance, the closer they will move toward concrete change. "Confusion" is usually an elaborated defense, not only against change, but also against awareness of the real sources of resistance to that change. Underneath confusion is usually fear. The process of dissolving resistance involves helping clients confront this fear directly, and staying in relationship with them as they learn to tolerate this experience.

When confusion is in the service of resistance, it is a mistake to confront it with information. This only leads clients in the opposite direction. It shores up the faltering defense of rationalization and frees them from having to confront their underlying fears.

A different scenario unfolds when a client is exhibiting idiosyncratic underlearning, as opposed to the resistance motivated by underlying fear outlined above. Sometimes clients really have no legitimate guess as to how the average person might approach a particular problem, since healthy behavior in this area was never modeled in their alcoholic families. At other times, they have a reasonable guess but no confirming experience. By asking the therapist how "normal people" would proceed (or simply by professing ignorance as to how to proceed), they may legitimately be seeking out new, or validating, information.

It is always valuable to explore with clients how they think the average person might approach a particular problem. In those cases where I believe the client's family of origin was disrupted enough in its functioning to leave a gap in her experience around a particular topic, I may not hesitate to confirm the client's correct guess as to how most people would behave. Or, if there is no guess forthcoming, I might share my experience by saying how I have seen other people confront the same problem.

While becoming the dispenser of sage advice courts disaster, it can nevertheless serve as an important evaluation tool. I think of such moments as direct interventions, the value of which stems from observing how clients use the information they have been given. The number of reactions is limitless. Some clients may denigrate my suggestion, perhaps because they are intent upon discrediting me, or because their pride does not permit them to need me. Others may ignore or argue against the direct applicability of my suggestion because it threatens their resistance, thus increasing their fear. Among the possible reactions, however, are those which suggest the presence of idiosyncratic underlearning: Some clients quickly put my suggestion to the test. Sometimes they are delighted with the results. Other times they encounter further barriers to change, but they don't waste time blaming the inadequacy of my suggestion. Instead, they remain hungry for information about how most people make their lives work.

One could respond to underlearning with an empathic connection to the frustration a client is experiencing. While this is not an incorrect response in any theoretical sense, and may be the correct response in specific cases, therapists should not restrict the range of their responses to this single possibility. By occasionally offering information to fill the gap in a client's experience, therapists also create the possibility of tapping into feelings that run deeper than frustration. More than one client has begun to experience the value of having a father figure (in the form of the therapist), and thus feeling more poignantly than ever the lack of a father in his family of origin. Without ever having experienced the help a father can provide, he was never aware of its absence.

Deprivation, as opposed to loss, is a much vaguer feeling. It may form the backdrop of one's life and go relatively unnoticed. It becomes the ground upon which a client stands, rather than the rock he suddenly stubs his toe on. The cautious use of directly correcting a client's underlearning may throw his underlying sense of deprivation into enough relief to enter his awareness.

TRANSFERENCE UNDERLEARNING

Recently I have encountered a deep level of underlearning, the significance of which I have yet to fully explore. I mention it here primarily for the purpose of completeness.

Several clients with totally absent fathers and father figures have had difficulty exploring their relationship with me. Some project qualities onto me which they imagined, as children, were the qualities of a father. But others have essentially learned to live in a world without fathers. Their projections are meager because, early in life they withdrew much of the psychic energy one ordinarily directs toward a father. I now see that their relationship with me has contained little specific transferential material, except for their inability to accept my continuous presence in the relationship with them. They have so firmly repressed any longings to have a father that the relationship with me has never taken on that symbolic significance for them.

I am not suggesting that transference cannot occur in cases of totally absent fathers. The presence or absence of a father in no way alters the existence of a child's normal interpersonal needs: the need to be seen and validated, and to have an ideal parent with whom to merge. For my clients, these needs still existed, and still matured along their individual paths. To the degree that these needs remain in their immature forms, they will be imported into the therapy and acted upon.

I am suggesting that deprivation can be so deep that it forms the background of one's life. While loss is reacted to, deprivation may simply be taken as normal. This results in clients having no specific experiences from their early relationship with a particular parent to "transfer" onto the therapist. In such cases, entering into a therapeutic relationship in which I symbolically occupy the role of a father may have nothing in the client's past to resonate with. It may not be recapitulating any previous experience. It may, quite simply, be the first time the client has ever entered into such a relationship. There is a gap in the transference due to a total lack of experience, which I have named "transference underlearning."

Although I am still exploring the treatment implications of transference underlearning, I assume that this problem must be approached from within the psychotherapy model. The lack of experience with a parent should not obliterate the normal human need, and desire, for parenting. The lack of total fulfillment of this need will often be experienced as a void within the client's sense of self. Exploring this void is difficult because of the infinite depth of grief which may be released.

The one aspect of the CD treatment model which probably holds the most promise in treating transference underlearning is its emphasis on spirituality. Stimulating clients to explore their relationship to God (as they choose to understand him or her) is a useful combination of abstraction and personalization. For many clients, only a being as infinite as God could contain the depth of pain that lies beneath disowning their most basic, and unfulfilled, need for a parent.

5

TREATING THE
CHEMICALLY DEPENDENT ACA

A great many ACAs find themselves in Pogo's shoes: "We have met the enemy, and they are us." As many as 50 percent of recovering alcoholics are themselves ACAs. Far from being distinct populations, ACAs and alcoholics have considerable overlap. This chapter looks at the special considerations that apply to those COAs who are also chemically dependent. Since these two identities are intimately related, treatment for one cannot ultimately be divorced from treatment for the other. This chapter explores how treatments for the two are related.

BASIC CONSIDERATIONS IN
TREATING CHEMICAL
DEPENDENCE

Chemical Dependence Is a
Primary Disease

The disease concept of alcoholism asserts that alcoholism is a *primary* illness, as opposed to a recognizable cluster of symptoms which derive from deeper causes. It asserts that individuals can reach a point where their past drinking produces effects which substantially contribute to the continuation of excessive drinking. Whether excessive drinking is initially due to genetic, psychological, or social reasons, once the process develops sufficient internal momentum to become self-sustaining, the disease of alcoholism exists. This momentum consists of various combinations of physical addiction, neuropsychological impairment, psychological defenses such as denial and rationalization, and/or social pressure. In lay language, "First the man takes the drink; then the drink takes the drink; and then the drink takes the man."

Once it is determined that alcoholism exists, the disease concept implies that it must be treated directly. Efforts to treat the underlying causes of a primary disease make no sense. For example, a person who is fatigued from overworking needs rest. But once the fatigue leads to contracting pneumonia, the lung infection can probably not be treated adequately by rest alone. The growth of bacteria has achieved such momentum that it will continue whether the patient rests or not. The proper antibiotics are now needed. The pneumonia must be treated as a primary illness if it is to be treated successfully. And, in many cases, the pneumonia must be treated before the fatigue can be overcome.

While many alcoholics are ACAs, their alcoholism must be seen as a primary illness. It cannot be adequately treated by addressing the ACA issues first, any more than an alcoholic with marital problems should have couples therapy first. In most cases, it is only after the successful treatment of a client's alcoholism that ACA, or marital, issues can be effectively resolved.

Abstinence Has a Role in Both Evaluation and Treatment

The basic question facing psychotherapists is whether an individual's drinking is problematic. When blatant physical addiction is present, the answer is clear. But many clients' drinking falls into a large gray area. This doesn't mean that therapists are left to flounder in the unknown. There are powerful techniques for flushing the truth into enough of a corner that it becomes revealed. Primary among these techniques is the direct invitation, from therapist to client, to participate in a mutual exploration of the question. Clients have as much stake as their therapists do in finding out whether their relationship to alcohol and other drugs is healthy. Assessing their willingness to explore this topic is a major step in their evaluation.

There is no better way for clients to explore this question than through a voluntary period of abstinence. If clients resist exploring their relationship to alcohol and other drugs, or insist that any period of abstinence is unacceptable, their reasons should be patiently and thoroughly explored. If clients agree to a period of abstinence and then violate it, they must be confronted with the possible implications of their behavior.

The underlying goal of abstinence is simple: As therapists, we want to provide precisely that therapy which has the maximum chance of helping our clients. When an ACA client would best be helped by focusing on her own drinking and drug use, it's our job to help her see that making chemical use the primary issue is in her best interests. Failure to do this (when it is the appropriate referral) misses a golden opportunity to intervene on a potentially deadly process, and simultaneously leads to inappropriate and generally unsuccessful therapeutic efforts. This is frustrating to client and therapist alike.

Fully 20 percent of clients who come to Genesis to deal with their ACA issues are using alcohol or other drugs actively enough for this to be problematic. To fall into believing that resolution of their ACA issues is even possible without abstinence, or that dealing with these issues is a way to affect their alcohol or other drug use, is to risk collaborating with their denial that their chemical use is problematic.

Reasons for Treating
Chemical Dependence First

There are three separate arguments for treating chemical dependence first when it exists in ACAs: 1) the genetic inheritance factor, 2) the potentially fatal nature of the disease, and 3) the impossibility of therapy in the face of active alcoholism.

• *Genetic inheritance.* ACAs have a propensity toward alcoholism that is genetically inherited. Individuals at increased risk for contracting any disease must always be approached with a high index of suspicion. Early signs of the disease are more likely to be accurate harbingers of later illness for them than for the general population. ACAs can ill afford to ignore early signs of possible alcoholism. While these signs could be innocuous and transitory phenomena in non-ACAs, in ACAs they may be life-saving warnings.

• *The potentially fatal nature of the disease.* It is well known that alcoholism is potentially fatal, whether through accident, neglect of general health, interaction with other diseases, suicide, or the direct toxicity of alcohol on such vital organs as the liver, the heart, and the brain. When not fatal, the decline in quality of life due to the disease can be significant enough to approximate death. Even in cases where the diminished quality of life is more subtle, treatment is the answer.

Alcoholism *is* treatable, and recovery can be miraculous. Left untreated, it is potentially devastating, both to alcoholics and to those around them. The consequences of failing to diagnose the disease are severe enough that professional ethics demand that every therapist achieve competence in this regard.

• *The impossibility of therapy.* Psychotherapy is virtually impossible in the face of active alcoholism. When alcoholism is present, it must be treated first before psychotherapy has any chance of being effective. This is true because psychotherapy requires a competent brain, and alcoholism compromises that brain. Attempting to treat alcoholism with psychotherapy, before abstinence begins, is a bit like treating a man's broken leg with physical therapy before putting it in a cast.

Psychotherapy is also markedly more difficult with clients in whom there is problematic, but not alcoholic, drinking. In discussing therapy with non-alcoholic ACA clients, I always require that they abstain from all use of psychoactive drugs for a minimum of 24 hours before and after therapy sessions. My reasons are simple: I recognize that psychotherapy has little power to directly influence people. Sometimes it feels like trying to move boulders with a feather. Even intermittent drinking can have a negative impact on therapy by creating emotional instability or aborting the important emotional reactions many clients have hours after a session.

Finally, in those cases where I have incorrectly evaluated the degree of a client's involvement with alcohol or other drugs, establishing a weekly 48-hour window of abstinence helps to keep the issue on the front burner until the correct diagnosis can be made.

THE DANGERS OF TREATING
ACA ISSUES TOO EARLY
IN RECOVERY

It has been said that an alcoholic is someone who can use up a year's supply of anything in a week. This includes recovery. I have seen many an alcoholic chafe against the impossibility of being a year sober in a week. It is all too common for alcoholics to take on more changes than they can handle early in their recovery. Some may stop smoking, cut out caffeine, and go on a weight-reduction diet while starting a program of physical exercise—all within the first month of sobriety.

There are two main reasons for such excesses in early recovery. First, the initial euphoria of being drug-free (the "pink cloud") can be an intense experience. New reservoirs of energy become available, both physically and psychologically. The action-oriented mode encouraged early in recovery would seem to suggest that this newfound energy be put to healthy uses. But alcoholics in early recovery are easily overwhelmed. The experience of being without one's chemical is enough deprivation to handle; it is not wise to encourage more.

The second reason alcoholics tend to bite off too much in early recovery is more sinister. It stems from disguised minimizations of alcohol's power. AA calls alcohol "cunning, baffling and powerful," and their literature is full of hard-won wisdom regarding the alcoholic's tendency to underestimate what it takes to free oneself from the prison of chemical dependence. This tendency contains vestiges of denial and pride. There is an underlying belief that the more easily one recovers from alcoholism, the less one is *really* an alcoholic. Acceptance that the disease has over-whelmed the individual and attained its own self-perpetuating momentum is still not complete.

The deepest layers of denial wear increasingly subtle and effective disguises, but pride always manufactures some way of feeling special. Pride leads individuals to see themselves as "different" from other recovering alcoholics. It leads alcoholics early in recovery to chafe against the requirements of time. While others may need a year to integrate the first year of sobriety, prideful alcoholics have this first year well under control within a few months! In their thinking, it's time to move on to the more "real" ACA issues.

In general, alcoholics early in recovery have little capacity to comprehend the depth of feelings unleashed by traveling back into childhood experiences. They minimize the amount of emotional energy needed to tolerate resolution of ACA issues and integrate these resolutions into their core personality—just as they underestimated the amount of time and effort needed to integrate their new identity as alcoholics. The danger of encouraging alcoholics to open up their ACA issues too early in recovery is that you inadvertently collaborate with, and reinforce, clients' denial and pride. When therapists become collaborators, it is usually because of ignorance (of the disease of alcoholism and its recovery) and/or countertransference (their own preference for working on ACA issues).

There are many consequences of entering into ACA issues too early in recovery from alcoholism. Perhaps the most acutely dangerous one involves relapse. Recovering alcoholics are at high risk for returning to their drinking if they are overwhelmed by feelings. Premature introduction of ACA issues, particularly early in recovery, when a new relationship to one's feelings is still being developed, is a prescription for relapse. This is not just a theoretical concern. I have frequently witnessed relapse in alcoholics whose therapists too zealously—and too early—led them into ACA issues.

In addition to relapse, premature introduction of ACA issues can lead to a superficial understanding of their impact on one's life. Until a client has solidified his recovery from alcoholism, it may be impossible from him to process and integrate childhood material with any effectiveness. Furthermore, the time and attention spent on these issues must be borrowed from working directly on one's recovery from chemical dependence. While this doesn't always lead to overt relapse, it may contribute to superficiality.

While there are no hard-and-fast rules for determining when recovering alcoholics are ready to begin exploring ACA issues, in uncomplicated cases I prefer to see a minimum of one year of abstinence before entering the counseling mode (two years before entering the psychotherapeutic mode) of exploring ACA issues. A recovering alcoholic should prepare for exploring ACA issues by working seriously on 1) integrating the identity of being an alcoholic, 2) readjusting her social network to support recovery, 3) exploring the role willfulness played in maintaining denial, and 4) establishing a healthier relationship to her emotional life.

There are few places where the AA axiom "first things first" applies more directly and literally than in the timing of introducing ACA issues during recovery from chemical dependence. The turmoil produced by entering into these issues will require all the recovery tools at one's disposal. This having been said, let's look at exceptions which prove the rule.

EXCEPTIONS

ACA issues should be introduced early in recovery from chemical dependence in cases of 1) youth, 2) fusion with an alcoholic parent, 3) relapse secondary to untreated co-dependence, 4) "contaminated label" (when the label "alcoholic" has been contaminated by unresolved issues), and 5) psychic numbing.

Youth

The younger the recovering alcoholic, the less "in the past" his ACA issues are. The need to introduce these issues early in recovery from chemical dependence reaches its extreme with adolescents, many of whom many still be living with an alcoholic parent. In such cases, "ACA issues" are synonymous with the CD recovery issues of "adjusting one's social network to support recovery." Adolescent treatment centers have discovered that as many as 80-85 percent of their clients come from chemically dependent families, and these issues must be dealt with simultaneously with abstinence issues.

Some recovering chemical dependents began drinking and using during their teen years, and now present purely adolescent dynamics despite being in their twenties. While they may no longer live at home, their "independence" may be a rebellion that perpetuates an intense emotional connection to their family of origin. Teenagers disguised by the mere passage of years, they have been prevented by their chemical dependence from completing basic adolescent developmental tasks. Once again, the earlier introduction of ACA issues may be helpful, especially when these issues have never submerged, but rather have been continuously present from childhood up to the present moment.

When ACA issues are introduced early in recovery from chemical dependence, this is rarely for the purpose of resolution as much as for the purpose of beginning detachment. For the adolescent currently living with an alcoholic parent, this detachment may be physical. For the young adult stuck in adolescence, this detachment is more emotional. In either case, the reason to explore ACA issues at an early stage of recovery is to protect the integrity of one's abstinence. Once the ACA issues have been dealt with sufficiently that they are no longer likely to result in relapse, it is best to put off deeper exploration and ultimate resolution of these issues until later.

Fusion with an Alcoholic Parent

It is not only teenagers who live with or remain fused to alcoholic parents. I have seen 50- and 60-year-olds who cannot maintain sobriety because they keep returning to strikingly unhealthy relationships with their alcoholic parents. When, upon discharge from an inpatient treatment program, an alcoholic is unable to entertain any option beyond returning to her actively alcoholic parents' home, it is time to begin breaking her denial about the destructiveness of such a relationship.

The more thoroughly fused the recovering person is with an elderly parent, the more difficult it becomes for him to refuse his parents' offer to nurse him back to health. It is seen as an impossible affront to the parent to consider a halfway house instead. Such untreated co-dependence on the recovering person's part is often complicated by a sense of guilt for having disappointed, or overtly abused, one's parent while drinking. There is now an opportunity, and even an obligation, to make amends. Since the making of amends is even prescribed by the program of AA, it can be extremely difficult to dislodge these clients from their plans.

Such clients can persist in their behavior only if they remain in denial of their feelings about having an alcoholic parent. Exposing them to ACA issues enough to crack this denial often uncovers deep pain, but it also creates one of the only available avenues for detaching them from a disastrous situation. It is very difficult to detach oneself from elderly, declining parents. But such detachment is sometimes necessary if abstinence is going to become a reality. There are few entanglements which require recovering alcoholics to go to such extreme lengths to achieve sobriety. Careful activation of ACA issues may provide the necessary motivation to go to whatever lengths are necessary.

Relapse Secondary to Untreated Co-Dependence

It often happens that recovering alcoholics abandon their self-centeredness by rushing headlong into its opposite. The narcissism of active addiction is disowned, and echoism emerges unbalanced.

This occurs with special frequency and intensity in ACAs with echoistic character structures predating the active alcoholism. In such cases, intoxication was their only avenue to re-owning their narcissistic needs. Without pharmacological access to these needs, and with an understandable tendency to associate them with being drunk, ACAs recovering from chemical dependence may develop a radically different relationship to their emotional life than what existed when they were actively drinking—different, but no healthier.

When co-dependence remains untreated, recovering alcoholics feel an intense need to be defined by the relationships they are in. They form relationships with people who have an overweening need to feel special, leaving the recovering ACA in an emotionally tenuous position. Without relationship, there is overwhelming despair. With relationship, there is continuous suppression of their feelings in the service of others. The mounting tension in the relationship is denied as well. Emotional sobriety—in the sense of emotional honesty with oneself and others, and the willingness to tolerate feeling experiences without being controlled by them or needing to gain control of them—is prevented by untreated co-dependence. Alcohol is the nearest available antidote to the psychic pain this engenders.

In a curious way, intoxication appears to move the client in the direction of health. It balances her excessive echoism by temporarily allowing narcissistic needs to be re-owned. A healthy character structure contains balanced amounts of (matured) narcissism and echoism. The problem with obtaining a semblance of this balance through intoxication is that alternating narcissism with echoism is not the same as integrating the two to the point at which they can be experienced simultaneously.

When ACAs recovering from chemical dependence have frequent relapses, and especially when these are occasioned by relationship difficulties, untreated co-dependence may be the cause. Since co-dependence in ACAs is usually engendered during childhood through destructive relationships with alcoholic parents, activation and exploration of ACA issues may be a necessary part of treating the relapses. In such cases, it is preferable to abort the relapse as quickly as possible to prevent long-term or severe toxic effects from the alcohol consumption, and to use the crisis of the relapse as an intervention on the client's denial of ACA issues. In the best of cases, such relapses are capable of propelling clients directly into deeper levels of psychotherapy.

Contaminated Label

At times, chemically dependent ACAs are caught between the rock and the hard place of knowing that they are alcoholic, but having such horrendous associations to that label that they are unable to fully identify with it. Loathing for their parents can place ACAs in an intractable dilemma. Either they must hate themselves for being alcoholic as much as they hate their parents, or they must accept that their parents had a disease (which they are not ready to do because their ACA issues are unresolved), or they must tolerate the conflict of loathing their parents while forgiving themselves.

The label of being an alcoholic has been so contaminated by unresolved issues with one's alcoholic parents that it interferes with accepting the reality of one's own chemical dependence. Recovery founders on the rocks of the past. The strategy I use for resolving this dilemma is to launch into dealing with ACA issues despite all the cautions I have previously presented. My goal, importantly, is not the ultimate resolution of these issues, but decontamination of the label "alcoholic." As soon as the client is able to identify, deeply and consistently, as an alcoholic, the ACA issues are put on the back burner again.

Deactivating ACA issues with such clients is usually easier than one might think. Once they have truly taken on the identity of being alcoholic, they will understand the need to postpone further work on ACA issues. It is therefore possible to enlist their conscious and active support for suspending further work in this area. In fact, their willingness to cooperate with such a decision is a convenient measure of how authentically they have entered into their new identity of being an alcoholic.

Psychic Numbing

In the early 1980s, I was medical director of a 28-day inpatient chemical dependence program run by the Veterans Administration. I was frequently confounded by the problem of helping recovering alcoholics develop a healthier relationship to their emotions when they successfully prevented any of their emotions from being felt. How could one practice tolerating feelings while still in the safety of a residential treatment program where no feelings emerged?

Since then, I have come to understand that such clients generally fall into two categories. One category characteristically suppresses their emotions. They also may pridefully state that they haven't had the slightest impulse to drink since becoming abstinent. The near-conscious control they exercise over their emotional life is transparent, takes an obvious toll in terms of psychic energy, and is best handled by confrontation from other clients who are also in early recovery.

The second category of clients without active emotional lives tends to exhibit psychic numbing, frequently resulting from childhood experiences in an alcoholic family (or, in the case of veterans, from combat duty in Viet Nam). Often, they long for their emotions to emerge, and experience their lack of feelings as an emptiness, a deadness. But their conscious efforts to activate feelings are useless, since psychic numbing reflexly deepens whenever emotional forces begin to stir. In such cases, I believe that experiential work designed to activate ACA issues is warranted—but only when the goal is to use the evoked emotions as material for developing a sober relationship with immediately present feelings. The goal should never be to reach for resolution of the feelings which arise. In fact, the lesson that one can experience feelings *without* having to act on or resolve them immediately lies at the core of the healthier relationship being sought.

Clinical Vignette:
The Veteran of Many Wars

During the discharge planning for Pete, a 35-year-old veteran, I became concerned that he was unrealistic about how thoroughly his life seemed in control. Although he was only 25 days sober, his emotional state was nearly placid. He felt unthreatened by prospects of being discharged and returning to the same living situation in which he had been actively alcoholic.

Knowing that Pete was an ACA who had been badly abused physically as a child (a fact which he had related upon admission without any emotional reactions), I chose to illustrate the dynamics of alcoholic families in a lecture by actively sculpting his childhood situation. As he chose other patients to represent his family members, I placed each in an exaggerated posture expressing the emotional realities of the relationships within his family of origin.

The largest man represented Pete's father. As I placed him on a chair, hand raised with a leather belt poised to crash down on the client's back, flickers of emotion finally began darting across Pete's face. I had him watch as the father brought the belt down in slow motion. Out of sight, I had removed my own belt and folded it into a loop, which I used to produce a loud "crack" near his ear just as the father swung past him. With concrete images of his family surrounding him and the unexpected sound of smacking leather, Pete was overtaken by tearful sobbing.

I immediately put my arm around his shoulder and focused his attention on the feelings of sadness which filled him at that moment. I dissolved the sculpture and maintained the focus on what it felt like to have the other patients see him crying. Eventually I was able to get him to open his eyes and look through the tears. I asked him to describe what he saw. He told me about the acceptance on other people's faces.

What made this event important was that Pete had openly experienced an active emotion in the company of others. By observing their reactions, he was also able to experience the totally new feeling of being closer to others precisely because his emotions were being expressed. This was the direct opposite of the message he had received from his family, where his father had been proudest of his son when he had been able to endure the most savage beating without a whimper.

The outcome of this experiential exercise was dramatic. Pete made some last-minute changes in his discharge plans which made his continued sobriety more likely. And it was a source of great pleasure to me two years later when he telephoned to let me know he had finished his training and started his first job as a CD counselor. He also asked my advice on how best to pursue his ACA issues, now that his sobriety was solidly in place.

Comments

The danger of pursuing ACA issues in the manner described above is that both patient and therapist may get the impression that resolving ACA issues is a necessary part of maintaining sobriety. It is not. Resolving ACA issues is more a part of increasing the quality of a sober life.

On the other hand, introducing ACA issues early in recovery can be useful, *if* it is clear that the purpose being served is one of working on sobriety issues.

6

PRINCIPLES AND TECHNIQUES
OF GROUP THERAPY
WITH ACAs

Group therapy has emerged as a powerful treatment modality for ACAs. But groups vary widely in their goals, structure, process, and techniques. What some therapists call "group therapy" falls at the counseling end of the treatment continuum, while other therapists' groups fall at the psychotherapy end. Both forms of group have value *if* the evaluation process outlined in Volume One has correctly matched individual clients' needs with the group best suited to meet them.

This chapter surveys the various types of group therapy, differentiates their usefulness (particularly with regard to the stages of recovery as outlined in Chapter 7 of Volume One), and illustrates groups currently being offered at Genesis.

GROUP THERAPY GOALS

The structure, process, and techniques of any therapy group should be directly related to the specific goal(s) the therapist has set. The more coherently the structure, process, and techniques support the group's goals, the more successful treatment will be.

By clearly delineating a group's goals from the beginning, therapists increase this internal coherence. Clarifying goals also greatly improves the therapist's ability to select the right clients for each type of group. When goals remain vague or too encompassing, criteria for client selection become diffuse, coalescence of the group into an effective working unit becomes difficult, and the therapist is more likely to remain a central figure throughout the group's lifespan, as group members remain confused about the purpose of the group and look to the leader for clearer guidance.

When applied to properly chosen clients, the following goals are all therapeutic: 1) education, 2) greater personal awareness, and 3) characterological change. Some therapists might include support as a fourth, separate goal. I do not, because support must be woven into the fabric of every group, although the techniques and processes therapists use to provide it will differ markedly from group to group.

The first two group goals, education and greater personal awareness, lie near the counseling end of treatment, while the third, characterological change, falls within psychotherapy. As with individual treatment, techniques appropriate to the counseling mode are often inappropriate in the psychotherapy mode. For example, directive techniques such as readings, meditations, and homework which educate group members and help them develop greater personal awareness may interrupt the interactive processes necessary for characterological change. Clarity regarding a particular group's goals is essential in order for the therapist to know when to use and when to avoid specific techniques.

Education

The Community Lecture Series outlined in Chapter 4 of this volume illustrates one kind of group in which the primary purpose is education. While this education combines both cognitive and affective levels, it's presented in such a way that audiences are completely free to respond at either level. They are also offered absolute safety and anonymity. No demands are made on them, because the speaker never focuses attention on any specific individual, unless he or she voluntarily asks a question.

Many ACAs are early enough in their recovery, or terrified enough of their issues, that educational settings are the most they can currently tolerate. The majority are emerging from the denial of the survival stage, or are working actively in the reidentification stage. While educational settings are not therapy, giving people information about the next steps they can take in their healing may help them consider more seriously the possibility of entering therapy.

The primary reason for viewing educational settings as groups is that it keeps therapists alert to the *experience* audience members are having, often for the first time, of sitting together with other recovering ACAs. This experience never comes from books, the other main source of education, and should be used to its best advantage to break audience members' sense of isolation.

Greater Personal Awareness

There is a big difference between knowing that alcoholic families keep secrets, and personalizing this information enough to be able to say, "The secrets *my* family kept are. . . ." Applying general information to one's personal life is the goal of the Genesis 18 Week Program. Similar groups designed to help ACAs increase their personal awareness of how growing up in an alcoholic family continues to affect their lives have sprung up in every community, and constitute a major force among ACAs early in recovery. We have designed our program specifically for ACAs who are in the reidentification stage, or beginning to move into the core issues stage.

Directive techniques facilitate client's search for greater awareness, and may include readings, homework exercises, journal writing, etc. The most powerful techniques include experiential work (e.g., Gestalt, psychodrama, guided imagery, meditations, etc.) developed largely within the human potential movement. When the goal is to retrieve memories, dismantle the denial of feelings, or evoke feelings toward past events, experiential techniques can be useful.

ACAs, especially those who exhibit stress-related characteristics, often benefit early in recovery more from facilitated discussions than from experiential groups, which can be too threatening. Additional cautions required in the use of experiential techniques are discussed in the section in this chapter entitled "The Genesis Intensive Weekend."

Characterological Change

Characterological change can occur in group psychotherapy as well as in individual work. In both cases, it's essential to activate clients' transference and correct the distortions such transference creates.

In addition to whatever transference develops between each group member and the therapist, a "family transference" develops as well, defined as "the tendency to view the group as the family of origin and to behave in the group as one once did in that first family."[1] In essence, family transference refers to two facts: 1) clients almost invariably recreate with the group members the same way of interacting that exists in their relationships outside the group, and 2) the characteristic pattern of these interactions can be traced back to defensive measures adopted and incorporated into one's personality when coping with an alcoholic family.

The goal of characterological change requires working within the transferences, and classical interactive groups[2] are specifically designed with this in mind. Interactive groups are rarely effective for people who have not entered into the core issues stage and require a structure, process, and set of techniques which are quite distinct from groups with counseling goals.

MATCHING GROUP STRUCTURE AND PROCESS TO GROUP GOALS

In order to achieve one's goals for any particular group (i.e., education, awareness, or characterological change), therapists must structure and run the group in ways which are consistent with the chosen goal. Groups are generally structured as either time-limited or ongoing, and the process can be organized primarily by either the therapist or the group members. The following considerations should help to clarify the decisions which must be made in designing a group.

Structure:
Time-Limited versus Ongoing

Time-limited groups create an entirely different mindset for clients than ongoing groups, and the consequences of this mindset should not be underestimated. For instance, it's common for time-limited groups to jump into intimate discussions more quickly than ongoing groups. The time limitation is like a set of parentheses around each member's behavior, containing it within a finite vessel.

Once people know that they will part company at a specific point in the future, they are freer to be vulnerable. We are all more likely to reveal a secret about ourselves to a stranger on an airplane than to the people next door on the day we move into a new neighborhood. This freedom is valuable and should be taken advantage of early in clients' recovery. Workshops represent the quintessential "let-it-all-hang-out" risk-taking that is made safer by a time-bounded structure.

At Genesis, we conduct 18 Week groups for people interested in exploring their ACA issues. This time-limited structure attracts many clients who are unable to consider entering an ongoing group because of the open-ended commitment required. The downside of time-limited groups is that the time eventually expires, and clients who have begun to develop intense bonds must then terminate, which is often very painful.

I resist the pressure to convert time-limited groups into ongoing groups, or to renew the contract for an additional period of time. I do this because 1) group members develop intense bonds in part because the experience *is* time-limited; 2) contracting to continue the group encourages the denial of feelings about termination (i.e., separation); and 3) there are consequences to entering into relationships without making a commitment to keep them going, and it's only when these consequences are experienced and understood that people reconsider whether to risk making longer-term commitments.

One powerful advantage of time-limited groups is that all members begin and end treatment at the same time. This allows their experience to be orchestrated, meaning that topics can follow a logical sequence, and discussions can build on experiences the group members have in common (i.e., everyone meets new people at the same time, and they face termination together). Topics or exercises which provoke the most intense emotional response can be followed by gentler experiences, and the hopefulness of recovery can be inserted whenever clients begin to despair. The more such orchestration is used to promote personal awareness through emotional experiences, the less appropriate the group might be for clients who are primarily in need of education.

Ongoing groups have the advantage of being able to sustain an intimate, therapeutic milieu indefinitely. While the level of vulnerability required for such intimacy may develop more slowly than with time-limited groups, it isn't based on knowing that contact with other group members will end on a specific date. Rather than basing relationships on artificial time constraints, the boundaries of relationships must be negotiated from the ground up. This explains why intimacy may take longer to develop, and why it can be sustained.

The Genesis long-term interactive groups require a minimum nine-month commitment from every new group member, which is long enough for them to become fully immersed in the group. A midpoint is reached where withholding oneself from the group can no longer be justified by still being the "new kid on the block," or by the imminence of termination. Only after people become immersed in the group can they take the leaps of faith necessary to start trusting other people enough to do the work they came to group for.

New members enter into a group which has seasoned and ripened into an effective working unit. While this can be stressful, it also permits the new member to hit the ground running.

The experience is similar to that of a person from a dysfunctional family marrying into a healthy one.

Process:
Therapist-Organized versus
Client-Organized

Whom do group events revolve around? Who organizes group interactions? In the case of the Genesis 18 Week group, a series of topics and a workbook determine group events. Less obvious organizers of group events exist: traditions such as check-ins and meditations, guided imageries designed to evoke intrapsychic material, exercises to provoke group interactions, or simply the gestalt therapist's style of addressing whichever clients wish to work on their material. While all these methods of organizing group are consistent with the goals of educating clients and increasing their personal awareness, they are contraindicated when the goal is characterological change through interactive group psychotherapy.

While it's true that interactive group therapists organize group work by consistently attending to group interactions, there is an important qualitative difference between therapist-organized counseling groups and client-organized (interactive) psychotherapy groups. For instance, clients in interactive groups are thrown back onto their own resources for initiating group events. When meetings fall into the doldrums, interactive group therapists explore how group members are experiencing the doldrums rather than orchestrate group interactions to pull them out.

The essence of interactive therapy lies in the relationships which spontaneously develop (or fail to develop) among group members. Who initiates interactions? Who avoids interacting? How do they avoid it? How does the group react to this avoidance? How does the group negotiate who speaks, when, for how long, about what, and so on? It's extremely important for therapists to be sensitive to the harm they can do to the interactive group process by openly or inadvertently organizing events, even if the group feels stuck or in trouble. Interactive group only exists to the extent that group members are truly left to their own devices to interact in their characteristic ways, even when push comes to shove. Once group members realize that a therapist will consistently intervene to circumvent moments when the negotiation process begins to break down, or when no one takes the initiative, everyone is released from being ultimately responsible for his or her own behavior in group.

Interactive groups work best if they are set up to be interactive from the start. Like delicate flowers, they are quickly damaged when therapists take over and get the group to revolve around their own agenda.

Clients who flourish in interactive groups have probably begun work in the core issues stage, and have the capacity to enter into the integration stage. Only a minority of ACAs seeking treatment should be referred to an interactive group. On the other hand, it's distressing to see clients who would benefit from interactive group psychotherapy complete a time-limited, therapist-organized group with the mistaken impression that they have experienced all that therapy has to offer.

THE GENESIS
18 WEEK PROGRAM

The Genesis 18 Week Program is defined as "a time-limited, therapist-organized group with the goal of greater personal awareness, using predominantly educational techniques (i.e., discussion and directed homework)." Clients accepted into Genesis 18 Week groups have been evaluated by the group therapist as being likely to benefit from an overview of ACA issues, to fill in gaps in their understanding, and to personalize this information further.

Evaluation interviews refer clients with active chemical dependence to more appropriate treatment, and suggest individual work rather than the 18 Week group for those who are in crisis, massively depressed, actively borderline, or who possess thought disorders. Clients with stress-related symptoms may be admitted to the 18 Week group unless their tendency to reexperience the trauma is extreme. Because group therapists are free to intervene when necessary to manage a client's excessive anxiety, this symptom is rarely a cause for referring clients to individual therapy rather than to 18 Week groups.

We encourage clients to expose themselves to Twelve Step meetings for ACAs before entering our program. Our primary rationale is that a certain percentage of clients will find their needs adequately satisfied through self-help groups, at considerably less cost. However, attendance at such meetings is never made a prerequisite for admission to our group, because many ACAs are so afraid of being overwhelmed by feelings that they feel safer entering a group facilitated by a therapist.

The Organization of the Program

Genesis 18 Week groups meet for 90 minutes, once weekly, with a maximum of ten clients (and a minimum of six) and one therapist. Chairs are arranged in a circle. Therapists take an active role from the outset of each meeting, thereby decreasing clients' anxiety about what will happen each week.

The first part of each meeting is usually devoted to asking group members to share what feelings and thoughts came up during the week as a result of the preceding meeting. Invariably, additional life events and crises are also reported, which gives the therapist an opportunity to respond empathically, but without moving to fix problems. In those instances when direct and focused counseling seems necessary, therapists explore whether the client has adequate outside support, and encourage an individual session when appropriate.

There is no magic in choosing 18 weeks for the length of our program. We initially met for eight weeks, but this unnecessarily rushed some of the topics. In addition, there was often a deepening of the connection among group members around the sixth week that seemed abruptly cut off by termination before it could be explored. Expansion to 18 weeks lets us devote more time to important topics and add a few additional topics, as well as some unstructured time toward the end. By including a three-hour Weekend Workshop after the ninth week, we have also deliberately intensified the bonding among members immediately before turning to recovery oriented topics.

The Program Workbook

A workbook developed by Genesis specifically for the 18 Week group is distributed at the first meeting. The purpose of the workbook is to increase continuity by incorporating homework into group members' daily life and preparing them for each week's topic.

Each weekly chapter has three sections. The first is an ongoing exercise in identifying and tracking emotions. The second includes exercises and readings designed to augment the previous week's topic and to begin stimulating thoughts about the upcoming topic. The third is a daily journal in which clients are asked to write down their delayed reactions to meetings, as well as retrieved memories and associations generated by being in the group.

Weekly Topics and
Program Overview

Each week has its own topic. While the topic serves to focus discussion, it is not designed to organize the full 90 minutes. This gives therapists the flexibility to attend to unexpected events which unfold in any given group. When possible, the aspects of such spontaneous events which illustrate the week's topic are highlighted. The topics for the first nine weeks are:

1. The experience of breaking the silence and speaking openly about being ACAs.
2. Detailed descriptions of each member's life with a chemically dependent parent.
3. The feelings of shame and guilt often stimulated by such public honesty, and how sharing these feelings can help them lose their sting.

4. Descriptions of ACA characteristics.
5. ACA characteristics seen in the context of having been developed as survival strategies.
6. Experiencing emotions that have long been suppressed by rules against feeling, by compulsive behaviors, and by psychic numbing.
7. The new awareness of a sense of loss and the need to mourn that experiencing emotions often leads to.
8. The role of control in one's life.
9. The control of anger, with an eye toward the price group members continue to pay for this strategy.

An initial foray into interactive group therapy is made in Week #8 as the therapist helps members identify ways they have carefully controlled what they reveal about themselves to other members of the group. The idea of a facade, existing in the here-and-now and affecting interactions within the group, is introduced, and clients are invited to identify a time when they have presented a facade to the group. Interactional issues are introduced to begin giving clients some experience with how an ongoing interactive group feels.

Our three-hour Weekend Workshop is inserted on a weekend between Weeks #9 and #10. In the space of eight days, group members meet three times for a total of six hours. The intensity of this contact greatly enhances their sense of connection.

The workshop provides an opportunity to review what people have experienced in the group up to this point, including which of their needs and expectations are being met and which disappointed. This discussion invites a deeper level of honesty between group members and the therapist than what has generally happened to date. The latter portion of the workshop involves an exercise in which people plan a concrete action geared toward advancing their recovery. Emphasis is placed upon the difficulty of choosing a small enough task that success is virtually guaranteed, without denigrating the action as being too small to be significant.

The topics for the remaining weeks are:

10. A follow-up of recovery plans developed during the Weekend Workshop.
11. Co-dependence (building on earlier discussions of control).
12. An open group: the group itself is responsible for choosing the topic.
13. Assertiveness.
14. Self-acceptance.
15. Play.
16. A review of what group members have experienced and learned together.
17. Any unfinished business.
18. Saying goodbye.

The lack of structure in the open group of Week #12 is designed to piggyback on the topic of co-dependence (Week #11), for the anxiety occasioned by lack of a topic is frequently a strong stimulus for co-dependent behavior. For example, there is often a rush to defer to the first suggestion made by a group member. The therapist allows group interactions to follow their own course for a time, but makes a few comments that are more typical of interactive group work, usually focusing on the group's efforts to negotiate the choice of a topic. Toward the end of the meeting, a transition is made back into the more educational mode. This labels the group's experience during this meeting as having been much closer to the core of interactive group work than is the goal of our 18 Week program—once again, expanding clients' vision of what therapy can be.

Regarding Week #13: While assertiveness is not a simple antidote, being increasingly assertive does challenge one's co-dependent stance. We frame assertiveness as an issue of trusting both yourself and others enough to reveal information about how you are feeling and what you are wanting. The ability to be assertive rests in part on self-acceptance (Week #14), which we look at in light of each group member's relationship to spirituality. Honestly sharing the role of spirituality in one's life takes assertiveness and often leads to a meeting in which there is great respect for a wide variety of different views. This respect in the face of diversity is commented on as the essence of how healthy family members treat one another.

After this difficult introspective work, it's time to take a look at play, the topic of Week #15. Rather than just talk about it, we give the session over to silliness, using tools like Mickey Mouse exercise audio tapes and the game of Pictionary. As group members process this experience, they often return to earlier topics, such as control issues and how hard it is to drop their facade.

Since termination is predictably a charged issue for ACAs, we devote the final three weeks to this issue. The "unfinished business" part (Week #17) can be especially fruitful. For example, a member may return to an earlier disagreement with another member which he had swept under the rug until now, when there is enough trust between them that the resentment can be spoken honestly and resolved.

The goal of the last week is for people to practice remaining present and experiencing their emotions as they part from one another. Keeping one's eyes open, even when it hurts, allows group members to honor the connections they have made with one another, and detach enough to move freely on to the rest of the day and potential connections with other people.

THE GENESIS
INTENSIVE WEEKEND

The Genesis Intensive Weekend is defined as "a time-limited, therapist-organized group with the goal of greater personal awareness, using predominantly experiential techniques."

Workshops are essentially time-limited groups which can be used to achieve either educational or awareness goals. Educational workshops do not differ substantially from the framework of lecture series, like the one we use to treat underlearning (described in Chapter 4 of this volume). Similarly, workshops designed to increase awareness through discussion and personalization do not differ substantially from the framework for the Genesis 18 Week program described above. It is when experiential techniques predominate—such as family sculptures and psychodrama—that a qualitative change occurs and additional considerations must be noted.

All experiential techniques attempt to bypass intellectual and verbal defenses and resistances by actively setting up situations (visualizations, interactive exercises, etc.) capable of evoking strong emotional experiences. These emotional experiences are then focused on.

At this point, I feel compelled to note my ambivalence about experiential work. I am ambivalent because of the great power experiential techniques possess—including both the power to heal, and the power to seduce clients and therapists alike into looking for quick fixes where none exist.

Experiential workshops for ACAs are often a lot of fun for everyone. Workshop leaders get to perform in ways that fall outside the normal therapist role. Client satisfaction is often high because what happens during these workshops—the "work" being done—corresponds to many clients' notions of therapy. In particular, it corresponds to the widespread belief that psychological healing occurs through the kinds of dramatic breakthroughs such workshops have earned a reputation for creating. But. . . .

The list of "buts" is too long for my comfort. First and foremost, experiential work is better at initiating change than sustaining it. Memories and emotions can be opened widely without any integration of the experience. As a result, some ACAs experience a temporary "emotional high," which rapidly fades without having produced any substantial changes in their lives. Other ACAs are overwhelmed by pain from their reopened wounds, and continue to hemorrhage long after a workshop is over. This is particularly true of clients who suffer from the post-traumatic stress disorder (PTSD) symptom of reexperiencing the trauma, which may only be worsened by continued exposure to such experiential workshops. Left with their raw pain, these ACAs become casualties for other therapists to treat.

It is the lack of follow-up which makes experiential workshops problematic. When clients open their feelings deeply, and then are left with them dangling, it can lead to their concluding that "See, feelings aren't safe; I'm overwhelmed, and now I'm abandoned." In the worst cases, people can literally reexperience the trauma of their childhood.

Second, experiential workshops are susceptible to becoming personality cults when their power is seen as stemming from a therapist's wisdom (or some other attribute) which is dispensed to clients. While this perspective may result more from clients' needs than from the needs of the therapist, experiential work is not the best environment for addressing such transference (although it may stimulate such transference to a greater degree than any other therapeutic setting). In the worst instances, when no screening of workshop participants has occurred, borderline and overtly delusional clients have latched on to experiential therapists in ways that either disrupt the workshop or give short shrift to the clients' distortions.

Finally, experiential workshops set a trap for many therapists to fall into their own narcissistic grandiosity, especially when clients begin to band together into celebration of the leader's powers. And, since I am personally not immune to such influences, I find myself quite cautious in this regard.

I would not be ambivalent about experiential workshops if there were not a positive side to them as well. In their training and professional work, psychotherapists are subject to a wide variety of intense experiences, many of which can be very valuable personally. For example, it's popular to attend Tavistock conferences, which can be very challenging personally, as part of one's training to do group therapy. There is no reason to assume that therapists are unique in their ability to make use of such experiences, or in their appetite for them. On the contrary, I have observed many ACAs respond positively, quickly, and lastingly to experiential workshops.

It would be denial on my part to dismiss the evidence that many clients get into long-term therapy, or deepen the level of therapy they are already in, as a result of experiential workshops. Without exposure to powerful experiential techniques, these clients might never have been able to move from an intellectual understanding of ACA issues to an emotional connection with their own life. Experiential workshops often help clients break through an impasse that has existed in their ongoing individual therapy.

Two factors stand out to differentiate those people who make great strides in experiential workshops from those who don't. First, I find that "workshop junkies"—people on a continuous quest for "aha" experiences—are far less able to receive lasting value from experiential workshops than ACAs who are having such experiences for the first time. The client for whom experiential workshops provide the first glimpse of previously unavailable feelings is the one who is most likely to benefit. The experience is one of a new relationship, whether to one's own feelings, to the past, or to others, which the client immediately recognizes is both possible and preferable. This is a very different dynamic from the "old pro" who goes from workshop to workshop like an addict looking for another fix. To such a client, workshops are less a glimpse of health and more a type of sustenance which he may be unable to produce internally through commitment to therapy.

Second, people who are most helped by experiential work tend to integrate that experience by continuing to explore it through long term psychotherapy. While "old pros" often perceive themselves as constant questers, they may in fact be avoiding the less dramatic and more disciplined therapy required to integrate their experience into real change.

The Organization of
the Intensive Weekend

I organize the Genesis Intensive Weekend for ACAs around a family sculpture, a form of psychodrama which occurs on the morning of the second day. The first day is a preparation for this psychodrama, and the second half of the second day is devoted to sharing reactions to the experience and attaining some emotional distance from it in preparation for ending the workshop.

The following set of beliefs provides the framework around which the workshop is designed:

1. It is valuable to be increasingly honest about the events in one's past.
2. It is valuable to allow painful feelings to be listened to, and not always resisted.
3. Sharing these feelings with others helps us listen to them seriously and respectfully.
4. The willingness to pay attention to negative feelings enhances the ability to experience positive feelings, which is one of the primary justifications for "dredging up the past."

The First Day

The workshop begins with everyone (maximum of 40 people, minimum of 15), in a circle, and with soothing music in the background (usually something from Windham Hill). People are asked to describe how it feels to be here in the group, entering into a full weekend with one another. Their hopes for the weekend are elicited. I encourage everyone to speak, if only a sentence about why they are here today. This gives each person the experience of being present and participating within the first hour of the workshop.

I then show *Mirror of a Child*, a videotape I made with the Johnson Institute that dramatizes one ACA's realization that her life is still being controlled by events from her childhood. The emotional reaction to this video can be powerful, and I help the group express their feelings. Inevitably, people begin telling stories from their own past.

The telling of one's story is something that never truly ends. Each stage of our lives gives us new perspectives and tools for relating new facets and depths. Such story telling should be seen as a process of making more and more meaning out of the painful aspects of one's life. It is through making such meaning that we take the sting out of our pain and transform experiences into strength.

To facilitate this process, I start by dividing the group into triads. Each person has at least 10-15 minutes to tell the other two people in his triad how it was when he was young. Next, I have participants tell one another, as honestly as possible, about the sources of pain in their lives today. What is it that brings them to this workshop? This question is meant to return some of the focus to how past experiences are leading to present day behaviors that are ineffective or harmful. Finally, I ask people to reveal something more personal about themselves than what they have said so far. This helps deepen the investment everyone is making in the weekend's work.

Much of the rest of this first day is designed to deepen the feeling level while maintaining a sense of safety, partly through my presence as someone who has done many such workshops, and partly by providing some cognitive structure for understanding how dysfunctional adult characteristics are produced by childhood experiences in an alcoholic family. The key here is a balanced approach between affect and cognition. This is in line with Irvin Yalom's point that "therapy is *an emotional and a corrective* experience. We must experience something strongly, *but we must also*, through our faculty of reason, understand the implications of that emotional experience."[3]

Toward this end, I explain the four categories of ACA characteristics, as we understand them at Genesis: Biology, The Wound, Poor Woundcare, and Underlearning. (For an overview of these characteristics, see Volume One, Chapter 1.) Emphasis is placed on the PTSD issue of psychic numbing and on co-dependence. Two exercises serve as focal points, a guided imagery and a mask exercise.

1. Guided imagery. Workshop participants are led through a guided imagery back into the childhood experience of playing on a slide. Suddenly, as people are sliding down, I introduce an alcoholic standing at the end of the slide, without any details to imply what the alcoholic looks like or is doing. In the ensuing discussion, I help the group describe first what they saw, and then what they felt.

This exercise helps people access the stereotypic images of alcoholics which they still carry within. It also provides an experience of the marked contrast between feeling free and the abrupt cessation of this feeling in response to an alcoholic's presence. Many people vividly describe psychic numbing at this point.

2. *Mask exercise.* Each participant draws a life-sized mask of the image she likes to project toward others. The group is then divided into smaller groups of ten or fewer, each with its own facilitator.

Each participant places her mask over her face, and the rest of the group gives her feedback on what they see in the mask. After listening to their comments, the person wearing the mask describes as accurately as possible what the mask is supposed to be portraying. When all have had the chance to hear feedback and explain their masks, everyone is asked to comment on what it really feels like behind their masks.

Next, still wearing their masks, participants are asked to write down something they are ashamed or embarrassed about. The papers are shuffled and randomly passed back to the participants. Each reads out loud to the group what is written on the paper he received. People are encouraged to own the statements they wrote, and to take off their masks when they do so. By this point, most participants are so uncomfortable with the masks that there is a palpable sense of relief in being honest. Participants who don't want to own their statements are given permission not to do so, but they are asked to keep their masks on while explaining the reasons for their reluctance. After this, they can remove their masks.

By the end of the day, I have had enough time to observe the workshop participants and consult with the other facilitators about which to enlist for our family sculpture the next morning. We use these criteria for choosing participants: 1) they should be able to demonstrate access to their feelings without great risk of being overwhelmed by them; 2) they should have clear memories of their family of origin, at least one sibling, and events in their past which lend themselves to easy dramatization, 3) they should be motivated to enter more deeply into their experience, and 4) they should be in ongoing therapy.

During the final break of the day, I speak with the workshop participant who seems to be the most likely candidate for the family sculpture. I tell him about the sculpture and discuss the possibility of focusing it on him. If he's willing to accept the invitation to be the central figure in the sculpture, I ask him to sleep on it that night and give me his final answer in the morning.

The Second Day

This day starts with a check-in regarding feelings that came up the previous evening, dreams people might have had, and the emotions they are now bringing into the room. We then move directly into the family sculpture. Because conducting this exercise demands nearly all of my attention, I arrange for a second therapist to monitor the audience while it is in progress.

I begin by extensively outlining the central figure's family tree on the board, asking him for names and a few adjectives to describe each relative's primary characteristics. The central figure then chooses other workshop participants from the audience to play the members of his family. He is instructed to make his choices on the basis of whatever associations occur to him—for example, a person's clothing, height, facial expression, mannerisms, etc. There is no need to explain why any particular choice is made. Meanwhile, audience members are given the absolute assurance that they do not have to be in the sculpture just because they are chosen, nor do they have to give any reason for refusing.

One of the assumptions of family sculpture work is that all participants intuitively begin to take on characteristics of the roles for which they are chosen. This is not mysterious. First, they have all seen the family tree, including descriptions and behaviors characteristic of their roles. Second, the central figure has undoubtedly chosen each audience member on the basis of similarities and resemblances to his actual family members, often with uncanny accuracy. Finally, playing any role for an hour or more has subtle effects on people. For example, playing a family member who is being excluded from interactions can quickly lead to feelings of loneliness, anger, and jealousy in someone who wanted to play an integral part in the family sculpture. These feelings are likely to parallel those the central figure's relative experienced in real life when she was excluded from being an integral part of her family.

Another assumption of this kind of work is that the sculpture begins at the moment audience members are chosen to play family members. As soon as I ask someone to step into the area being used for the sculpture, the central figure starts reacting. For example, when the "father" moves into the sculpture, the central figure may begin to bristle. His body stiffens slightly with fear. His breathing changes. He shifts his stance. He may move slightly away from the father. All of these reactions are important information to be used immediately or later during the sculpture exercise.

During this process of choosing audience members and setting up the initial configuration of the sculpture, I stay close to the central figure and begin to make physical contact with him, often with a light hand on the shoulder or back. I do this for several reasons. Later, it will be for reassurance, and to guide him as he walks in and out of the sculpture. For now, physical contact helps me to monitor his subtle reactions to what is happening around him.

Once the sculpture is set up, I walk the central figure in and out through the scene, instructing him to monitor his emotional reactions as he comes close to each family member. At times I ask him to stop and look into the eyes of a particular family member. The purpose of the sculpture is to make the past so concretely real that it becomes palpable. Any number of techniques can be used to facilitate this, from having the central figure take another person's place within the sculpture, to setting the sculpture in motion (often using another facilitator to feed participants appropriate dialogue and actions), to taking characters out of the sculpture and sitting them down for one-on-one discussions with the central figure.

It's vital to monitor the emotional reactions of everyone in the sculpture. Often the most important work is not done by the central figure whose family has been recreated, but by a member of the audience who has been asked to play a particularly propitious role. I don't hesitate to deviate from the original "script" to attend to emotionally important events.

For example, in one sculpture, the central figure was placed in a re-creation of a time when he had been physically abused. Although he was unable to have an emotional reaction to the scene, the woman playing his sister, who had been sent to her room and forced to listen to the beating all by herself, had a tremendous outburst of rage. The sculpture put her in touch with her own sense of anger at having been powerless to keep her father from battering her mother. The focus of the sculpture shifted to help her explore her unexpected experience of rage. The other participants got as much out of this as they would have gotten from the central figure's story, and the central figure was confronted with the damage his psychic numbing continued to do to his life.

It's also necessary to help each person decompress from his or her participation in the sculpture. I do this by gradually dismantling the sculpture, person by person, and allowing each individual to talk about his or her experience during the exercise. Emotional reactions can be very intense, and people must often be aided to return to the here-and-now. The opportunity to describe the feelings which came up while playing a particular role facilitates this.

Finally, the central figure has often been through a harrowing experience. I advise him to take it easy for the rest of the day. He has just done his major piece of work for the weekend and should relax from this point on. I also offer him the opportunity to have his therapist contact me if this is useful, or to contact me himself if necessary. This offer recognizes that the family sculpture has activated powerful forces, and that I have some responsibility for this as the facilitator and the authority figure. Reactions to this event may continue to emerge for days, even weeks afterward. I must be prepared to help people respond therapeutically to these reactions, without interjecting myself between them and their therapists.

By the end of the sculpture, there are often many members of the audience who are in tears and needing to talk. To attend to this, we break into facilitated groups of ten or fewer.

The afternoon is devoted to two exercises. The first, a recovery planning exercise, is concrete, undramatic, and meets participants' need for action: People are asked to identify sources of their low self-esteem and plan an action that would improve this one area of their lives. The focus is on the future ("What's going to happen after this weekend is over?") and on the task of choosing a goal which is almost certainly achievable.

This exercise accomplishes several things. It helps participants begin the process of decompressing from the weekend workshop. It helps bind some of the emotions activated by the sculpture. And it confronts ACAs with their tendency to see achievable goals as insignificant because they don't take care of the "whole problem."

The second exercise takes place after the final break. Participants return to a darkened room in which the chairs have been placed in two concentric circles. A guided imagery is used to bring them into the presence of a little child at play, presumably a picture of themselves in the past. They are led to focus on their emotional reactions to the child's free play, and to condense these feelings into a single statement that they would like this child to know about himself or herself. Before they are able to speak this sentence to the child, they are brought back into the current moment, still clutching that sentence in their memory. The inner circle is then instructed simply to listen and receive, while the outer circle slowly rotates, whispering their sentences to each person in the inner circle. After helping both groups describe their experience, the circles change places and the process is repeated.

The point of this exercise is to give people the experience of more openly receiving spontaneous messages about their core worth without having to do anything in return, and to help them understand that this openness is made possible by the painful work they have been doing in the workshop. In other words, opening up to real feelings about real events in the past leaves people better able to feel good about themselves now, and to trust that others may feel the same about them. At its best, this is a dramatic *experience* of the three healing forces at work: honesty, experiencing feelings, and entering community. It is also, we hope, a kind of "reward" for working so hard all weekend long.

Toward the end, we talk about the emotional "high" that participants are likely to feel from this weekend. I point out that friends and relatives who have not shared this experience are not likely to understand this "high." I remind participants that, while we were in the workshop, wrapped in a special cocoon of our own making, our other family members were probably doing ordinary, everyday things—watching TV, caring for children, mowing the lawn, shopping. I caution them to be sensitive to whether the people in their lives are even interested in hearing about their weekend. The best approach is to pay attention to what it feels like to be telling someone about it, and simply to stop if it feels uncomfortable.

Finally, I make sure that participants understand that their emotional "high" will fade—guaranteed. This isn't because the "high" is unreal or unimportant. It's just in the nature of things that such emotional intensity cannot be sustained. The task now is for everyone to find some other place, most often a Twelve Step group or therapy, to begin the long, slow process of putting into perspective what has happened during the past two days. Hopefully, people will achieve some clarity on what behaviors and feelings led to the "high," and find ways of continuing to put these into action in their daily lives. Our workshop, in the end, is little more than a vision of the possibilities that recovery offers.

GENESIS INTERACTIVE GROUPS

Genesis interactive groups for ACAs are defined as "ongoing, client-organized groups with the goal of characterological change."

Groups designed to bring about characterological change lie toward the psychotherapy end of the counseling-psychotherapy continuum, and work primarily by focusing on the here-and-now relationships which develop in an ongoing, client-organized group. For carefully chosen clients, such groups provide a powerfully rich milieu which is qualitatively different from what is attainable within individual therapy.

Chapter 3 of this volume describes individual therapy as being the most effective approach to problems with hierarchical relationships, the prototypic relationship being with one's parents. Group psychotherapy, on the other hand, is more effective in approaching problems in peer relationships, such as those with a spouse, friends, and co-workers. This distinction between how individual and group therapy approach hierarchical and peer relationships is a matter of degree only, and should not be given a black-and-white interpretation.

Interactive groups are designed to give clients the greatest possible opportunity to sort out questions of responsibility in relationships. For example, many ACA clients complain of some version of the following: They are unable to figure out to what degree their angry outbursts at a spouse are justified by the spouse's abusive behavior, and to what degree they are an overreaction to old issues triggered by innocent behavior on the spouse's part. An interactive group helps the client sort out what is actually happening and why by setting up the following social experiment: An unbiased observer (the therapist) brings the client together for weekly meetings with several other people, none of whom know each other. No contact outside the group will be made without being reported back to the group. Interactions among group members will be allowed to take their own course, with a minimum of interference from the group leader.

Now, when the client spontaneously experiences a subtle re-creation within the group of the confusing interactions which occur with her spouse, several important things can happen. First, there will be little doubt that the client had some hand in bringing about this re-creation, although there will probably be some resistance to seeing this. The fact that interactions have been allowed to take their own course will remove many of the rationalizations that prevent the client from taking seriously her own role in the re-creation.

Second, a host of more or less unbiased and supportive peers in the group will have been privy to the entire sequence of events comprising the interaction. Each will have different views of what has occurred. As flawed as their individual perceptions may be, the confluence of their viewpoints will provide an important opportunity for the client to begin sorting out precisely what has occurred. Has she been abused, or mistreated, in the group? Is she overreacting? What has she unconsciously done to help create the situation? What are her feelings in the midst of this situation, and which are reminiscent of the past, especially of her family of origin? The very fact that there is an environment where these questions can be explored begins to break the pattern of merely reacting to perceived threats. New behavior can be laid down and practiced. Interactive group therapy has accomplished its purpose.

I believe that 50 percent of the work of running interactive groups is done before the group ever meets—through evaluation, selection, and careful preparation of clients. This is a labor-intensive process for therapists. (Our usual procedure is to have interactive groups led by co-therapists, and in such cases both therapists must be present during evaluations.) To begin with, clients should meet the following criteria:

- they have entered into at least the core issues stage of recovery;
- they are able to tolerate anxiety without relying on the therapist for active containment;
- they have minimal borderline symptoms;
- they have demonstrated the ability to introspect, with some access to feelings;
- they have appropriate expectations of how the group is run, and what it can accomplish for them.
- they are able to describe current relationship problems; and
- they have no active chemical dependence.

Because setting reasonable expectations is so crucial and so difficult for interactive groups, we begin doing this from the very first instant of client contact. We screen prospective clients over the telephone before the evaluation interview, focusing on what they are looking for in group, and steering them to other group styles when appropriate. For the evaluation interview itself, we follow the format outlined in Chapter 8 of Volume One, with one exception: During the final ten minutes, we describe the interactive group, emphasizing its lack of structure and stressing that the therapist will focus on whatever process emerges, rather than actively organizing the group's efforts.

We then hand clients a written Group Agreement, which repeats the description and stipulates several points which we ask each member to voluntarily agree to. These points include matters of confidentiality, payment, refraining from verbal abuse, an abstinence rule covering 24 hours before and after each group, a nine-month commitment with at least four weeks' notice of termination, and a rigorous obligation to report outside contact with other group members.

We don't make firm decisions about accepting clients at the time of the evaluation interview, except in cases where it's clear that a client is not going to be accepted. It's best to let this be known face-to-face, since it is frequently interpreted as rejection. We try diligently to be clear with clients that our task is to pre-scribe what we believe to be the most effective treatment for them. When interactive group is not the answer, we must refer them somewhere else. The fact that Genesis has 18 Week groups, as well as couples and individual therapy, makes it possible to offer an immediate alternative to interactive group. While some clients are wounded by their perceived rejection, many others are relieved that they will be saved the trouble of beginning a therapy for which they may not be completely suited. Those who persist in feeling rejected are often painful to deal with, but this only reinforces our opinion that interactive group is not the treat-ment of choice for them.

A second interview may be necessary to complete the evalua-tion. If so, we make another appointment at the end of the first interview. Otherwise, we set up a follow-up phone appointment for a few days in the future. For clients who are already in therapy, this gives them the chance to meet with their current therapist and discuss our group. It also gives us the chance to contact their therapist, with the client's permission. We have no intention of interfering in an existing therapeutic relationship (for example, by cooperating with a client's acting out against his current therapist by terminating prematurely in order to join our group), or of blithely waltzing into position as the next in a long line of therapists who have been defeated. Taking this latter risk may be acceptable in individual therapy, but it should not be allowed to put a whole group in jeopardy.

We have two reasons for arranging a follow-up phone appointment with clients: First, it allows co-therapists to discuss a client, to mull over their observations, and to seek consultation when needed. Second, it allows clients an opportunity to have delayed reactions; for example, realizing once they are out of the therapist's presence that they are too anxious to enter interactive group. Entering group is a major decision, not to be taken lightly. It's prudent to give oneself a few extra days to decide about such a large commitment.

Once an appropriate client has decided to enter group, the final step is to exchange names. The client is given the first and last names of the other people in the group (with their permission), and her name is given to them. In the event that anyone recognizes another person's identity, the extent of their prior contact must be explored to avoid bringing people together who have any previous complications in their relationship. This prevents unpleasant surprises and emphasizes from the very outset the importance of group members reporting all contact with each other outside of meetings. For interactive group to be successful, everyone must have access to all the information about interactions among group members. When this is violated, even a little, doubt creeps in, trust is broken, and people begin censoring their comments to each other. Interactive groups are seriously jeopardized when two or more members begin responding to each other in ways that no one else understands as a result of outside contact.

In the first interactive group for ACAs, co-led by Dr. Stephanie Brown and myself,[4] issues of trust, personal needs, responsibility, and feelings all arose. Permeating each of these issues, and giving them a common intensity and poignancy, was the underlying issue of control. In more than a decade of working with ACAs in interactive groups, the same issues have continued to emerge as the focal points around which treatment turns.

Group Issues:
Control

Issues of control exist on both interpersonal and intrapsychic levels. On the interpersonal level, group members fear that either they may tend to control the meeting by talking too much, or feel controlled when others talk too much. They frequently see group as a sort of pizza pie, in which there are just so many pieces of time to go around. Whenever anyone takes more than their share, other group members are denied. Silences are used to gain control of the group's attention, at the same time the internal withdrawal during these silences is an effort to gain control over one's own feelings.

Questions from others are felt as demands to speak. The transition from one group member's speaking to another is often quite difficult, as people are not practiced in the art of negotiating interactions. The question "Are you finished?" is often perceived as "You ought to be finished." Everyone walks on eggshells, and direct negotiations are either avoided or transpire with such speed that they are like handing off a hot potato. Constructive feedback is often seen as a command to change and evidence of rejection ("I can't do anything right."). An uncomfortable sense of being "one down" often permeates the group.

The transference here is from family interactions, where issues of power are continually just below the surface (e.g., in unspoken rules about who is allowed to comment on realities in the family, and what events must be denied). The therapist's role is to embody, rather than teach, the possibility of healthier interactions. For example, in the face of the pizza-pie model, therapists must radiate confidence that there is plenty of time and energy for everyone to get enough of their legitimate needs met in a group that is functioning well.

On the intrapsychic level, members use denial, suppression, and repression in an effort to keep tight reins on their own outward expression and inward awareness of emotions. Most group members eventually acknowledge problems in expressing anger, which is avoided by projecting a facade of having themselves under control. A client's projected image of being under control is a counterbalance to the alcoholic's being out of control. It is seen as having value in and of itself, while allowing genuine spontaneity and intensity of feeling is seen as akin to the wildly out-of-control behavior of the alcoholic. In a homogeneous group of ACAs, this distortion receives silent, but profound, confirmation by each group member's behavior. Clients mistakenly believe that healthy, mature behavior comes through more effective control.

It is extremely important for therapists not to overtly or covertly reinforce this belief, or it becomes doubly hard to change.

Group Issues:
Trust

Issues of trust are significant on at least two levels. First, group members do not naturally trust one another, even in the face of evidence that trust is possible. They continuously exert control over how much of themselves they allow others to see. Trusting another person is tantamount to giving him control over you. As one group member explained, "If I trust you, I give a piece of myself to you, and I can't be sure what you'll do with it." Implicit in this is a distrust in one's ability to defend oneself against being controlled by others.

Second, group members lack self-trust, as evidenced by constant questioning of the validity of their own feelings and perceptions. Events that merit attention (such as inappropriate or nervous laughter after a member cleverly puts herself down) may be ignored as group members unconsciously fall back into old behaviors (e.g., responding to pressure from their alcoholic parents to avoid commenting on embarrassing events). One way to ignore direct experience is to call one's perceptions into question ("Did I really hear that?") for the sake of maintaining a facade of normality.

The wretched nature of trust issues for ACAs is summed up in one group member's explanation of why she couldn't trust the others: "I can't believe they're really interested in listening to me, because maybe I want them to listen just so I can manipulate them. And when I ask them to listen, they feel obligated, so I can't trust their response anyway."

Group Issues:
Acknowledging Personal Needs

Acknowledging personal needs, so integral to healthy relationships and a working interactive group, can be anathema to ACAs. Group members experience this as a source of guilt, assuming that others are powerless to avoid the imposition of their needs (since they themselves feel powerless to avoid responding to others' needs). They equate it with being vulnerable, since others can use their request against them. And they equate it with being dependent, a one-down position that is inimical to feeling in control.

For many ACAs, an important means of survival during childhood was to be dependent only at carefully controlled times: when dependence was demanded, or when others were free to attend to their needs. Acknowledging their needs (such as the need to be comforted when scared) was uncoupled from internal realities. They developed the ability to postpone getting their needs met until circumstances were more prudent.

As a result, honesty about personal needs feels extremely dangerous. There is constant pressure to keep a cap on the intensity of their needs, and to control when and how they are expressed. However, once this degree of control has been attained, the possibility of ever expressing one's needs becomes remote. In a group setting, this translates into a sort of impasse: Everyone is willing to permit everyone else's needs to get attended to first.

Group Issues:
Responsibility

Group members have a pervasive tendency to take responsibility for other people's feelings and actions. This is caused by the deep confusion of boundaries within their families of origin, where the alcoholic parent disowned responsibility and the co-dependent parent inappropriately accepted it. There is a reluctance to bring too much painful feeling into the group for fear that this will ruin other people's moods. There is little sense of mature empathy—of being able to listen attentively to another person's feelings, respond intimately to them, but remain impervious to taking them on.

Group leaders play a critical role in modeling how such empathy works. In particular, therapists must be able to tolerate the dissatisfaction that periodically envelops a group when it plateaus or gets stuck in its work. Likewise, therapists must sometimes tolerate group members' anger toward them for being unable, or unwilling, to fix uncomfortable interactions within the group.

Group Issues:
Feelings

In general, feelings are experienced as bad, despite group members' intellectual protestations to the contrary. Most clients enter therapy convinced that catharsis is an important part of therapy, if not its very essence. But, in the here-and-now, when push comes to shove about actual feelings, group members are almost always reluctant to let them show. Negative feelings are resisted for fear that they will get out of control or even be contagious, in which case the group member having the feelings must take responsibility for how they affect other group members. Positive feelings are capped for fear that they will leave other group members feeling worse by comparison, or because expressing them will somehow place the feelings in jeopardy, or because neither the group nor the good feelings can be trusted.

Invariably, the group member with the most intense feelings is regarded ambivalently. He is both admired and feared—admired because of the general acceptance that awareness and expression of feelings is healthy, feared because such freedom with feelings resembles the alcoholic's behavior, and thus runs the risk of hurling the group out of control.

The Therapist's Tasks: Facilitating Awareness and Working Within the Transference

Once an interactive group is formed and the issues outlined above begin to develop, therapists face two tasks which must be undertaken simultaneously. One task involves facilitating group members' awareness of when the same dysfunctional behavioral patterns which affect their relationships outside the group are being imported into relationships inside the group, often in very subtle ways. Once group members have this awareness, they can begin to see group interactions as part of their real lives, rather than discounting them as artificial.

The other task involves working within the transference—recognizing and reacting to distortions which arise from group members' family of origin experiences. Therapists in interactive groups are "group members with a special status." Within the family transference framework, they are clearly parental figures. They must recognize the transference projections being placed upon them and steadfastly avoid identifying with these projections (which would only confirm them). They must also take a stance within the group which models the healthy role of a parent.

Given the personal histories of group members, it is inappropriate for the therapist to adopt a position which is too detached and aloof, since this risks reenacting the very trauma which has brought people into the group in the first place. It also misses the opportunity to correct substantial and important elements of underlearning among group members. For many ACAs, the therapist's behavior will be the first and only image of healthy parenting they have ever seen. For the therapist to remain aloof and intervene only with crisp, intellectual interpretations of the transference may be appropriate in certain individual therapy cases, but not in group. Instead, the therapist should model interactions with a parent who is emotionally present but has firm boundaries.

Such modeling represents a substantial personal challenge to the therapist's maturity and authenticity. It makes interactive group work both exciting and profoundly difficult. One of the most common mistakes I have observed among interactive group therapists is underestimating the degree of this difficulty.

The concept of family transference carries within it the kernel of another idea: It implies a similarity between interactive group therapy and family therapy, which emphasizes the systemic focus group leaders must maintain. Interactive group is an arena where individual issues are always present. Leaders must continually respond to the context in which these issues arise—the group itself—and not give in to the temptation to deal predominantly with individuals. In other words, rather than exploring the issues themselves, the therapist's primary material should be the effects these issues have on the group as a whole.

For example, it is possible to focus on one member's excessive need to attract the group's attention and miss the fact that this 1) serves a group purpose (e.g., by keeping group meetings "hot"), 2) may serve other members' purposes (e.g., by keeping them from having to initiate discussions of their own concerns), and 3) certainly could not occur without the tacit approval of the rest of the group. Every event in an interactive group is an interaction, if only through its passive acceptance by group members. Such passive acceptance is frequently a dysfunctional behavior, learned in alcoholic families where it was too dangerous to challenge the existing order. The rule of thumb guiding therapists should be that any group member's defenses which are not being challenged by the group are being entered into by the group. It is best to focus on the group's behavior in this regard, rather than the individual's.

Group therapists must approach their work with the unshake-able belief that individuals have their best chance to change in healthy ways when the health of the whole group is attended to. The group itself is the agent of change.[5] Everything the group does affects each individual, and each individual's behavior affects the group. The implied message must be that it is impossible for people to withdraw from being in relationship without this having some effect on their relationships. Silence in the group is just another form of relating, and often a powerful one.

The more openly group members can be drawn into exploring what events and interactions create a vital and healthy group, the more the therapist can deal with the basic assumptions and transference projections group members have about interpersonal relationships. This work is best done by focusing on the negotiation process—or, frequently, the lack of negotiation—which sets the rules and expectations within the group. For example, how is it that the group decides to be terminally polite? How is it that the group remains focused on one individual until the topic under discussion is absolutely exhausted? That it focuses more readily on people's bad feelings than on their positive feelings? That it's willing to let the more silent members sit, week after week, without comment? That meetings gravitate toward taking turns, rather than vibrant interactions where people occasionally talk over each other in their enthusiasm? That all discussion stops as soon as it appears the therapist might have something to say? That interactions in the waiting room are more spontaneous than anything that occurs once group meetings begin? And so on.

In the group agreement used at Genesis, we clearly state that it is the responsibility of group members to monitor whether the terms of the agreement are being adhered to. As a result, the therapist is rarely the final arbiter of such thorny issues as, "What constitutes excessive outside contact among members?" Instead, this question becomes a group negotiation.

To give an example of how this works, consider a group where two members have outside contact. This is duly reported to the group. The therapist innocently asks how those group members not involved in the contact react to hearing about it. It's remarkably therapeutic for people to register their discomfort publicly. Perhaps someone feels jealous or left out. Perhaps someone else is suspicious that the full extent of the contact can never be adequately reported. Invariably, differences regarding this issue arise. Now the issue becomes one of how the group will handle such differences. What is it like to be stuck in seemingly incompatible points of view? Do they look to the therapist for a solution? The therapist may empathize with how uncomfortable negotiations are when they bog down like this, but she will throw the question back on the group, perhaps stimulating group members to talk about their frustration.

Many group members will belittle the importance of discussing the rules in this way. Others will try to end the discussion by proposing a rigid rule for everyone to follow. People may begin feeling that the group is not working, or that the discussions are keeping the group from doing its "real" work. Wrong! For many ACAs, the experience of open negotiations, with differing points of view, is alien and uncomfortable. At first, the therapist must work to help group members tolerate this experience, in the faith that it is an early step toward developing a healthy group culture. Later, the therapist may point out patterns in the positions different group members take whenever such discussions arise, and ask the rest of the group how these patterns are affecting them. This leads to a deeper level, one on which the group negotiates about how it will conduct its negotiations. At this point, the very essence of interactive group psychotherapy is present.

Guidelines for
Interactive Group Therapists

Exactly what do therapists *do* when they lead interactive groups? This can neither be adequately described nor taught through didactic means. To be learned, it must be observed, experienced, practiced, and supervised. There are few, if any, universal rules or concrete techniques. There are only general guidelines, which must continually be tailored to the present context, generated by the ebb and flow of group events.

Irvin Yalom's[6] discussion of the general tasks and techniques important to interactive group therapists provides a framework for approaching the question of what interactive group therapists do.

• *First, therapists set group norms, both through their technical expertise and as model-setting participants.* The primary norms to be set include encouraging group members to monitor their own behavior (e.g., regarding regular and prompt attendance), to value self-disclosure, and to see themselves as the agents of change.

Therapists are also responsible for setting certain procedural norms, such as confidentiality and payment procedures.

• *Second, therapists emphasize the here-and-now.* Attention is continually refocused back on what is happening, or not happening, during the meeting itself, why it is happening, and how people are reacting to it. This emphasis on the immediate present is accomplished in two ways, emotionally and cognitively.

On the emotional level, therapists work to activate group members' here-and-now awareness. For example, in the midst of an overly intellectual discussion, a group member may make an off-color remark which everyone else reacts to with embarrassment before quickly returning to their rational discussion. Therapists activate here-and-now awareness by inquiring into what emotions everyone just felt during the brief, and somewhat stereotypic, reactions which followed the off-color remark.

On the cognitive level, therapists emphasize the here-and-now by focusing attention on the group process, which Yalom defines as "the relationship implications of interpersonal transactions."[7] For example, when a group member laboriously tells every detail of a family argument, the therapist might bring as much attention to the way in which this information was delivered to the group as to the information itself. He might ask the other group members, "How did the way this story was told affect you?"

• *Third, therapists work within the transference.* Remembering that clients must come to the point of seeing for themselves the misperceptions caused by their transference (as opposed to having the therapist disabuse them of these misperceptions by teaching them out of the transference), therapists have different tools for working in the transference in group than in individual therapy. As in individual work, a willingness to enter into relationship with clients (what Yalom calls "therapist transparency") permits therapists to model here-and-now behavior. When such behavior does not conform with clients' transference expectations, the chance exists for corrective emotional experiences.

Unique to group is the opportunity to use consensual validation—the pooling of observations by all members of the group. Many transference induced misperceptions can be accepted as such by clients only because the rest of the group gently insists that none of them share the same perceptions of, understandings of, or emotional reactions to specific events in the group. For example, consider the client who continually feels judgmentally dismissed by the therapist. He may be helped to see that this is a misperception when the therapist turns to the rest of the group, asks for help understanding how she is doing this to the client, and is told that no one else sees this happening.

Unless attention is paid to the transference in interactive groups, the possibility that group members will experience characterological change is remote. The primary sources of transference onto therapists (outlined in Volume One, Chapter 4) will stem from archaic echoistic needs for an ideal parent with whom to merge, archaic narcissistic needs to have one's developing capabilities seen, and fear of retraumatization by the capricious behavior of authorities one is dependent upon. This leads to paradoxical demands that leaders be both "more human" and "more than human."

The primary source of family transference will be the role each group member played in the dynamics of his or her family of origin. In other words, those clients who heroically "rescued" younger siblings will tend to be overly protective of other group members.

Working within the transference means that the therapist must avoid either circumventing client projections (i.e., acting as though they don't exist) or directly disabusing clients of them (i.e., rejecting the projections before they have an opportunity to be optimally frustrated). While the traditional manner of working with transference involves interpretation, this is less the case in interactive group psychotherapy. Individual interpretations invariably place therapists in too authoritative a role, bending the group process toward members' competing for wisdom from the leader. The most effective way to work with transferential issues is through consensual validation and increased therapist transparency.

Seeking consensual validation in the face of transference projections is often anxiety-provoking for therapists, but results in excellent modeling. By encouraging clients to check out their perceptions with one another, everyone in the group becomes responsible for contributing to reality testing. For example, consider a group in which everyone shares one member's perception that the leader is being too cold and aloof. At this point, it is particularly valuable to have a co-therapist with whom to discuss the possibility that one *is* being a bit more aloof than necessary, or to confirm that both therapists believe the group as a whole is making the same projection.

When one of my clients feels that my encouraging him to check out his perceptions with the whole group is an effort to gang the group up against him (after all, I am perceived as having the most influence over the group's perceptions), I take the initiative myself, explaining my own need to hear whether the distortion is mine or the client's. Even when everyone aligns against me, claiming that I am too aloof, I can respond by empathizing with their disappointment and frustration. The fact that I may be the source of their discomfort doesn't mean that I can't genuinely empathize with their feelings.

This process is usually alien to the experience of ACAs, and is not easily trusted. I must content myself with the hope that I am *optimally* frustrating the group's need to have a perfect therapist/parent—i.e., I am providing reality testing about my limitations without abandoning my relationship with group members.

Therapist Self-Disclosure

Therapist self-disclosure is one of the areas of greatest confusion among group therapists. I make a distinction between indiscriminate disclosure, especially of factual information about myself, and the use of my here-and-now reactions. The latter form of self-disclosure facilitates group work by providing clients with information about how the therapist feels in response to the group's perceptions of him or her, or in response to how those perceptions were communicated (e.g., angrily? calmly?). While such self-disclosure is problematic, this is no excuse for abandoning it as a legitimate therapeutic tool—especially with ACAs. When problems do arise, it is usually because therapists have inadvertently introduced their own misperceptions and agendas into the group's dynamics (i.e., countertransference).

How do therapists justify revealing their feelings at one point and not another, to one client and not another, on one day and not another? How do we avoid allowing our own sensitivities to mold the group's norms about what perceptions are important, or even correct? Traditional arguments in favor of maintaining a blank screen are powerful precisely because questions like these are so difficult to answer. Obviously, practicing with a co-therapist offers substantial opportunity to gain some objectivity, but even this isn't foolproof, since co-therapy relationships are often made up of teacher/student pairs (with tendencies to defer to authority) or long-term partners (who tend to become a self-reinforcing system).

Despite the many legitimate questions surrounding this issue, the fact remains that self-disclosure by therapists about immediate events is a necessity with ACAs. It is unacceptable, when one group member inappropriately and abusively hurts another, for the leaders to sit impassively. Much of the healing for ACAs in group involves *reacting*—feeling abused when they are abused. If the leaders behave as though nothing out of the ordinary has happened, group members are thrown into immediate doubt about their own reactions.

When I am leading a group, and when the people in the group treat each other inappropriately (and especially when they treat me inappropriately), I allow myself to react, most often with confusion. I register uncertainty about what to do next, distress about what a group member's actions might mean, or sadness when people are being cruel or unfeeling. These expressions are often purposefully vague and lack the impact that expressing anger or delight might have (although it's useful to display these emotions too, at times).

I never fake an emotional reaction, which would be manipulative in the worst sense. I must be genuinely feeling whatever I permit the group to see. And I never allow extraordinary events to pass by without some reaction, although it's important for me not to push my reactions to the forefront when other group members are reacting as well.

"Presence"

For me, the guiding principle in interactive group therapy is "presence," both for therapists and clients. Presence is an elusive but nevertheless very real quality. It exists in varying degrees in all human interactions. It implies an empathic connection between the interactants, and an emotional responsiveness on each of their parts. Attention is focused on the here-and-now. Dissociation is at a minimum. Facades are at a minimum. Communication is from human being to human being. Boundaries are clear. Manipulation is at a minimum. People are speaking from a deeper level of their experience than usual. An electricity fills the air. It takes no effort to listen and pay attention. More energy is gained than expended by being a part of the interactions. My experience is balanced on its edge.

For example, clients have less presence when they talk about being sexually abused but don't experience any of the feelings they have about this. Listening to them tell the story is little different from reading the same information in a letter. As a therapist, I may *know* the importance of what the client is telling me, but I don't *feel* it. When clients allow their feelings to respond to what they are relating to the group, they are more present. The more spontaneously they allow their feelings to respond to their full intensity, the more present they are. This presence is communicated to others who are in here-and-now relationship to the client, and is generally experienced as a heightened sense of aliveness.

People can become increasingly sensitive to the quality of presence. When it begins to exist in group, I call people's attention to it by asking whether they noticed anything different about the group (during the period of time when I experienced greater presence). I help them to explore their own experience of this quality. I eventually label it. People become intrigued by it. They wonder what creates it, and how they can attain it more frequently. They consciously begin to seek it, and use its absence to note that something is missing from the group interactions. Intellectualization and defensiveness are seen to destroy it.

Eventually, intimate relationships are seen as settings where people can agree to seek presence as a goal in and of itself. When this happens, I know that I have helped the group to develop norms which will nurture greater health for those members who are capable of attaining it.

7

PRINCIPLES
AND TECHNIQUES
OF INDIVIDUAL THERAPY
WITH ACAs

The evaluation process (described in Chapter 8 of Volume One) frequently leads to a recommendation that ACAs pursue individual therapy. The primary indications for recommending individual therapy are:

- clients in crisis,
- clinical depression,
- intense anxiety (especially to the extent of phobias and panic attacks),
- psychological disturbances unrelated to being an ACA (e.g., schizophrenia or manic depressive illness),
- post-traumatic stress disorder (PTSD),
- vacillations between co-dependent and narcissistic personality disorders,
- resistance to group,
- clients with intense unresolved issues with parents,
- most borderline clients,
- some chemically dependent clients (especially if their denial requires individual attention),
- as an adjunct to group or couples/family therapy, and
- clients who specifically choose to work individually.

Once the decision has been made to refer a client to individual therapy, it is important to assess which specific treatment modalities would be most helpful. The reasons for recommending individual therapy are so varied that no single treatment method applies to all clients. As with group therapy, individual therapy is a collection of modalities, ranging from those with a behavioral focus to pharmacological interventions, counseling techniques, and transferential psychotherapy, to name a few.

It is here that the framework for healing and recovery developed within the chemical dependence field is invaluable.[1] Depending on their current stage of recovery, ACAs entering individual therapy face different tasks and respond to different forms of treatment. For example, behaviorally oriented treatments are most helpful for the client who is still deeply enmeshed in an alcoholic family and/or out of control with his own compulsions (such as eating). On the other hand, transferential psychotherapy is more useful for the client who has entered into the core issues stage of recovery and is questioning the role of willpower in her life. The recovery framework sorts treatment modalities for ACAs into a rational continuum, rather than viewing them as contents of an eclectic grab-bag.

The important point is that therapists can use different modalities to "meet clients where they are" without falling into a meandering course of therapy *if* their actions are informed by a developmental framework of healing and recovery. This keeps them flexible enough to respond to a client's current recovery task while continually guiding the client toward future tasks. Awareness of the form such tasks take, and of their general sequence, is part of the expertise clients seek from professionals.

Especially in treating alcoholism, it is clear that clients' rapidly developing capacities as they progress through the stages of recovery require shifts from one treatment modality to another. Pharmacotherapy may be appropriate during acute physical withdrawal but unnecessary once the client is capable of being drug-free without seizing. Education, with an emphasis on behavioral goals, may be appropriate next, until clients develop the capacity to enter into intimate relationships without being overwhelmed and relapsing. Interpersonal support becomes increasingly accepted and valuable once the capacity to maintain interpersonal boundaries is present. Eventually, once the capacity to introspect is developed, insight and exploration of feelings are in order. Finally, many recovering alcoholics become able to make use of transferential work.

It isn't necessary for therapists to confine themselves to one treatment modality, handing clients off to the next therapist once a client's recovery has advanced. By being aware of the treatment task at hand as well as the next task likely to be encountered, therapists can continually plant seeds that come to therapeutic fruition later.

For example, during the most acute phase of withdrawal, therapists can educate clients about the Valium they are taking to prevent seizures. Once the client is able to comprehend and remember this information, therapists can shift the educational focus to more general information about the disease concept. Or, when clients are mechanically attending AA meetings, therapists might begin encouraging use of a sponsor as a means of facilitating the development of interpersonal support. Once this support is in place, clients are better able to tolerate thinking about their feelings, and therapists can begin inching toward the next task. In this way therapists can slide from one treatment modality to the next, continually and gently challenging clients to push forward in their healing.

There are at least two reasons why the recovery-sensitive, developmental model for treating alcoholics also works with ACAs. First is the primacy of treating active chemical dependence before stress-related characteristics, and the need to address both before attempting the transferential psychotherapy necessary for characterological change. Second is the relevance of a CD recovery framework to ACAs' denial and distorted relationship to willpower, both of which were learned from an alcoholic parent. Both points are illustrated in the case history, "The ACA Architect," presented later in this chapter. Before turning to that, it's helpful to consider the three stages of individual therapy.

INDIVIDUAL THERAPY:
AN OVERVIEW

Individual therapy has three stages: *initiation, sustaining therapy,* and *termination.* Each stage has different dynamics and requires different techniques. After reviewing these stages, a case history will be presented to illustrate them in greater detail.

Initiation

The initiation stage is usually undertaken when ACAs are still locked into pathological patterns of behaving, feeling, and thinking. Until characterological change occurs, these patterns cannot be changed in any sustainable way. But, since characterological change is the anticipated *result* of therapy, the initiation process must occur within the context of the client's current mixture of strengths and weaknesses. For many ACAs, the successful initiation of therapy is the bulk of work which must be done, and occurs in gradual layers.

It is an extraordinary thing for ACAs to enter into therapy—a human event which is remarkable to the extreme. People learn from their experience. For many ACAs, their total experience of being vulnerable to an authority figure has been painful. It has, in fact, been the primary source of pain in their lives. So why would any ACA voluntarily reenter this kind of relationship, even on a symbolic level? This commitment invariably represents a nearly miraculous leap of faith, a return to the lion's den without assurance that the outcome will be any different. Such is the power of human hope—or such is the power of pain as a motivator!

Initiation may involve a prolonged period of counseling, during which clients undertake a variety of tasks, from looking at their own relationship to alcohol, to resolving many of their stress-related characteristics, exploring and personalizing information about ACAs, and successfully entering into Twelve Step work. Many clients will terminate at this point, grateful for the help they have received but uninterested in exploring the relationship which has developed (or failed to develop) between themselves and the therapist.

In most cases, therapists should bless the work a client has done up to this point and allow the termination, unless the client's leaving is so obviously in the service of his denial that interpreting or confronting it has a chance of leading to meaningful insights. It's important to understand that some clients may experience substantial improvement in their lives without ever moving beyond the counseling level of treatment. Further growth may take place elsewhere, if it is even needed.

Therapists are often called upon to undertake considerable preparatory work to facilitate clients' commitment to enter therapy beyond the counseling level. Here is where familiarity with Twelve Step recovery and counseling techniques can be most valuable. Successful initiation represents a step, both symbolic and actual, toward rapprochement, the developmental stage during which truly healthy relationships first become possible. It occurs when the client becomes willing to explore the relationship with her therapist, with all the anxiety, vulnerability, dependence, and transference projections this relationship entails. Questions reminiscent of rapprochement issues arise, such as how client and therapist can relate to each other across the hierarchy which divides them.

Sustaining Therapy

Once therapy has been initiated, the transference can be explored and worked through. The dynamics of sustaining therapy through this difficult process differ from those which underlie initiation. While the counseling mode used during initiation allows the therapist to use certain techniques without exploring how they affect the client-therapist relationship, this is no longer possible. At times during the second stage, actions taken by the therapist intensify the transference, and the dynamics necessary to sustain therapy call upon the therapist to allow the client to explore her perceptions of the therapist's behavior.

For example, charging a client for a missed session might be handled very differently, depending on whether therapy is in the initiation stage or the sustaining stage. During the initiation stage, the therapist may try to avoid transferential reactions to the charge, perhaps by offering to reschedule the session for later in the week, at no additional charge. During the sustaining stage, however, the transference issues regarding being charged for a missed session become the central material for therapy. The therapist might even withhold logical explanations for the charge to keep transferential reactions on center stage. He might make an empathic connection with the client's reaction, but avoid "acting in" (i.e., taking actions within the therapy to diffuse tension resulting from transferential distortions). Such actions should only be taken when clients are unable to tolerate the intensity of transference and are about to flee therapy, to their detriment.

The goal of the sustaining stage of therapy is the resolution of rapprochement issues. With ACAs, this resolution results from optimally frustrating, and thereby facilitating the maturation of, clients' archaic echoistic needs, and validating their archaic narcissistic needs until they are re-owned. Characterological change occurs as a result of symbolically reworking this developmental process at as deep a level as possible.

Termination

The final stage of therapy embodies yet another set of dynamics. This is a post-rapprochement period, following the relational shift described in Chapter 3 of this volume. Termination involves processing a client's newly developed autonomy by exploring its implications for the client-therapist relationship. By entering into a new relationship with the client, in which the therapist acknowledges and responds directly to the client's greater autonomy, termination helps solidify the client's characterological changes.

Termination should explore the fact that separation, as opposed to abandonment, has become possible for the client for the first time in her life. While this will likely raise uncomfortable memories of past abandonments, it differs from those events in three important ways: 1) the client *chooses* termination, 2) willfully (if grudgingly) accepts its inevitability, and 3) experiences the process from an entirely new perspective based on her greater level of autonomy. Termination involves exploring clients' feelings about ending therapy, sorting through those which are left over from the past, solidifying new ones that arise, and undertaking this entire process in a more collaborative way than was possible before the relational shift.

CASE HISTORY:
THE ACA ARCHITECT

I first met Jody W., a 35-year-old architect, through her husband, Ron. Ron sought consultation with me because he was concerned about Jody's drinking. Although I ascertained that Ron himself had issues worthy of therapy, it was clear that he had no desire to begin individual work, and that significant marital issues existed. I invited Jody to schedule an individual session with me in preparation for beginning couples work, if this proved agreeable to all parties.

This began a specific course of individual therapy with Jody that illustrates the points introduced above and may provide a clearer sense of the structure which underlies an entire course of treatment.

Initiation Part 1:
When Active Alcoholism
Is Present

During the individual evaluation session I scheduled with Jody, she was composed, emotionally constricted, earnestly in denial about her drinking, highly intellectual, and willing to take the "identified patient" role—but beneath her placating exterior, she was intensely rageful and blaming toward Ron. Despite her pervasive defensiveness, I felt an empathic connection to Jody's basic experience of feeling misunderstood and ignored. It was only in the context of sensing this connection that she was eventually willing to let me see her pain.

A brief period of couples therapy ensued before Jody concluded that she needed to be seen individually. During the six couples sessions, the focus was not restricted to Jody's drinking, although there were ample opportunities to point out connections between her drinking behavior and the strife that existed between her and her husband. Jody initially attributed this strife to the "excessive sensitivity of her over-controlling husband." The fact that Ron quickly escalated his concern about Jody's drinking into sharp and global judgments about her basic character whenever he was faced with her denial simply confirmed her belief that he was overreacting. I was able to loosen her grip on this perspective by acknowledging the possibility that Ron was in fact being excessively sensitive and over-controlling, but that such accusations from her left him feeling unlistened to—an experience Jody frequently had herself, and was able to feel some empathy for, perhaps because I was showing empathy for her own sense of having her painful feelings go unnoticed.

Evaluation of this couple's issues could not be separated from evaluations of each individual's issues. It was clear that basic communication skills were lacking in their interactions, but this assessment only scratched the surface of their problems. The lack of firm boundaries between them contributed in no small part to their difficulties in communicating. Clearly, these difficulties could not be resolved until their boundaries became firmer, and for this to happen, individual work would be necessary.

For Jody and Ron, initiation consisted of continuing to gather data while simultaneously working toward whatever improvements in communication could be attained. I instructed them to practice concrete communication exercises (e.g., repeating what the other had said to his or her satisfaction before responding). The goal was to decrease the intensity of the most toxic interactions, while inching each person toward working on his or her individual issues.

For Jody, the immediate issue was the willingness to explore her relationship to alcohol. At this point in therapy, I saw no evidence that she was physically addicted, but her use of alcohol was clearly interwoven throughout the couple's problems. I needed to get a better idea of how much alcohol use had pervaded her personality, and to find a way of disentangling the couple's issues from her alcohol consumption.

For Ron, the immediate issue was to help him de-escalate his anger regarding Jody's drinking, as well as to bring into better focus what the anger was really about. I suspected that his own family of origin issues were being triggered by Jody's emotional unavailability when intoxicated, but I didn't have a sufficient therapeutic alliance with him to pursue this further.

I arranged to see each of them individually again, with different assignments for each. Ron was to attend an Al-Anon meeting and discuss his reactions with me. Jody was to read a booklet on alcoholism I gave her and discuss her drinking with me. I believe that she accepted this recommendation because I clearly had no foregone conclusions. Our discussion was going to "clear her name," in her words, if she was in fact not alcoholic.

My individual session with Jody began with her spontaneously giving an analysis of the booklet's information. She criticized the "simplistic" style in which it was written and offered several examples of negative evidence (i.e., since Jody did not exhibit some of the behaviors which were ascribed to alcoholics in the booklet, this was taken as proof that she was not alcoholic herself).

Rather than enter into debate about the booklet, which Jody would have greatly enjoyed, I explored her attitudes toward alcohol, alcoholism, and alcoholics. Since her own father had been alcoholic, I used history taking as an opportunity to observe these attitudes in action, as well as to find out more about her basic beliefs about the disease. She exhibited a pattern often seen in ACAs: she was simultaneously quite judgmental about alcoholics, generally lacking in knowledge about the disease, and consciously indifferent about her father's alcoholism. Such a pattern complicates the process of dismantling denial about one's own alcoholism, because the label "alcoholic" is contaminated by feelings toward one's parent, and because any decrease in denial will eventually challenge the indifference toward one's parent.

Jody was able to tolerate exploring her relationship to alcohol because it was only one part of my efforts to understand her. I was meeting some of her narcissistic needs by being an attentive, worthy audience. She also enjoyed the intellectual pursuit of minutely dissecting the effects of even small amounts of alcohol on her feeling states. By the end of the session she was much less defensive regarding the process of looking at her drinking, and was willing to abstain for the next week to explore what this experience might be like.

Two events transpired in the next few weeks to break Jody's denial. First, she was able to abstain from alcohol, but did rummage around in her medicine chest to find some Valium she had stockpiled a few years ago. Not only did she take this on a couple of occasions, but she initially hid this information from me. When Jody eventually revealed her use of Valium, she felt deep shame. I empathized with her shame, rather than confirming her own harsh judgments about herself, which allowed her to pursue what this deception meant. Jody rapidly used this event as symbolic of how deception pervaded her life. She spoke touchingly of how often she hid her emotions from Ron, even when he guessed correctly what she was feeling.

We decided to meet individually for several weeks, during which we explored how such deception touched her day-to-day life in innumerable ways. I allowed Jody to pursue this topic because it was, indirectly, laying the groundwork she needed to look more honestly at her drinking.

The second event occurred after Jody resumed drinking. She reported a bout of intoxication, including a blackout, but passed this off as not having any significance. Instead, she viewed this behavior as "play"—relaxation after several weeks of abstinence. The next week she entered my room in obvious distress. She had found an empty bottle in her dresser drawer! Jody was stunned. Hiding or sneaking drinks had been one of the pieces of negative evidence she had used to establish that she was *not* alcoholic. There was no way she could imagine the bottle having gotten there unless she was trying to deceive Ron about the amount of her drinking. She even entertained the idea that she had been trying to deceive herself—the very definition of denial in the booklet I had given her earlier. I continually praised Jody for her willingness to grapple with the meaning of this hidden bottle. At times I even pointed out how easy it would be to pass this event off as meaningless. She insisted that this could lead to a complete loss of integrity. Soon afterward, Jody agreed to attend her first AA meeting.

Although Jody never connected very deeply with AA because of her deep fear of becoming dependent on others, she did use it to begin taking a less moralistic stance toward her disease. She also committed herself to individual therapy with me at this point. The couples work was put on indefinite hold, with heavy emphasis being placed on Ron's continuing to attend Al-Anon. For the next six months, Jody and I concentrated on maintaining her abstinence. She successfully achieved this goal, but felt more miserable than on the day we first met.

Initiation Part 2:
When Dissociation Is Present

It quickly became apparent that Jody had come to rely on alcohol for many things. Chief among these was relaxation, particularly in social and intimate situations. Without alcohol, she floundered at the mercy of her stressful job situation and felt increasing tension in her marriage. Unable to relax when she got home, she was more irritable with Ron. Fights were more frequent, and sexual contact fell to nil. The psychological problems which Jody's drinking had obscured were becoming open, sensitive wounds.

In therapy, Jody was preoccupied with a litany of complaints about her inability to relax and the escalating friction with her husband. Her primary way of containing these feelings was to convert them into critical anger, directed toward her boss and Ron. I was expected to listen to, and validate, her scathing attacks on how others treated her harshly.

It was clear that Jody was in a state of feeling narcissistically wounded. She felt deep inadequacy and invalidation as a result of acknowledging her alcoholism. I needed to form an empathic connection with the only feeling which leads to the narcissistic client's getting into psychotherapy—pain. Therefore, whenever Jody described someone's mistreatment of her, I listened carefully for the pain lying just beneath her anger, and invited her to talk about this feeling as well.

An important event in Jody's therapy occurred when she was relating a story from her past. As a school girl, she overheard her mother bragging to a wealthy friend about her report card, which was almost straight A's. But all Jody's mother said directly to her was, "Why did you get an A-minus?" (The most revealing story Jody ever told me about her mother was that, whenever anyone asked her religion, she replied, "I'm a narcissist.") After listening to Jody criticize her mother, I asked her to imagine how she would feel if she saw a 13-year-old neighbor being treated the same way by her own mother. Jody immediately felt the deep pain such treatment would create. However, when she tried to gain access to this pain in herself, Jody went numb. She was stunned by her inability to remember what we had been talking about before losing contact with her feelings. This event became the prototypic example of her dissociation.

A thorough exploration of Jody's experience of dissociation led to two things: First, we developed a mutual language for discussing an aspect of her life which she had never shared before. Second, we were quickly confronted with the absolutely pervasive presence of such dissociation. Without alcohol, Jody had to substitute a psychological mechanism to cushion herself from her pain. She felt great relief at my seeing the depth and breadth of her suffering, but was completely unable to tolerate experiencing her pain. Whenever difficult emotions began to arise within a therapy session, Jody went numb.

I wasn't yet able to work within Jody's transference, and therefore couldn't help her symbolically retrace and complete the developmental steps necessary to nurture her growth. I knew that until she became better able to tolerate her immediate experience, she would always flee into the safety of dissociation. Furthermore, until the dissociation improved, she would not be able to deal with all of her feelings about being alcoholic. My intermediate therapeutic goal needed to concentrate on helping her develop the discipline and faith to tolerate her experience. This would build a foundation for two things: solidifying her identity as an alcoholic, and setting the stage for entering into transferential psychotherapy.

Since Jody's pain was more accessible through discussion of the past, I frequently encouraged her to tell me about her childhood. Her father was a passive alcoholic from whom she occasionally felt genuine warmth, but only when her mother was not present. She recalled sitting in her father's lap as he read the Sunday comics, only to have him stiffen and put her down when his wife entered the room unexpectedly. Jody's mother rarely showed feeling. Born with only a partial left arm, she had developed an aloof stance toward the world. Her most intense emotions always revolved around the pain or inconvenience which others caused her.

Jody had great difficulty acknowledging the impact which her early family environment had on her, both as a child and as an adult. Whenever long-repressed feelings arose, she was amazed all over again that emotions should live so long or be so strong. The process of retelling the story of her childhood took several months. This portion of the therapy was augmented by having Jody participate in the Genesis 18 Week Program (a time-limited, structured group described in Chapter 6 of this volume), in addition to her individual therapy. Our work together often served to highlight the group work. She brought in a family photo album to make old memories more concrete and real, called relatives to fill in gaps in her childhood memories, and eventually revisited her childhood home and her father's grave site.

During this stage, three therapeutic goals were being pursued simultaneously. First, denial about the past was being lifted, and this was laying the groundwork for more intense and conscious development of the transference. Second, direct education about alcoholism was taking place; as we explored her father's drinking, especially how it helped him to remain emotionally passive, we were also applying this information to Jody. And third, each time past memories triggered their associated emotions, we had an opportunity to observe Jody's dissociation. By learning to identify her dissociation at the time it occurred, revealing to me that she had become numb, and identifying the triggers of this experience, Jody was developing an increased capacity to tolerate her immediate experience on a feeling level.

I knew that Jody's dissociation was diminishing when an important series of events occurred. Until this point in therapy, much of Jody's avoidance of pain was in the service of denying the depth of her longing for her father. Her relationship to this longing (which turned out to be a primitive echoistic need) changed in the process of reestablishing contact with a paternal uncle. As a young adult, Jody had moved some distance from her family at the same time she had left the Mormon Church. Communication with anyone other than her nuclear family dwindled to almost nothing. She had not visited any member of her extended family since her father's death nine years ago. She assumed that they rejected her for leaving the church.

In the search for family photos, Jody wrote to her Uncle Ray. He responded with such warmth that her assumptions about being cut out of the family were challenged. She remembered that her uncle had lived with the family for a year when she was a youngster, and wrote to him a second time for help filling in some of her lost memories. Again, his long, discursive letter moved her. She was also surprised to learn that her father's drinking had been severe well before she was born. For Christmas, Jody sent her uncle a current picture of herself, and asked for one in return. Uncle Ray took the initiative to send her the latest picture from a family reunion as well, with each relative identified on the back.

With each step taken in reestablishing contact, we monitored Jody's emotions and expectations. There was a striking discrepancy between the depth of her reactions to evidence that she was accepted by her uncle, and the degree of longing for this acceptance which she could allow herself to feel.

On New Year's day, Jody took the risk of telephoning her uncle. His tearful response to her voice choked her up to the point that she had to hang up and call again later in the day. She was clearly finished with the treatment of her dissociation. She had not gone numb in response to her uncle's tears. She had not yet been able to tolerate her feelings for very long, but she had not gone numb. She had told her uncle that she was choked up and had to call back. And then, once she was off the phone, she had broken into sobs. It was finally clear to her how important it was to feel accepted by her family. She could acknowledge the depth of her longing to belong.

I suspected that the initiation stage of Jody's therapy had been completed when another sequence of events occurred. Once Jody was able to own her need to belong, I reintroduced the idea of visiting AA meetings. She responded hesitantly again, but was now open to experiencing and exploring this hesitation. What came up was her fear that she would not "fit in," that even here she would not "belong." We gradually worked to put this to the test. At first I had her drive by an AA meeting while it was in progress, but not go inside. We explored the feelings which arose during this exercise. Next, I had her walk past the meeting, and again we explored her feelings. Eventually Jody entered the meeting (partially in defiance of the slow measures I was suggesting). The more she used the meetings as an opportunity to develop a more accepting relationship of her own feelings, the more fond of the meetings she became. Ultimately Jody experienced a sense of belonging in AA, but throughout the therapy, discomfort with her own spiritual impulses put a limitation on how much she used Twelve Step programs.

The day Jody told me she was beginning to enjoy meeting people in AA, I wondered aloud whether she ever felt that she would not "fit" into individual therapy, or that she would not "belong" in the sessions with me. When Jody immediately acknowledged such feelings and spontaneously began talking about them, I recognized that she was ready to work in the transference with me.

Sustaining Therapy:
Working in the Transference

After nearly two years of therapy, during which far more attention was paid to her alcoholism than what I have been able to detail above, it became possible to enter into directly working in the transference with Jody. By this I don't mean to imply that our task at this point was to openly discuss her transference projections. I knew that if that time ever came, it would probably be quite a bit later. I also don't mean to imply that the transference had not been present from the start; it had. What I mean by "directly working in the transference" is that the two of us were now sufficiently engaged in relationship with each other that I could begin moving her back through developmental tasks. This can happen only after the process of engagement is complete, since it is engagement which sustains clients during therapy by allowing the therapist to support them even while frustrating their archaic needs.

Abstinence in and of itself had brought about considerable change for Jody. She had learned about the disease of alcoholism (both as it related to her father and herself), had begun to explore the experience of being a child with an alcoholic parent, had freed herself from most of her tendency to dissociate, and had developed some tools for tolerating her immediate experience while sober. My counseling during this time, in combination with my awareness of her transference issues, had enabled her to engage with me at an increasingly deep level. She had become emotionally attached to me and was willing to start acknowledging this. She was also at the threshold of trusting that what happened to her mattered to me.

Another important event had taken place during her abstinence—an event akin to a characterological transformation. As Jody's active alcoholism started fading into the past, what had appeared to be her narcissistic character structure lifted. An overlay of the alcoholism (both its direct pharmacologic effects, and the lifestyle of denial that accompanies chronic alcohol use), her narcissism gradually gave way to her underlying character structure, which is primarily echoistic (co-dependent). In Jody's case, the narcissism induced in her by chemical dependence had been the complement of her more basic echoism, effectively defending her against the primitiveness of her urges to be symbiotically dependent on perfect others for her sense of identity and self-worth. By the end of the second year of therapy, Jody had switched from seeing me as the audience she was entitled to have, to assuming she had to be an admiring audience for me. Her own narcissistic needs were once again disowned, and her primitive echoistic needs were in the ascendancy. Her transferential projections now caused her to see me as narcissistically self-centered, the way both of her parents had been (to different degrees and for different reasons).

Jody began to idealize me out of her archaic echoistic needs. Having read my book for ACAs, she tried to conform quite concretely to my descriptions of recovery. Whenever she became confused, she probed me for rules and answers which she could follow. She studied me in the therapy session and tried to model herself after me as much as possible. In interpersonal situations outside therapy, she continually asked herself how I might act and tried to imitate her images of me. Such conscious efforts to imitate is a normal process in young children who are searching for their identity by copying parents.

Simultaneously, Jody assumed that she would feel worthwhile only if I loved her enough. Since she saw me as pervasively narcissistic (an accurate impression of her parents which she had transferred onto me), she assumed that the more completely she mirrored me, the more completely I would love her. Understanding this transference dictated the path therapy had to take. Not frustrating her primitive urge to fuse with me would recapitulate her experience as a child, when her parents encouraged her archaic echoistic needs (out of their own needs to feel special). But I knew it would be a mistake to disabuse her too quickly, or too directly, of the belief that my love could make her feel complete.

First, she needed to experience optimal (i.e., gradual) frustrations of her impulse to become whole by merging with me. By confronting her with the proper amounts of frustration, I hoped to help her mature her echoistic impulses. This maturation needed to occur in manageable steps. Jody's constant (though unconscious) fear was that I would suddenly, massively, and traumatically frustrate her desire to fuse with me before she was ready to give up this archaic dream on her own. Lack of empathy on my part for her fears of abandonment ran the risk of such massive frustration that the therapeutic bond between us would rupture and even push her in the direction of disowning her echoistic impulses (rather than maturing them) in order to avoid the pain of their disappointment.

Second, there *was* no way to directly disabuse Jody of her transference projections that she would be saved by becoming a reflection of me. She would experience my efforts to reason her out of her projections as further "wisdom from the master," much as the student seeking answers from a guru accepts as an answer the guru's assertion that there is no answer.

I responded to Jody largely by avoiding any actions which would confirm her belief that I could love her enough to save her, or that copying me had any value for her. I let it be known that my regard for her was not based on her ability to be like me. I continually probed for an increasingly accurate and detailed account of her experience, especially regarding her relationship with me. Focusing on the interpersonal events between the two of us was my primary shift in response to Jody's successfully completing the initiation stage of therapy.

Jody was reluctant to reveal the reality which lay behind her facade of compliance and imitation. She feared that this reality would establish that she was not my perfect mirror, and I would stop loving her and potentially abandon her. The most powerful therapeutic stance I could take at the moment was to continue pressing her to share her deep experience, demonstrate an interest in who she really was, and invite her into a deepening empathic connection with me. I accepted the differences between us, but she was threatened by them. I began a patient waiting game.

A watershed in Jody's therapy occurred when she encountered me unexpectedly in a department store. I greeted her pleasantly, chatted superficially for a few moments, and took my leave without calling my wife over to meet her. This deeply affected her. She felt betrayed and abandoned.

While her reaction could be interpreted as narcissistic rage at not being treated as the center of my attention (as occurs regularly within therapy sessions), I also saw it as the final straw that broke through her primitive echoism. She would never be able to focus her entire life around me, as there were other people who obviously commanded my primary attention. She had to abandon her symbiotic position. She felt separate from me. The challenge now was to see if we could build a new foundation for our relationship based on her maturing echoistic needs (i.e., rapprochement), a relationship in which she voluntarily remained vulnerable to me despite the knowledge that this would never lead to the depth of salvation she had always thought it would.

Jody didn't give up her primitive echoistic impulses without a fight. She tried to make me "bad" for having abandoned her by accusing me of being indifferent toward her, of being incapable of the intimacy I demanded from her, even of leading her into an intimate relationship for the primary purpose of assuring a steady weekly income from her. I knew that people feel abandonment when they lose their parent (or therapist) before experiencing the parent's (or therapist's) empathy for their loss. It was crucial that my engagement with Jody be reinforced at this point.

If I had considered her primarily narcissistic, I would have worked to keep an empathic connection with her pain and disappointment at having "lost" me. In fact, there was no difficulty getting her to be in touch with and to express these feelings. But I considered her primarily echoistic, so I worked instead to empathize with her fear of abandonment, her longing to be dependent on me, and the loss of self which she experienced when she felt this connection was broken. The goal was to have her re-own her narcissistic needs, which she spontaneously did when her echoistic needs were thwarted, and *to mature her primitive echoistic needs.*

To nurture this maturation, I needed to validate her echoistic needs and keep them activated through empathizing with them, and I needed to provide a context which gradually shifted more and more toward reality. There was nothing wrong with Jody's impulse to be dependent or to merge with me. It simply needed to be subjected to the limitations of reality. Jody was facing a critical question: How much can any person borrow an identity from another, whether by mirroring or by being loved? This was a question she had to answer more and more realistically, if she was to continue growing. Ultimately, she needed to recognize the limited success that can be achieved by seeking a sense of self from others, and to recognize that these limitations are not due to the inadequacy of others or to their arbitrary withholding.

Jody seriously considered leaving therapy during this time. This period was the eye of the needle. I helped her talk about it indirectly by using discussions of the past which paralleled current events between us. She spoke of all the disappointments she had felt with her parents. Every time she defended her decision to protect herself from them by retreating behind a facade and hiding her own identity, I validated the value of such a strategy for children who are confronted by self-centered parents. I also helped her see that she had eventually lost the choice of whether to submerge her real self beneath a thick exterior, or to allow others to meet her as she really was.

When Jody began talking more about the lack of freedom she felt in this regard, I knew that some level of rapprochement was eventually possible between the two of us. She accepted that I could understand her experience of feeling that she had lost me. Our empathic connection moved to a new level. Having set aside the illusion that she could achieve an identity through me, she was nevertheless choosing to remain in relationship with me.

Now it was time to negotiate more directly the parameters of that relationship. This negotiation process would pass many times through her belief that I was withholding and inadequate, and that these "bad" qualities about me were what determined the parameters. I knew that the goal was for her to explore her experience of these parameters and to continue negotiating them until she would eventually begin seeing that most relationship boundaries result from the human condition itself. Only a few were being set by my withholding and inadequacy, and even these she eventually accepted as having nothing personally to do with her. They had more to say about my own unique personality, and certainly were no reflection on her.

Jody's transference represented the primary barrier to two important developmental steps: maturing her echoistic impulses, and achieving and accepting a realistic view of how much an individual's sense of identity and self-worth can be derived from relationships with others. Every time she felt I had abandoned her, I used her feelings as an associational bridge to the past. She then explored past events which led to the same feelings. When appropriate, I was able to validate for her the abandonment which had occurred at those times. It was important to return our discussion to the present as well, for her sense of being abandoned by me was also a real event which needed to be explored.

Sometimes Jody could see differences between past and present events that led to her feeling abandoned. At other times she remained convinced that I had abandoned her in the same way her parents had. I never contradicted her, for to do so would have challenged the legitimacy of her feelings. Instead, I reminded myself that the empathic connection I was making with Jody's feelings of abandonment provided a different context for our relationship than what she had experienced as a child with her parents. Simultaneously, her willingness to trust this connection enough to talk openly about her feelings was a different action than she had ever taken with her parents. I had to be content with knowing that a good part of therapy is practice. We were practicing relationship at a new level, according to an altered set of rules, than what Jody had grown up with. I had to allow sufficient time to pass for this practice to be fully integrated, and for the maturation process to occur.

In therapy, being on a plateau may indicate a stall in the therapeutic process, or it may be a necessary pause to allow growth to occur and be consolidated. This is one of the greatest uncertainties plaguing therapists—how to tell the difference between a stall and a pause. Ultimately, a quantum leap in growth may be the only way to confirm that healing forces were hard at work during the plateau. Ultimately, there is no way to be certain that a relational shift is going to occur until it does. There are no hard-and-fast rules about whether the process should be trusted at one point or pushed at another. Perhaps the best a therapist can do is to let his or her own clinical experience be the guide, rather than personal issues and temperament.

In Jody's case, there was a time when responding to transferential issues clearly stimulated the maturation of primitive echoistic needs. It happened between sessions, after we had been discussing her marital difficulties for several months. I was 400 miles away when I checked with my office and learned that Jody had called in some degree of panic. She had been told I was out of town and might not be reachable. An hour later she called again to say that there was no need for me to be in touch with her after all. When I returned the call anyway, she was amazed. She was so accustomed to having to cope with life on her own that she had quickly given up on the idea that I would be of any support during her current crisis.

I knew that Jody's call to me contained elements of being dependent upon me rather than her husband, Ron. However, I chose to respond for two reasons. First, she didn't yet seem ready to become more vulnerable to Ron, who was still acting out some of his hostility issues on her. Her dependence on me seemed like a safer, indirect half-step toward becoming more vulnerable, and taking that half-step with her therapist seemed an altogether appropriate action. Second, her transference onto me up to that point was that I wouldn't be there for her if she became too needy. The forces I had to bring to bear in stimulating the maturation of Jody's echoistic impulses included not only optimal frustration of their primitive expression, but also reward for their more mature expressions. I felt as though Jody's call to me was a new level of risk for her. It was an appropriate request to make of a therapist, so I wanted to meet this request in as timely a manner as possible. I saw myself as rewarding her growth and simultaneously validating what might have been the initial re-owning of some of her narcissistic needs.

When Jody and I next met face-to-face, she was much more direct in her appreciation of me than she had ever been. I had met her need to talk at a time when it had taken some effort on my part. She saw this as concrete proof that I cared for her. Since this was an accurate assessment of my behavior, I noted that a relationship with some emotional importance had obviously developed between the two of us. After she had a moment to digest and acknowledge this, I indicated that her therapy could move to a deeper level if she were willing to focus primarily on our relationship.

At the end of this session, she asked if we could exchange hugs. This is not a routine practice on my part, but I do hug clients occasionally, especially when it is useful for the engagement process or when it is likely to open up new areas for exploration. She gave me a longing gaze just before the embrace. I noted that this could soon serve as an avenue for deepening the therapy. (In my personal vocabulary, the more intensely the transference has been activated, the more likely I am to call a "hug" an "embrace.")

Jody avoided looking at our relationship for several weeks. The therapy seemed to be drifting. She expressed some need for direction, and I repeated my belief that the therapy could go deeper by attending more to the relationship she had with me. Jody suddenly became helpless. She expressed ignorance as to how to look at our relationship. As we explored this, she acknowledged her fear, and eventually touched on the possibility of having to face the fact that I am a man and she is a woman. I took the opportunity to agree that our relationship was undoubtedly affected by our being of opposite sexes. She heard this as my saying that our relationship was "adversely" affected by the sexual difference, and went into feeling betrayed.

I upped the ante by bringing to her attention the gaze she often gave me just before an embrace (using that word). She immediately knew what I was referring to. I said that it didn't seem wise to continue exchanging embraces as long as we weren't sure of the sexual implications being activated. Again, Jody felt betrayed. From her perspective, I was arbitrarily restricting her, rejecting her, and taking care of my own needs before considering hers. In other words, she had returned to seeing me as narcissistic. Given her recent willingness to be vulnerable enough to call me in between sessions, she felt doubly taken advantage of and abandoned.

As her response escalated under its own steam, I sought consultation and questioned my timing. Although I was trying to empathize with her feelings, she grew increasingly angry. She spoke of feeling intruded on by me, which I couldn't relate to the actual behavior between the two of us. It seemed to me as though I had done the opposite of intruding, since I had put a limit on acting on our feelings toward each other in favor of talking about them. On the other hand, I had taken the initiative to identify the sexual component of our behavior. Eventually I could see that this acknowledgment had been the intrusion. Jody perceived me as inappropriately sexualizing what she saw as innocent behavior. To her, the adoring gaze she gave me was a form of hero worship; *I* was the one who imposed a more sexual connotation onto it.

Several elements in Jody's response hinted at the possibility of childhood sexual trauma: the way her anger escalated into vengefulness, her strong association of intrusiveness with sexuality, and the insistence on her "innocence" as opposed to my "badness." I suggested that she amplify her feelings further, and then asked her what age she felt. Jody immediately responded that she felt 12 years old. This age corresponded to two events: entrance into puberty when she first menstruated, and developing her first awareness that her father was alcoholic.

Sexual abuse is a matter of perception as much as behavior. I have come to believe that elements of sexual trauma exist in almost every woman's past, if only as a combination of the girl's fear of being sexually vulnerable and the father's insensitivity to this fear. COAs are at greater risk than other children[2] of being sexually abused, and those who are not directly abused still feel in danger. Parental loss of control may never spill over into the sexual area. But, for a girl entering puberty, natural sexual fears compounded by a parent's general loss of control and chronic self-centeredness can destroy her sense of safety. It is the lack of safety at one's parents' hands which is the most damaging aspect of sexual abuse, and frequently occurs even in the absence of blatant sexual behavior.

With Jody, I shifted the focus away from the sexual aspects of embracing and turned it to how she felt about my being intrusive. She recognized that she had never hated me before this, and sensed that some of the intensity of her reaction had to be coming from the past. She spontaneously explored the possibility that her father had abused her sexually. No memories arose. For the next couple of months, I worked with her primarily as a trauma victim, a style of work which looks more at whether dissociation is present than at the current state of transferential events.

When Jody reported a dream about her parents having intercourse, she remembered two important events. First, she recalled a time when she was inserting a tampon and her father drunkenly entered the bathroom and started urinating. Afterward, he left without any comment or acknowledgment that he had interrupted anything. Jody had been mortified, but had no way of talking about the feeling. The event was never discussed. Second, she suddenly recalled that arguments between her parents, which happened almost exclusively when her father was intoxicated, frequently ended with lovemaking. Her father was uninhibited in his vocalizations at those times.

For years, Jody had to lie in her bed and listen to her parents making love in the next room. Again, this was never discussed. (When Jody eventually did discuss this with her mother, toward the end of her therapy, her mother had a revealing series of responses. First she claimed not to remember anything about it. Eventually she said that she thought the children had all been asleep. Finally she acknowledged that she had been too embarrassed to ask her children whether they had heard anything. These responses were the final confirmation Jody needed for her belief that her mother's self-centeredness was a form of chronic abandonment.)

Jody probably never experienced overt sexual abuse. But the

combination of her parents' insensitivity to her sexual fears and her father's lack of control when drinking had left her with many of the same issues seen in sexually abused girls.

These issues having been brought into the open, I could now return to working within the transference. I asked Jody how it felt to consider the possibility that our embracing each other had a sexual component. She expressed dislike for this, but no longer accused me of being the cause. I encouraged her to explore this feeling of dislike. My goal was to help her accept her side of this sexual component, and to demonstrate that I accepted it as well. When I explained that abstaining from embracing made therapy a safer place for exploring whatever sexual feelings she had toward me, Jody could see that voluntarily restricting herself contributed to the safety and richness of our relationship. By not acting on our sexuality, we could accept and discuss it. The mutuality of this dynamic seemed appropriate to how father and daughter might best deal with the new sexual realities brought about by the onset of puberty. Another developmental task had been reworked, more successfully this time than the first time around.

I see therapy as an opportunity for people who had an unsatisfactory relationship with their parents to demonstrate their own capacity to have been more successful, given a more healthy environment. By fully entering one's transferential projections with a therapist, and working them through to a more successful conclusion, clients have the experience of being "good enough children."

When parents are dysfunctional for whatever reason, this dysfunction creates caution and defensiveness in their children. Under these circumstances, the children cannot achieve their potential, and are left with questions about their own competence. There is nothing mysterious about this. A baseball player on a series of bad teams with bad coaches may be left not knowing how good he might have been. The same goes for children in dysfunctional families. A successful therapeutic experience (i.e., being a "good enough client," in one's own eyes) can't change what happened in the past. But it can release people from the belief that they were incompetent as children. Successful therapy can demonstrate this competence and enhance it in ways that transform their adult character structure.

Facing the sexual component of our relationship brought Jody to the threshold of completing her rapprochement with me. Through exploring the sexual aspects of her longing for me, she began to soften. I felt a new tenderness from her. When Christmas came, she brought in some cookies as a gift. In discussing this, she celebrated feeling that this was more of a choice than on previous Christmases, when she had agonized over what to bring me. This year she was aware that no gift would be special enough to win me over. No gift was going to substantially change the relationship between us. In fact, her decision to bring me a present seemed devoid of any significant effort, conscious or unconscious, to affect our relationship. Jody was using the gift as an acknowledgment to herself of what our relationship had already become, not as an effort to transform it into something new.

She began speaking of how the relationship was something she had longed for much of her life. Instead of letting the gift alone speak for her, she made the effort to tell me directly that I had become very important to her. She did not seem to be scared to let herself be vulnerable to me in this way.

A relational shift had occurred. Its presence was a palpable experience for me. I no longer sensed the same need to monitor all the implications of my every action, expression, and communication. I no longer felt the possibility that Jody's transference would distort my intentions in unexpected ways. In other words, I no longer had to monitor her response to me in order to understand and define her transference. The vast majority of her transference had been revealed to me. I could now reliably predict when and how she might misapprehend me.

I understood the relational shift as the interactional manifestation of an intrapsychic, characterological change—the goal of therapy. In response to the shift, which Jody had initiated, I shifted my style of working with her. Her sense of self had coalesced on a new and deeper level. It was no longer endangered by incompatible feelings. She had become able to tolerate such feelings as paradoxical instead of seeing them as antithetical forces threatening to rip her self apart. She had achieved a developmental step which permitted rapprochement on an entirely new level. Like any "parent," I needed to be open to this level, not just theoretically, but by my very presence. I needed to meet her in a new way and respond to her increased capabilities by entering into relationship with her on a new basis.

None of this had to threaten my position as her therapist, just as a child's maturation doesn't have to endanger his parent's identity as his parent. But I knew that unless the relationship itself matured, I would eventually be rejected as an inhibitory influence. Jody and I had to rediscover a new way of being in a client-therapist relationship, and the effort to forge this new relationship had to be embarked on more mutually than it had been in our past.

My purpose now became to work with Jody to solidify her growth. After the relational shift takes place, this solidification process occurs primarily by reviewing the course of therapy up to that point, interpreting transferential events (i.e., providing the intellectual framework to aid integration of the client's experience in therapy), and more actively laying the groundwork for successful termination.

Termination of Therapy

Termination is a bittersweet experience for clients and therapists, although the emotional intensity of this complex event varies widely from client to client. The bitterness naturally comes from losing contact with a human being with whom one has shared a great deal. Emotions have become intertwined, and the client's fate has come to matter greatly to the therapist. This doesn't mean that the therapist's own identity or self-esteem depends on the client's actions. All it means is that therapists have usually come to care deeply about the client's happiness, pain, and health. It is simply the therapist's burden to know, like parents after a couple of decades of sharing their children's lives, that it is best for independence and autonomy to become fuller. It is an act of love to let go at the right point. It is an act of incompletely matured narcissism and/or echoism to hold on longer than is good for one's charge.

The sweetness of termination comes from watching a long-term client blossom. An elementary test of whether a client is ready to terminate involves measuring his willingness and ability to explore and tolerate his feelings about leaving you. Is he able to conceive of his termination in concrete terms? Does he let it be real, or does he ignore it, minimize it, or deny it by insisting that he will see you again in some setting? Does exploring termination open a new facet or deeper level of the transference? If this is the case, then treatment must concentrate on working this through before proceeding with termination.

A touchstone of successful termination is whether enough characterological change has occurred to allow the relational shift to continue throughout termination and even beyond. In other words, has the client achieved enough rapprochement with the therapist that termination is experienced as a loss, but not as an abandonment? When clients have reached this level of health, they are able to move through termination at whatever speed the process dictates, keeping their eyes open despite the pain they feel at losing what has been one of the most significant human relationships they will ever have.

In Jody's case, termination began with the coming of the new year, when she wondered openly what work was left for her in therapy. I reflected the question back to her, adding my own about what areas of dissatisfaction remained in her life. She spoke for several more months of the discomfort she still experienced in her marriage. Eventually she asked her husband to enter couples work with her, but he refused and entered individual therapy instead. Jody was content to allow this to run its course, with the hope that Ron's personal work would soon pay some dividends for the relationship. As soon as this topic was exhausted by Ron's entering therapy and Jody's realizing that she was willing to remain in the marriage for the time being, Jody immediately returned to questioning her continuation of therapy.

I tested her readiness for termination by asking how she felt about the possibility that she might stop seeing me in the near future. Jody used this opening to talk about the love she had developed for me. In particular, she felt that I had come to support her in ways her father never had. She revealed that, while she had had sexual fantasies about me earlier in the therapy, she was surprised by the fact that these had passed. With some trepidation, she told me that I was not the type of man she is traditionally attracted to. Since I am considerably shorter than Jody, and carry enough extra weight that I am perceptibly less athletic than her lovers tend to be, I felt she was trusting me enough to reveal the actual degree of sexual attraction she felt for me, as opposed to that which her transference had generated. This was perhaps the most convincing piece of evidence that a relational shift had occurred at a deep enough level to be lasting. I marveled that she had been able to reveal her lack of sexual attraction to me without fearing I would punish or abandon her.

Jody explored the sadness she felt at thinking about leaving me, and allowed herself to cry during the session. Several tender moments passed between the two of us with a minimum of embarrassment.

At this point Jody voiced her disappointment that therapy had not helped with a problem she had intermittently brought up during the three years we had spent together. Although she was far less tense than when I first met her, she continued to experience a series of physical complaints, from headaches, neck spasms, and shoulder pain to intermittent difficulty getting to sleep. It was clear that her underlying character structure continued to keep her autonomic nervous systems activated, and to involve her musculature in whatever psychic tension she experienced.

I acknowledged that the style of therapy I practice would not necessarily target these symptoms very effectively, and suggested that an alternative form of therapy might be useful at this point.

Jody indicated an interest in pursuing this, but was thunder-struck when I replied that I could make an appropriate referral, and that termination of our therapy would be necessary if she chose to follow through with this. She quickly recovered from her shock and minimized her reaction.

Jody began the following session by expressing surprise that I had the temerity to suggest she discontinue seeing me in order to begin body work. We quickly reestablished the facts of how this interaction had been my response to her questions. Jody then expressed her dismay that I had sounded so ready to send her on her way—in essence, to get rid of her. She was hurt by my appar-ent unwillingness to fight to keep contact with her. At one point she insisted that I conduct the body work with her. As I patiently explained that I choose not to work in this style, and thus it would not be in her best interests for me to attempt a therapy for which I had not adequately trained myself, Jody began to understand: There were limits to what I could do. There were even limits to what I wanted to do. Her needs and interests had grown until they no longer matched my talents and interests. The inevitable had happened, and it was out of caring for her that I was willing to recognize this, rather than hold on to her to meet my own needs.

The fullness of the bittersweet experience of termination began being present, and we shared it together. This was goodbye, for no other reason than that our time together was complete. This was the point we had been striving for from the moment of initial contact. It just didn't conform to how Jody had imagined it would feel. Of course, her original image of termination had been formed when her sense of self was less firmly and broadly developed than it was now. From her less fully matured perspec-tive, she had imagined that termination would be easy. Her image of greater health had involved the absence of negative feelings. Now that she was actually within the experience of ter-minating, she found that pain was still with her whenever some-thing of value was lost. The difference was that she was feeling the pain when it first arose, and that it was neither tinged with fear nor resonating strongly with past, unresolved pain.

During our last session together, Jody imagined how she would look back on our experience together twenty years hence. It was clear to her that she would think very kindly of me. She teared up, but did not break eye contact. I had become part of her family. This may have begun symbolically, but it had left the symbolic realm somewhere along the way. I was a real part of her family now, because she knew her feelings for me would not die, just as emotions from her childhood had not diminished in intensity with the passage of time.

Some therapists might say that Jody had developed "object constancy." Others might say that she had successfully incorporated me as a "self-object," or that she had achieved "authenticity." However it is expressed, I saw her as reaching the point where she was open to both her own deep experience and to the relationship with me, without blurring boundaries in order to make the experience more intense.

During the succeeding months, Jody dropped me a couple of notes and called me to ask for a referral for a friend. To myself, I interpreted these actions as efforts to keep me in her life, despite having terminated. When compared to the actions of a grown child who chooses to maintain a channel of communication with a parent, in part to maintain the human connection and in part to honor the importance that parent has played in his or her life, Jody's behavior seemed more an expression of her health than a sign of unfinished business.

Conclusion

While I hope that the preceding case history is both illustrative and informative, I realize that long-term individual psychotherapy is impossible to explicate in a single example. The sustaining and terminating stages, especially, require more individualization than other modalities described in this book. Even long-term interactive group psychotherapy tends to have a more consistent form and process, because group dynamics do not vary greatly as individuals cycle through the group.

Additional vignettes would contribute to a richer picture of individual psychotherapy's potential for healing, but might also generate confusion around why different tactics were taken with different clients. Such considerations can only be addressed effectively through direct supervision of specific cases, which raises the question dealt with in the following and final chapter: How are people best trained to treat ACAs?

8

TRAINING AND COUNTERTRANSFERENCE

The problem of training therapists to adequately treat ACAs is no different from the problem of training therapists to adequately treat any client. I use the word "problem" to stress that such training is difficult, complex, and not standardized.

In many cases, the trainer's concept of therapy ultimately determines the curriculum which is presented to students. When the goals for therapy are narrowly conceived, the training of therapists is more easily codified. For this reason, counseling techniques appropriate to working within the CD model lend themselves to being taught with some success in lectures and texts. On the other hand, when the goals for therapy are more broadly conceived and include characterological change, the training of therapists is vastly complicated. Teaching people to work within the transference requires the time-honored and labor-intensive technique of apprenticeship, called "supervision" in the mental health field.

In general, the tools needed by therapists evaluating and treating ACAs include the following:

1. *Knowledge Base*
   - factual information based on research
   - comprehension of major theoretical frameworks

2. *Sense*
   - common sense: the ability to elicit and recognize significant clinical data
   - analytic sense: the ability to apply theoretical frameworks to specific clinical data

3. *Self-Awareness*
   - clarity re: personal boundaries, temperament, and limitations
   - authenticity

4. *Clinical Experience*
   - breadth
   - depth

This chapter looks briefly at the process of providing therapists with these tools. The metaphor I use to picture the relationships among these tools is a three-legged stool. No single tool is "the foundation" upon which the others rest. Rather, if any one tool is weak or missing, the entire stool tumbles under its own weight. An adequate knowledge base is one leg. The second leg is a composite of common and analytic sense, with neither being strong enough to support the stool without the other. The third leg is self-awareness. Clinical experience permits each of the three legs to thicken and strengthen, if the therapist has the ability to integrate this experience and continue growing.

KNOWLEDGE BASE

Information is the easiest tool to teach. Lectures, videotapes, and texts are cost-effective ways of transmitting factual information to large numbers of students. Information is also the easiest tool to assess. Multiple-choice tests can be administered to screen masses of candidates wishing to practice therapy.

Precisely because information is so easy to gain, it's often overemphasized in training programs, and serves as the primary hurdle students must jump in order to become licensed. Such an approach, narrow as it is, has demonstrated sufficient worth that no one seriously advocates its abandonment. Perhaps the reason for its success lies in the fact that lack of sense (common and analytic) and the absence of self-awareness are formidable barriers to gaining a knowledge base in the mental health field. These barriers, rather than any lack of intelligence, are far more often the cause of a student's inability to demonstrate comprehension of the necessary knowledge base.

The knowledge base required of therapists working with chemical dependents in early recovery and secondary co-dependents is less extensive than that required of therapists undertaking transferential work. For the former, counseling techniques which effectively elicit healthy facets of clients' personalities are the mainstay. This includes education, communication skills, assertiveness training, confrontation of denial, and support for attitudes and behaviors which extract the client from dysfunctional systems. For the latter, extensive familiarity with child development and personality theory are necessary as well.

Any suggested curriculum for therapists working with ACAs will immediately spawn debate and controversy. Once these responses are understood as valuable and constructive, the process can begin with some degree of equanimity. As a first approximation, I would suggest that therapists interested in providing the full range of treatment services to ACAs be familiar with at least the following works or their equivalents. In all cases, familiarity with these texts is only complete when the journal articles mentioned in each have been explored as well. Also, these books represent goals to be reached. I do not attempt to list more fundamental and historical works which usually need to be comprehended first.

Chemical Dependence
Knowledge Base

• *Al-Anon Faces Alcoholism*, Second Edition (Al-Anon Family Group Headquarters, Inc., New York, 1984).

- *The Alcoholic Family* by Peter Steinglass *et al.*, (New York: Basic Books, Inc., 1987).
- *Alcoholics Anonymous*, Third Edition, referred to as the "Big Book" (Alcoholics Anonymous World Services, Inc., 1976).
- *Diagnosing and Treating Co-dependence* by Timmen L. Cermak, M.D. (Minneapolis: Johnson Institute, 1986).
- *I'll Quit Tomorrow* by Vernon Johnson (New York: Harper and Row, 1973).
- *Is Alcoholism Hereditary?* by Donald Goodwin (New York: Oxford University Press, 1976).
- *The Natural History of Alcoholism* by George Vaillant (Cambridge, MA: Harvard University Press, 1983).
- *Not-God: A History of Alcoholics Anonymous* by Ernest Kurtz (Center City, MN: Hazelden, 1979).
- *Treating The Alcoholic: A Developmental Model of Recovery* by Stephanie Brown (New York: John Wiley and Sons, Inc., 1985).
- *Treatment of Alcoholism and Other Addictions: A Self-Psychology Approach* by Jerome D. Levin (Northvale, NJ: Jason Aronson Inc., 1987).

ACA Knowledge Base

- *Another Chance* by Sharon Wegscheider (Palo Alto, CA: Science and Behavior Books, 1981).
- *Children of Alcoholics*, edited by Margaret Bean-Bayog and Barry Stimmel (New York: The Haworth Press, 1987).
- *Children of Alcoholism: The Struggle for Self and Intimacy in Adult Life* by Barbara L. Wood (New York: New York University Press, 1987).
- *Children of Chemically Dependent Parents: Academic, Clinical and Public Policy Perspectives*, edited by Timothy Rivinus (New York: Brunner/Mazel, Inc., 1991).
- *The Drama of the Gifted Child* by Alice Miller (New York: Basic Books, Inc./Harper Colophon Books, 1979).
- *Evaluating and Treating Adult Children of Alcoholics*, Volumes 1 and 2, by Timmen L. Cermak, M.D. (Minneapolis: Johnson Institute, 1990, 1991).

- *Group Psychotherapy with ACOAs* by Marsha Vannicelli (New York: The Guilford Press, 1989).
- *Guide to Recovery* by Herb Gravitz and Julie Bowden (Holmes Beach, FL: Learning Publications, Inc., 1985), reprinted as *Recovery: A Guide for Children of Alcoholics* (New York: Simon and Schuster, 1987).
- *Post-Traumatic Stress Disorder in Children* by Spencer Eth and Robert Pynoos (Washington, DC: American Psychiatric Press, Inc., 1985).
- *Psychological Trauma* by Bessel A. van der Kolk (Washington, DC: American Psychiatric Press, Inc., 1987).
- *The Psychologically Battered Child* by James Garbarino, Edna Guttman, and Janis Wilson Seeley (San Francisco: Jossey-Bass Publishers, 1986).
- *Stress Response Syndromes* by Mardi Horowitz, M.D. (Northvale, NJ: Jason Aronson Inc., 1976).
- *A Time to Heal* by Timmen L. Cermak, M.D. (Los Angeles: Jeremy P. Tarcher, Inc., 1988).
- *Treating Adult Children of Alcoholics* by Stephanie Brown (New York: John Wiley and Sons, Inc., 1988).

Psychodynamic Psychotherapy Knowledge Base

- *Adaptation to Life* by George Vaillant (Boston: Little, Brown and Company, 1977).
- *The Analysis of the Self* by Heinz Kohut (Madison, CT: International Universities Press, 1971).
- *The Interpersonal World of the Infant* by Daniel Stern (New York: Basic Books, 1985).
- *The Narcissistic and Borderline Disorders: An Integrated Developmental Approach* by James Masterson, M.D. (New York: Brunner/Mazel, Inc., 1981).
- *Object Relations Therapy* by Sheldon Cashdan (New York: W. W. Norton & Company, 1988).
- *The Psychological Birth of the Human Infant* by Margaret Mahler, Fred Pine, and Anni Bergman (New York: Basic Books, Inc., 1975).
- *The Theory and Practice of Group Psychotherapy* by Irvin Yalom (New York: Basic Books, Inc., 1975).

SENSE

Writing about common and analytic sense is difficult enough, but how do they get taught? Clearly, their essence will never be captured in texts nor transferred in lectures. There is only one arena for sharpening these skills: clinical practice.

Common Sense

"Common sense" is an excellent phrase, for it implies interfacing with the real world. Books and ideas can exist entirely within one's head, but clinical data exists outside of us. I have witnessed fellow medical students who learned the most complicated facts about streptococcal bacteria, then looked right into patients' throats and couldn't recognize the significance of what they saw. Common sense implies that looking at and listening to real people requires an ability to "get out of our head's idea" of how the disease process should appear in order to recognize actual diseases.

I once watched a brilliant medical student take a history from a man who was actively bleeding from his ulcer. As the student walked away, pondering why the patient had seemed so reluctant to give his history, we all saw the man lean out of his bed and vomit a stomach full of red blood. To bring the discussion closer to home, it isn't at all uncommon for therapists with book knowledge about alcoholism to miss its presence in a client they have seen in therapy for years.

In order to bridge the gap between basic knowledge obtained from books and the classroom and actual clinical situations, therapists require extensive supervision. Ideally, therapists in training should be directly observed (through a one-way mirror or on videotape) as they practice their interviewing and evaluation skills. Supervisors can point out events which escaped a student's attention, were never uncovered because of fragmented, leading, or mechanical questioning, or were controlled by the client's behavior. With persistent practice, therapists can greatly enhance their perceptual skills, just as students of bird watching eventually begin to see birds which only their teachers noticed previously. Without increasing these skills, therapists may be extremely intelligent, but burdened by a lack of common sense.

Analytic Sense

Once all the clinical data is obtained, how is it understood? Our analytic sense is involved in synthesizing, reframing, and turning clinical data over and over until it begins to reveal its theoretical implications. The most valuable exercise for developing analytic sense is the diagnostic process.

I continually ask students what they think is going on psychodynamically to explain a client's particular behavior. How do our theories help us understand the clinical data before us? For example, is the client's inability to relate childhood memories the result of lying, forgetting, suppression, repression, dissociation, etc.? The answer we give to this question has diagnostic, and therefore treatment, implications.

Many students of psychotherapy possess great powers of common sense, but resist understanding what they see and hear. As I mentioned in Chapter 1 of Volume One: *Evaluation*, the fear that clients can be violated by forcing observations about them into procrustean beds of theory has merit. It's also true that over-reliance on theoretical perspectives can color and even block our perceptions. Nevertheless, we all venture best guesses about what is making a client suffer. The diagnostic process is simply a disciplined effort to bring these best guesses into full awareness, to subject them to the scrutiny of our knowledge base of theory, and to coordinate our diagnostic impressions with our treatment plans.

Again, supervision of students' clinical practice is the most powerful means of sharpening their analytic sense. Teaching the diagnostic process only occurs when students are actively involved with real clinical data. This humanizes the process and adds urgency to performing it well.

The following texts are useful references during the early stages of practicing interviewing, evaluation, and diagnosis:

• *Disorders of Personality: DSM-III, Axis II* by Theodore Millon (New York: John Wiley and Sons, Inc., 1981).
• *Handbook of Neurological Examination and Case Recording* by D. Denny-Brown, especially "XI. Examination of Intellectual Function," pp. 67-80 (Cambridge, MA: Harvard University Press, 1967)
• *Learning Psychotherapy* by Hilda Bruch (Cambridge, MA: Harvard University Press, 1974).

SELF-AWARENESS

The only "tool" one has for doing therapy is oneself. Master craftsmen have a loving and demanding relationship with their tools. They are able to get the best possible performance out of them, while also taking care not to damage one by using it inappropriately.

Supervision plays a role in developing self-awareness among students of psychotherapy, but it must usually be augmented by personal therapy and familiarity with Twelve Step work as well. There is a difference between supervision and therapy. While supervision will identify when a therapist's personal issues are distorting his perceptions and motivating his actions, it is rarely appropriate for supervisors to help students resolve these issues. Such resolution should occur in a therapeutic atmosphere, where development of the transference is appropriate.

Supervisors may point out when students are transferring old, unresolved conflicts into the relationship with them, but this disrupts the supervision process. The transference must be contained (preferably by dealing with it elsewhere) in order to protect the supervision. In other words, supervisors help students develop greater access to their health and competence. In this respect, supervising is a form of counseling. When it becomes therapy, the value of the supervision is diminished. For example, students may resist a supervisor's suggestion, not on the basis of the suggestion's merit, but rather on the basis of the student's unresolved authority issues.

Personal therapy yields benefits on several levels. It provides an important *experience* of the process, which contributes to empathy with clients. It can expand a therapist's very concept of what therapy has to offer. It can increase the quality of one's personal life. And it can be a valuable aid to surviving a very demanding profession.

While there are many ways in which personal therapy can enhance a therapist's skills, two seem to me especially important: it provides clarity regarding one's boundaries, temperament, and limitations, and it increases one's authenticity.

Self-Awareness and Clarity

One of the primary tasks facing therapists, and one of the primary contributions made to a client's therapy, is the ability to keep one's own personal issues on the back burner.

The classical way to keeping the therapist's material separate from the client's is the psychoanalytic tradition of being a blank screen. When a therapist remains expressionless, remains totally unknown to clients, and even sits outside her clients' field of vision, this gives clients the opportunity to imagine the therapist to be any way they please. When the transference is thrown up on as blank a screen as possible, it is theoretically as undistorted by the therapist's individual idiosyncrasies as possible.

The technique of confronting clients with a blank screen has fallen into disfavor with most therapists today. Now that the human relationship between therapist and client is seen as one of the curative forces in therapy, the blank screen is revealed as an interaction capable of recapitulating highly abnormal relationships in a client's dysfunctional family of origin. For example, a client with a tendency to reexperience the trauma may react to a blank screen with a worsening of his stress-related characteristics, particularly if his parents were emotionally unavailable to him when he was a child.

Object relations therapists teach that the healing force of therapy lies within the client-therapist relationship. For therapists to work effectively within this framework, they must themselves be able to enter into mature, intimate relationships. They must also be able to keep track of the contributions they are personally making to relationships with clients, even as the clients are actively involved in their transference projections. Therapists don't have to remain inactive to keep tabs on their contribution. They can allow the screen to move. And if the therapist is aware of the motion he or she is creating, this contribution can be subtracted from the client's behavior, leaving a relatively clear picture of the client's material.

Personal therapy is the premier way to develop a strong, coherent sense of self, clearly defined boundaries, awareness of the underlying temperament with which one was endowed by birth, and a realistic appraisal of one's own personal limitations (as well as the limitations inherent in the human condition itself). These attributes are necessary to withstand the pervasive and often intense pressure clients exert to identify with, and thereby confirm, their projections.

Self-Awareness and Authenticity

Authenticity is the wellspring of power in human relationships. This quality implies an important attribute which goes beyond clarity regarding one's boundaries. Authenticity also involves vulnerability.

Therapists must be capable of being vulnerable to their clients. Without this quality, therapy remains just a set of techniques. It is the therapist's ability and willingness to be authentically present in the relationship with clients which gives validity to its "symbolic" nature. The therapist-client relationship can never be reduced to a symbolic recapitulation of parent-child interactions when the therapist is authentically present, because her presence imports the power of the moment as well.

Therapists' facility with knowing their emotional responses in real time, combined with their ability to confront clients with coherence between their inner and outer self (when appropriate), draws clients powerfully into actual relationship, rather than passively leaving them within the symbolic context. Both symbolic and present realities are occurring. With time, the present relationship between two people, one of whom is in the therapist's role, predominates. This is the essence of the relational shift. The more authentically therapists can approach clients, the more the power of their person will draw clients into greater health.

CLINICAL EXPERIENCE

There is no substitute for practicing therapy over long periods of time. Many aspects of the therapeutic process, from basic concepts to subtle refinements, cannot be fathomed by students with only a few years of experience. For example, it's difficult to gain much experience with the process of terminating long-term individual clients early in one's career. How long does a therapist have to practice before having terminated 20 long-term clients—those with at least three years of therapy?

Complicating this is the fact that, once a therapist has gained such experience, it will undoubtedly deeply affect the way he views therapy from its inception. How different will termination of long-term clients be after a therapist has *begun* his therapy with the lessons learned after watching his first 20 long-term clients? There is simply no substitute for experience.

Two facets of clinical experience are particularly important for therapists interested in working with ACAs: breadth and depth.

Breadth of Clinical Experience

Therapists training to work with ACAs should have direct experience with at least three populations: ACAs, chemical dependents, and clients in a general mental health setting. Without this breadth of clinical experience, the training is lopsided.

Experience with clients in a general mental health clinic is an important protection against interpreting everything ACAs bring into therapy as being unique to their history with an alcoholic parent. This experience should also sharpen therapists' diagnostic skills by presenting them with the full range of human pathology. It is very difficult to recognize someone with manic-depressive illness if you have never seen anyone with this diagnosis.

Experience in the general mental health field is valuable for three obvious reasons: 1) it enables the therapist to recognize the full range of pathology in ACAs and to assure that appropriate therapy is recommended; 2) it is difficult to reassure a client that he or she is *not* manic-depressive if the therapist has never seen someone who is; and 3) therapists who have had hands-on experience with the full range of human pathology usually sit more confidently in their offices, knowing that they have the capacity to recognize and respond appropriately to almost anyone who walks through the door.

Direct clinical experience with chemical dependents should be a prerequisite for treating ACAs. Therapists who do not take advantage of the opportunity to work with chemically dependent clients should feel obligated to explore their reasons for avoiding the experience. Oftentimes, such avoidance indicates important countertransferential issues. I have seen a surprising number of therapists treating ACAs who are still afraid of, or angry at, alcoholics. This is so unfortunate that it is tantamount to being unethical. Therapists may have the choice of whether or not to deal with their issues regarding alcoholics, but their ACA clients do not.

How can therapists feel their integrity is intact when they avoid dealing with these issues themselves, even as they attempt to help clients do what they have avoided? It must be remembered that, whatever the feelings therapists may have toward alcoholics, these are the feelings which they have toward their clients' mothers and fathers. If your hope is that ACA clients grow to keep their boundaries clear while dealing with their parents (or their parents' memories), that they detach from their parents' behavior, and that they find freedom from the anxiety and fear they associate with alcoholics, then you must walk the same path. This seems so self-evident that it hardly requires emphasis.

Depth of Clinical Experience

By depth of clinical experience, I am referring to two things. First, I believe that the best foundation for doing psychotherapy is familiarity with classical approaches. These approaches, whether they are ultimately the way a therapist practices, are a backlog of experience, gathered and communicated by very well-meaning and intelligent people. Doing the best they could, often from within the confines of their particular social/cultural contexts, these people have much to teach us, not the least of which is humility.

For example, psychoanalysis was once the radical cutting edge. Were any of us practicing in Vienna at the turn of the century, we would undoubtedly have been excited about its innovations. If we now find ourselves attracted to theories which we feel improve on psychoanalytic theory, this is more an accident of the era in which we are born, and has nothing to do with our innate intelligence. It appears to me that those therapists who begin their training by specializing, especially in nontraditional approaches, become more limited than necessary in their skills. There is plenty of time for specialization and branching into nontraditional areas, and choosing these options on top of a more traditional foundation generally serves to increase one's effectiveness.

Second, I believe that, while theories are selective windows, they are all looking at the same phenomenon. There is great value in pursuing one theory far enough to slice into the heart of the human experience. Which theory you choose will probably be determined more by a combination of your temperament, unresolved childhood issues, unique sensitivities, and the vagaries of luck than by any intellectual path, although we all tend to point to this latter explanation when we are rationally explaining ourselves.

The discipline to understand and pursue one theoretical stance long enough to break through the surface of human behavior can transform a therapist's random clinical experiences into a coherent perspective. Once this transformation occurs, all theories are seen in a new light, one in which their strengths and weaknesses are differently assessed.

For example, choosing to treat ACAs within an interactive group framework eventually generated enough depth in my clinical experience that I was able to begin understanding more of the essence of object relations theory and self-psychology. This understanding was not generated within the first couple years of working with this population.

COUNTERTRANSFERENCE AND THE ACA AS THERAPIST

At Genesis, I have hired both ACAs and non-ACAs as therapists. There are advantages and disadvantages to both. The more traumatized an ACA has been, the more likely she is to trust that only another ACA could understand the intensity of her experience. On the other hand, there is often a poignancy to ACAs realizing that they are able to communicate their experience with sufficient clarity that non-ACAs can affectively attune to them.

The disadvantages of being an ACA treating ACAs fall into three categories: a tendency to understand too quickly, thereby missing the client's unique individuality; contamination of the therapy by the therapist's own issues; and burnout.

A Tendency to Understand Too Quickly

Although I have emphasized the critical role of empathic connections between therapists and their ACA clients, I now need to stress that it is possible for this empathy to be too quick and too intuitive. Even when it is accurate, overly rapid empathy aborts an important process and can even lead to clients feeling unseen.

For example, an ACA therapist may "understand" what is painful about having an alcoholic parent before the client has described his own unique experience in any depth. Part of the value of telling one's story lies in the client's hearing it themselves. When ACA therapists empathize too quickly, on the basis of their own experience, clients may be left with the feeling, "I know you are on my side, but you don't know what my side is yet." Of course, this awareness is more likely to be subliminal. But even when fully conscious, it is rarely discussed with a therapist early in the relationship.

I find that the most effective questions I ask are often the simplest, even the dumbest, ones. When clients describe their childhood experience as being very lonely and isolated, I quickly remind myself that, while I do know my own experience of loneliness and isolation, I don't know how they may experience these feelings. I ask them what their loneliness is like. The more fully I remember that I am not inside another person's head just because we use similar words to describe our experience, the more deeply respectful I become of a client's uniqueness.

The ACA therapist can be tempted to join the client's rush to be understood and validated, and end up missing the concrete details. I remember listening to my own father tell me how proud he was of me, knowing that he had no idea of who I was. There is a danger that ACA therapists can create this same, empty feeling within their clients. For clients to feel heard, they must first be helped to talk.

Contamination of the Therapy

The number of ways in which ACA therapists can contaminate therapy with their own unresolved issues is incalculable. But this doesn't differentiate them from non-ACA therapists. Whatever uniqueness exists here lies in the frequent confluence between therapists who are ACAs and ACA clients regarding triggers for one's issues, and the defenses which these issues activate.

It should suffice to say that for ACA therapists and their ACA clients, the single most powerful trigger in the universe for personal issues is the same thing: relationship with an alcoholic. Countertransference exists whenever therapists possess attitudes or ignorance about alcoholics or active symptoms of posttraumatic stress disorder (PTSD) and co-dependence that impact the therapeutic process. This impact often comes from blind spots. The worst blind spot may exist in those ACA therapists who continue to deny their own parents' alcoholism, or to minimize the effect this had on their own lives. Other blind spots may exist when psychic numbing intrudes on the development of intimacy within the therapeutic relationship, or when therapists' own primitive echoistic needs cause them to lose sight of their competence during periods when clients are rejecting them.

More active distortions may also appear in the countertransference. Clients usually present therapists with far more material than they can explore. The questions therapists ask, and the responses they give to a client's answers, are powerful positive reinforcements. This is particularly pernicious when therapists unsuspectingly encourage certain feelings in clients while subtly discouraging others by inattention to them. The business of therapy is to facilitate clients' awareness of themselves, not for therapists to substitute their own issues. When this occurs, clients become unwitting stages upon which their therapists' unresolved feelings play themselves out.

Although my descriptions of this process obviously express distaste for the impact of such countertransference, this is not intended to imply that therapists are ever able to prevent countertransference. In fact, ACA clients with co-dependence will actively participate in identifying with even the subtlest countertransference projected upon them, making the total avoidance of this dynamic impossible. However, despite the inevitability of countertransference, therapists do have the responsibility to minimize its impact whenever they can. There is no better way to remain aware of countertransference than by continuously subjecting oneself to the scrutiny of a trusted supervisor.

The complementary nature of narcissism and echoism provides an additional setup for activating significant degrees of countertransference. In some cases, ACA therapists cannot tolerate the transferences projected upon them. Their countertransferential response is to abort or negate the transference. In other cases, therapists may not be able to give up the transferences made upon them. Their countertransferential response is to nurture an immature relationship with the client, blocking the client's efforts to progress through her needed developmental tasks.

These two examples might take the following forms: In the former case (intolerance of transferences), a co-dependent client's assumption that the therapist needs to be the center of attention may violate the therapist's primitive echoistic need to avoid being the center. Countertransference may motivate the therapist to explain too directly that therapy is the responsibility of the client, and the therapist cannot be looked to directly for answers. Rather than allowing the client to experience that the therapist has no magic answers, he has run the risk of causing the client to hide her desire for one.

In the latter case (inability to give up transferences), a narcissistic client may assume that the therapist's role is to be an audience. When the therapist's own co-dependence accepts this role, the client's grandiose exhibitionism may be stimulated. In the name of validating the client's self-esteem, the therapist may never help the client to mature her narcissistic needs.

Burnout

ACA therapists who have yet to recover from their own issues are in danger of over-extending themselves in the precise settings which are the most powerful stressors for their own unresolved issues. Daily doses of taking on other people's feelings (which occurs when countertransference distorts the process of empathy), while having memories of one's own childhood in an alcoholic family stimulated, are not without effect. Propelled by a need to help others take seriously in their own lives what the therapist's family has yet to take seriously is a recipe for disaster.

There may be no better way to prevent burnout than active participation in Al-Anon Twelve Step meetings, since this program is specifically geared toward helping people avoid being overwhelmed by other people's problems. This raises the important issue of how therapists treating ACAs relate to the self-help movement.

THERAPISTS IN
TWELVE STEP PROGRAMS

Although much has been written about Twelve Step programs, the best way to achieve an intimate knowledge of their philosophy and benefits is by active participation. This holds true for therapists as well as for co-dependents and other ACAs seeking recovery.

How do therapists handle the question of their participation? In my experience, that depends on the therapist. On one end of the continuum are those who completely avoid attending meetings in order to maintain their privacy (and sometimes, unfortunately, to maintain their own personal denial and/or professional arrogance). In the middle of the continuum are those whose participation is time-limited (e.g., preceding major involvement in treating clients who actively use the program), or limited to a small home meeting, or even to a meeting closed to anyone but other therapists. On the other end of the continuum are those who participate actively and openly without regard for minimizing their self-revelation to clients (or potential clients) who are also in attendance.

Such self-revelation is a two-edged sword. On the one hand, it is extremely valuable for all therapists treating ACAs to find some way of personally working the steps and participating in meetings. On the other hand, there are two groups of therapists whose unrestricted participation in Twelve Step meetings might be problematic: 1) those who are in denial about the fact that their unguarded self-revelation has powerful consequences, usually negative, in their relationship with clients who attend the same meeting, and 2) those who place the responsibility for such consequences wholly on the client while militantly safeguarding their own right to participate in the program. While the first group may be operating partially out of ignorance of how psychotherapy works, both attitudes undoubtedly reflect a significant degree of countertransference as well.

CONCLUSION

There are few professions as fascinating, and personally challenging, as being a therapist. Like French trappers of old, we set out on each adventure with little more than our own wits to sustain us. Our training comes mostly from experience, and results in confidence that we will be able to find whatever we need along the way. Our path is determined by a few basic principles, knowledge of our own limitations and strengths, and an ability to understand the terrain which immediately surrounds us.

Training to work with adult children of alcoholics is an exciting choice, due in part to the fact that the field is still actively defining itself. Already, it is apparent that this particular population demands a broad range of therapeutic skills. Not since the chemical dependence and mental health fields parted company has there been such a need to reunite the two disciplines. Expertise in psychodynamic psychotherapy, developmental issues, trauma theory, and the phenomenon of chemical addiction are all required, and must all be synthesized with each other. The concept of co-dependence holds great promise to clarify traditional beliefs about narcissism and child development, and perhaps to illuminate small facets of the human condition itself. Training to be a therapist in these areas must be taken very seriously, and undertaken as a professional way of life.

Finally, working in the ACA field is a high risk/high gain equation for therapists who are themselves ACAs. The ACA therapist has much to offer and much to gain. Prudence would dictate that personal therapy, intimate experience with Twelve Step programs, and ongoing supervision are absolute requirements for anyone embarking upon this path.

Appendix I

APPLYING THE TWELVE STEPS
TO CO-DEPENDENCE

THE TWELVE STEPS

The Twelve Steps, shown in Figure 1, are a condensation of wisdom from across the ages, tailored to lives which have been disrupted by obsession with alcohol (in the case of the alcoholic) and alcoholism (in the case of the co-dependent). They are built around the assumption that our minds and our hearts can heal, but that this healing cannot be forced any more than we can force water to flow directly toward the sea. We can deepen the existing river bed, and sometimes straighten it a bit to allow the water to flow more freely, but it is useless to try to make water flow uphill.

Like water, healing flows through channels which are etched through the structure of our minds. Any efforts to encourage healing must move through these natural channels, and not try to force growth along paths which do not exist.

Just as the body heals a cut if we keep the wound clean, there are actions we can take to facilitate the natural healing forces within the mind. When consistently practiced, they expand the channels through which healing and growth must move. The Twelve Steps lead people to practice three disciplines: rigorous honesty, a willingness to accept feelings as legitimate parts of our lives, and a commitment to enter into community with others. Each discipline unlocks the potential for inner healing. The steps are especially effective when brought to bear against problems resulting from excessive denial, an unrealistic relationship to willpower, and obsessions—i.e., the "ism" of alcoholism, and the core of co-dependent personality disorder.

Figure 1
The Twelve Steps of Alcoholics Anonymous

1. We admitted we were powerless over alcohol—that our lives had become unmanageable.
2. Came to believe that a Power greater than ourselves could restore us to sanity.
3. Made a decision to turn our will and our lives over to the care of God *as we understood Him.*
4. Made a searching and fearless moral inventory of ourselves.
5. Admitted to God, to ourselves, and to another human being the exact nature of our wrongs.
6. Were entirely ready to have God remove all these defects of character.
7. Humbly asked Him to remove our shortcomings.
8. Made a list of all persons we had harmed, and became willing to make amends to them all.
9. Made direct amends to such people wherever possible, except when to do so would injure them or others.
10. Continued to take personal inventory and when we were wrong promptly admitted it.
11. Sought through prayer and meditation to improve our conscious contact with God *as we understood Him,* praying only for knowledge of His will for us and the power to carry that out.
12. Having had a spiritual awakening as the result of these steps, we tried to carry this message to others, and to practice these principles in all our affairs.

The Twelve Steps are relevant to co-dependents in the following specific ways.

• *The First Step* ("We admitted we were powerless over alcohol—that our lives had become unmanageable").

Until they accept the First Step, many co-dependents continue to feel guilty that they are not clever enough or strong enough to get the alcoholic in their life to stop drinking. It may never occur to them that it is literally impossible to *make* other people stop drinking. It *is* possible to *ask* that they stop drinking, to *suggest* that they stop drinking, to *refuse* to be around them when they are drinking, to *confront* them with the damage they have done to their own lives and the lives of people who love them, to *invite* them to spend some sober time with you, etc. But none of these approaches has the power to *force* them to stop drinking. The alcoholic has been given all the power he will ever need to continue drinking, if that is what he is going to do.

The first half of the First Step challenges the co-dependent's basic beliefs about her efforts to control an alcoholic parent. The second half offers the same challenge to her efforts to control the rest of her life. It suggests that she is compounding her problems and wasting her energy trying to control what is beyond her limits, and then feeling shamed by her failures. It says that the reason she cannot keep parts of her life under control isn't because she is inadequate, but because those parts of her life lie outside the ability of any human being to control.

When taken seriously, the First Step relieves co-dependents from having to be superhuman by confronting their denial about what is and isn't under their control. Implicit in this is the suggestion that a person's emotional life is not under his conscious control, so it makes no sense to be ashamed of one's feelings, no matter what those feelings might be. This is analogous to the release from shame alcoholics feel when they first accept that alcoholism is a disease, not a character flaw.

However, acceptance of the First Step also eliminates a cornerstone of the co-dependent's identity: the sense that she exists only because she is needed. This can create considerable anxiety.

• *The Second and Third Steps* ("Came to believe that a Power greater than ourselves could restore us to sanity," "Made a decision to turn our will and our lives over to the care of God *as we understood Him*").

These steps suggest that an individual's conscious mind is not the pinnacle of creation, nor is it obliged to stand alone against the stresses of the world. The leap of faith these two steps require creates a new sense of belonging and a greater acceptance of one's feelings.

The single most effective way to recapture the *capacity* to belong is through a leap of faith toward God (or whatever you may wish to name your Higher Power). The important point is that you leap toward where you feel God might be. Whether you are right or wrong is of secondary importance to your *willingness* to act on your belief. Communion with God, however you conceive such a Higher Power, reopens the capacity to belong and to feel "at home"—two feelings with which co-dependents have lost touch. The capacity to belong affects our relationships with both the outside and the inside worlds. It permits us to enter into friendships with a feeling that we are welcome. It also permits us to enter into a new relationship with our own emotions. As we feel at home within ourselves, we can begin welcoming our feelings as legitimate parts of who we are.

• *The Fourth and Fifth Steps* ("Made a searching and fearless moral inventory of ourselves," "Admitted to God, to ourselves, and to another human being the exact nature of our wrongs").

The inventory of Step Four is an exercise in self-honesty. The Fifth Step suggests that this inventory is complete and objective only when you share it with someone else. The ultimate goal is to stand before your God and speak the truth about yourself, as best you know it, without dramatizing your shortcomings or understating your virtues.

These two steps require rigorous honesty, particularly when it comes to evaluating your virtues, as most people are convinced that they will recover faster if they give special emphasis to the harm they have done to others. Such emphasis is merely a form of manipulation by which we attempt to impress our Higher Power.

• *The Sixth Step* ("Were entirely ready to have God remove all these defects of character").

This step suggests that you become "entirely ready" to have God remove all your defects of character, which requires another great leap of faith. Whenever paralysis from fear of the unknown ensues, as it often does at this point, Al-Anon advises starting over again with the First Step, as a reminder that you are powerless to erase fear of the unknown. Such fear is normal, but you don't have to handle it alone. You can rely on their Higher Power to help you move through it.

Refusal to rely on a Higher Power may be one of the character defects listed in your Fourth Step inventory. Admitting it to yourself, another person, and God will probably move you one step closer to being "entirely ready" to be free of it. The Twelve Steps are a continuously self-reinforcing process of becoming more honest, accepting your feelings, and entering into community—all of which promote the healing which is gaining momentum even before it has begun creating concrete behavioral changes.

• *The Seventh, Eighth, and Ninth Steps* ("Humbly asked Him to remove our shortcomings," "Made a list of all persons we had harmed, and became willing to make amends to them all," "Made direct amends to such people wherever possible, except when to do so would injure them or others").

These three steps continue the process of rigorous self-honesty, turn it into a way of life, and deepen the willingness to bring new levels of honesty into current relationships.

• *The Tenth Step* ("Continued to take personal inventory and when we were wrong promptly admitted it").

Once the past has been dealt with honestly, the Tenth Step is a commitment to keep the slate clean. You will never again accumulate a backlog of guilt—as long as you continue to be honest in the here-and-now about your actions and promptly acknowledge any harm that you do.

The Tenth Step gives you a solid internal foundation upon which to base your self-esteem. Your willingness to deal honestly with yourself becomes the guiding standard for your life, not whether you make mistakes. Your own sense of integrity becomes more important than the impressions others have of you. Such a way of life runs in the opposite direction of active co-dependence.

• *The Eleventh and Twelfth Steps* ("Sought through prayer and meditation to improve our conscious contact with God *as we understood Him*, praying only for knowledge of His will for us and the power to carry that out," "Having had a spiritual awakening as the result of these steps, we tried to carry this message to others, and to practice these principles in all our affairs").

The final two steps bring fullness to one's spiritual life, and thus bring fullness to one's healing. They solidify a sense of identity which includes the *capacity* to belong. This is in marked contrast to the tendency of active co-dependents to borrow their sense of identity from their partners, yet still feel deeply isolated from others and their own feelings.

COMMENTS

The Twelve Steps are of value to both primary and secondary co-dependents. Concrete behavioral changes, leading to detachment and detoxification from stresses which intensify co-dependent traits into a full-blown, disabling disorder, are gently supported by other members of the fellowship. But beyond this, a disciplined adherence to the Twelve Steps also promotes characterological change, which can create a shift in the very foundations of one's identity.

The Twelve Step fellowship gives the co-dependent a safe place to rework the foundations for his identity. Strengthened by the Twelve Steps and the Twelve Traditions, the relationship with his Higher Power, and peer relationships with other group members, he feels secure enough to abandon the roots of a dysfunctional identity and leap into the unknown. The psychological events which are stimulated by active participation in a Twelve Step recovery program can be of such profound significance that a therapist's failure to comprehend them may render the therapy relatively irrelevant.

Appendix II

A TIME TO HEAL

I was fascinated by Huckleberry Finn from the moment I met him through Mark Twain's writing.

To all appearances, my own life was quite different from his. Huck lived during a time of feuds and flimflam men in rough-and-ready pre-Civil War America. I attended an average school in Ohio during the 1950s, studied diligently, and had never met a real criminal. Huck took off on his own and rafted the wild Mississippi River. I rode my bike to school occasionally. Huck's mother was dead, and his father beat the tar out of him. My parents got divorced when I was thirteen, but I was never left without a roof over my head.

On the surface, Huck's life and mine were worlds apart. So why have I always responded to him as though he were a twin brother? When I reread Twain's book as an adult, I finally understood the bond. My fascination and sense of kinship with Huck made complete sense at last: We are both children of alcoholic fathers.

The Adventures of Huckleberry Finn leaves no doubt about Mr. Finn's alcoholism. "Every time he got money he got drunk; and every time he got drunk he raised Cain around town; and every time he raised Cain he got jailed." He drank so much that his face was drained of color and white—"not like another man's white, but a white to make a body sick, a white to make a body's flesh crawl." He drank until he hallucinated and lost all memory.

In one frightening episode, Huck witnessed his father screaming about imaginary snakes crawling up his legs and biting him on the neck. Later that night, Huck relates, "He chased me round and round the place with a clasp-knife, calling me the Angel of Death and saying he would kill me."

Huck's father was a violent man who beat Huck until the boy was covered with welts. He was a bitter man who blamed all of his misfortune on others. He was a spiteful man who resented Huck's "school learning"; he vowed to take Huck down a peg for putting on airs and tore up an award his son had received from school. He was a public disgrace, the acknowledged town drunk. When a new judge in town naively took Mr. Finn into his home to reform him, Huck's father promptly stole enough money to get drunk, rolled off the porch roof, broke his arm in two places, and almost froze to death before sunup. Today, we recognize Mr. Finn as a very sick man. The disease of alcoholism ruined his life and led him to a premature death.

In his drunken view of the world, Mr. Finn saw Huck as his personal possession. He terrorized Huck to get drinking money (which Huck quickly gave him in order to avoid getting a beating). Whenever Huck showed any independence, his father literally held him hostage. At times he would not let Huck out of his sight for days; at other times he would simply take off, leaving the boy locked up in their remote cabin. Huck had no right to exist, except to make his father's life easier. When the widow who cared for Huck during his father's year long absence asked to have protective custody of him, the courts refused to interfere. The judge said that he did not want to separate families if he could avoid it.

Huckleberry Finn was the child of an alcoholic (COA), and this experience profoundly affected his life. Beneath his bravado was fear. Under his bubbling enthusiasm was a boy who knew enough depression and loneliness to almost wish for death at times. He suffered from guilt far out of proportion to anything he had done, and he felt responsible for others' misfortune. Whenever his life lacked drama, Huck would become bored and would long for change of any kind. He lived behind a facade of fabrication so pervasive that telling the truth felt strange. His strategy for getting through life was to escape, to keep out of quarrels, to let other people have their own way, and to keep the roots of commitment to anyone or anything from sinking too deeply. Throughout it all, he wrestled with his own sense of self-worth.

There is a lot of Huckleberry Finn in every child of an alcoholic. You may recognize the kinship you feel with him without understanding its source. His experience is a mirror in which you may see many of your hopes and fears reflected. You may see your own deep sense of being an outsider, your own unrelenting drive to survive. And you may see yourself on the run, trying to get away from a past that can never be left far enough behind.

By and large, the effects of being raised by an alcoholic parent have not changed much in the last hundred years. In the beginning of the book, Huck found himself in a dilemma, bouncing back and forth between two intolerable situations. Whenever he spent time with the widow as his guardian, life became boring. He attended school, was taught religion, took daily baths, and had to stop cussing and smoking his pipe. Life seemed empty without the drama of surviving his father's drunken binges and the adventure of fending for himself when his Pap disappeared for days at a time. On the other hand, whenever he fled the widow, Huck became a hostage to his father's beatings and insanity.

On the terrifying night when his drunken father chased him around the cabin with a knife, Huck grabbed a rifle off the wall and held him at bay until he finally passed out from the alcohol. Sleep eventually overtook Huck as well. The next morning, he was awakened by his father, who, with no memory of the night before, demanded to know why Huck was sleeping crouched by the door with the gun across his knees. Huck immediately judged that it was best not to tell the truth. "Somebody tried to get in, so I was laying for him," he said.

Today, such creativity in a person's survival instincts is called "street sense." In the middle of the last century it was called "river sense." Huck instinctively understood that his father had no memory of what had happened the previous night (such episodes are called alcohol-induced memory lapses, or blackouts). He therefore took the opportunity to make up a different version of reality, one that felt safer than the truth.

Most people living with an out-of-control alcoholic learn not to make unnecessary waves. Reality becomes what the alcoholic is willing to accept as reality. Huck's response to a world that was out of his control and that cared little about who he was as an individual symbolizes the response of most COAs.

Freedom through escape made the most sense to Huck, and the only way he felt able to escape was by staging his own death. When his father was away, Huck smashed down the door of their cabin with an axe and rummaged around for provisions. Then Huck shot a wild pig and smeared its blood on his bed covers and on the axe. He pulled out some of his own hairs, stuck them to the axe's blade, and tossed the axe into the corner as evidence of his murder. Finally, he conspicuously dragged the pig's body down to the water's edge, leaving "evidence" that his own body had been tossed into the river. Then he disappeared on his adventures down the Mississippi.

Huck's trip down the Mississippi River serves as a metaphor for the journey made by children of alcoholics as they attempt to leave home and make lives of their own. This journey is largely motivated by the dream of escape, and it is all too frequently bought at the price of cooperating with one's own death—emotional, spiritual, or even physical.

Huck's creed for life is expressed in his thoughts on how to have a successful raft trip. He felt that there must be no conflict; his way of dealing with negative feelings was to say nothing, never to let on, to keep things to himself. "It's the best way; then you don't have no quarrels, and don't get into no trouble." He tells us, "If I never learnt nothing else out of Pap, I learnt that the best way to get along with his kind of people is to let them have their own way."

When two swindlers hitched a ride on his raft, Huck knew they "warn't no kings nor dukes at all, but just low-down humbugs and frauds." But if they wanted Huck to call them kings and dukes, then he had no objections, " 'long as it would keep peace in the family."

Being a COA, Huck understood that the perfect way to disguise yourself is to let other people see in you whatever they want to see. Up against uncontrollable forces, Huck learned to take on a chameleon-like quality. No matter whom he fell in with, he could take on their characteristics or mold himself to get what he needed from them. In the course of his adventures, Huck was befriended by a whole gallery of characters, including feuding Southern aristocrats and confidence men. At one point, Tom Sawyer's Aunt Sally mistook Huck for Tom, who was expected to arrive momentarily for a summer vacation. Huck, in need of a good meal, played the part perfectly before he even knew who the woman thought he was. When she introduced him to his "cousins" as Tom Sawyer, Huck was stunned: "It was like being born again, I was so glad to find out who I was." From that point on, he simply became Tom Sawyer.

Children of alcoholics tend to have the chameleon nature that Huck so often showed. While this trait can be charming and useful, it can also become such a habit that it turns into a prison from which a person's real identity never fully emerges.

Being an underdog throughout his life, Huck had sympathy for underdogs everywhere. He befriended a runaway slave and repeatedly risked his own safety to keep his friend free. At another point, he put himself in great danger to foil a plot to swindle three newly orphaned girls out of their inheritance, cleverly leaving the con men to argue between themselves over which one was to blame for losing the money.

Huck's heart softened each time he saw someone down on his luck. He understood from his own experience how easily this could happen.

Huck's kindheartedness also stems to some degree from the exaggerated guilt experienced by so many adult children of alcoholics (ACAs). He frequently felt guilty for things, even when he knew he had done nothing to cause the misfortune. "But that's always the way; it don't make no difference whether you do right or wrong, a person's conscience ain't got no sense, and it just goes for him anyway." When Huck was caught in the middle of two feuding families and saw one of the boys get shot, he knew he could not go near that family's house again, "because I reckoned I was to blame, somehow."

Toward the end of the book, Huck learned that his father had died. Huck no longer had any reason to keep on running and could safely return to Hannibal. What happens in the book's last half-page tells us a lot about Huckleberry Finn.

Running had become a way of life. Rather than settling down to a relatively normal life and allowing himself to be adopted by Tom Sawyer's aunt, Huck said that he had heard of some excitement up in Indian country (probably Oklahoma), and he reckoned he would light out for there in search of further adventure. Although this warms the heart, and the reader roots for Huck to remain forever a boy in search of excitement, it also represents another way in which Huck had been molded by his experience of growing up with an alcoholic parent. It was not only the thirst for freedom that burned brightly in Huck's breast; fear also propelled him to seek escape as a way of life.

At the end of the book, Huck's strategies all seem to be working, but Huck is still a child. It is unlikely that his way of accommodating to life's problems provided a firm foundation for a full, rich, and satisfying adult life or for successful intimate relationships. For Huck, as for so many millions of other COAs, running had become the goal. He had to keep running, if he was to feel safe. But, as with so many ACAs, Huck would certainly have run out of gas at some point and had to face what it was he had been running from all those years. He would have discovered that he had begun by running from his father but ended up running from himself. Living in a survival mode is one of the major characteristics of ACAs.

The final two paragraphs of the book also illustrate how distanced Huck had become from some of his emotions. On hearing of his father's death, he had absolutely no reaction. Had he come to have no feelings whatsoever for his father? More likely, he was not aware of what his feelings were. One is left to wonder how many years it would be before Huck would finally allow himself to react to having lost his father.

In an interesting deviation from Mark Twain's book, a Public Broadcasting System movie of Huckleberry Finn chose to have Huck learn of his father's death much earlier in the story. The PBS version had Huck immediately deny that his father had ever treated him badly. Huck also concluded that he might have somehow been responsible for his father's death. Although these reactions were not contained in the original book, they certainly depict how a child of an alcoholic might respond.

If Huck was ever to heal the wounds suffered at his father's hands, it would have been through the rigorous honesty he possessed. During his deepest crisis of the spirit, he was confronted with his tendency to try to escape the consequences of his misdeeds by keeping them hidden. He tried to excuse himself for this by saying he had been brought up to be wicked, but he recognized that he could have gone to church and set this right. He knelt to pray, but no words would come. It was then that he realized his deepest flaw. He had been playing double, trying to pray for something when he knew deep down it was a lie. Huck discovered that "you can't pray a lie." It was this willingness to see his own denial that gives me the most hope that Huck may eventually have been able to stop running.

If Huck never found a way to stop running, it would have been because he cooperated with his own death. The elaborate staging of his own murder symbolizes the way in which COAs often obtain an element of freedom in their lives by accepting their own unimportance. By going into hiding, by being less than what they normally would be, by opting out of the reality they have been placed in, COAs obtain some sense of control over lives that are otherwise taken over by others and thrown into chaos.

Mark Twain gave us no idea of what eventually became of Huckleberry Finn. I prefer to imagine that he traveled with the Buffalo Bill Wild West Show or joined the Yukon gold rush. But I have nightmares of his lying drunk and destitute in a back alley of Hannibal, Missouri, still a loner, compulsively seeking excitement until the end. Huck did say, "I'd druther been bit with a snake than Pap's whiskey"—but what COA hasn't made such a statement?

There are lessons of universal value to be learned from the struggles of COAs. Above all is the lesson that healing begins with honesty. Huck Finn demonstrated such honesty when he had the integrity to admit that he was trying to pray a lie; he knew his deepest flaw was that he played double with life. This flaw can only be dissolved by making the discipline of recovery a part of daily life.

From Timmen L. Cermak, M.D., *A Time to Heal*
Los Angeles: Jeremy P. Tarcher, Inc., 1988, pp. 1-8.

REFERENCES

CHAPTER 1

1. Stephanie Brown, *Treating the Alcoholic: A Developmental Model of Recovery* (New York: John Wiley and Sons, Inc., 1985), p. 28. Dr. Brown describes this characterological change as "a change in attitude toward and consequent interpretation of self and others."

2. George Vaillant, *The Natural History of Alcoholism* (Cambridge, MA: Harvard University Press, 1983), pp. 217-235.

3. Brown, p. 28.

4. Harry Stack Sullivan, *The Psychiatric Interview* (New York: W. W. Norton & Company, Inc., 1954).

CHAPTER 2

1. Such a framework is similar to Freud's early work with Charcot. At that time, hysterical symptoms were seen to be the distorted outcroppings of repressed impulses. This seemed to be verified by sudden cures brought about through hypnosis. Freud became cautious when it became apparent that some "repressed memories" cathartically expressed under hypnosis were of fabricated historical events. The truth contained in the patient's "screen memories" was restricted to the emotional level, and often did not lie in their literal detail. This confusion lies at the base of the debate between drive theory and trauma theory (see Volume One, *Evaluation*, Appendix I).

2. Alice Miller, *The Drama of the Gifted Child* (New York: Basic Books, Inc./Harper Colophon Books, 1979), p. 75.

3. Miller, p. 10.

4. Miller, p. 67.

5. Miller, p. 69.

295

6. Erwin Parson, "The Role of Psychodynamic Group Therapy in the Treatment of the Combat Veteran," in *Psychotherapy of the Combat Veteran* (New York: SP Medical and Scientific Books, 1984), pp. 153-220.

7. Spencer Eth and Robert Pynoos, *Post-Traumatic Stress Disorder in Children* (Washington, DC: American Psychiatric Press, Inc., 1985), p. 173.

8. Miller, p. 85.

CHAPTER 3

1. For further information on the process of intervention, see Vernon Johnson, *Intervention*, (Minneapolis: Johnson Institute, 1986).

2. Sheldon Cashdan, *Object Relations Therapy: Using the Relationship* (New York: W. W. Norton & Company, 1988), pp. 53-78.

3. George Vaillant, *Adaptation to Life* (Boston: Little, Brown and Company, 1977) p. 160.

4. Margaret Mahler, Fred Pine, and Anni Bergman, *The Psychological Birth of the Human Infant* (New York: Basic Books, 1975).

5. Daniel Stern, *The Interpersonal World of the Infant* (New York: Basic Books, Inc., 1985), pp. 138-161.

6. Cashdan, p. 23.

7. Heinz Kohut, *The Analysis of the Self* (Madison, CT: International Universities Press, 1971).

8. Stern, pp. 37-68.

9. Irvin Yalom, *The Theory and Practice of Group Psychotherapy* (New York: Basic Books, Inc., 1975), p. 28.

10. This definition was written jointly by a symposium of faculty members at the First National Conference on Co-dependence, Scottsdale, Arizona, September 6-9, 1989.

11. Cashdan, pp. 81-146.

12. James Masterson, M.D., *The Narcissistic and Borderline Disorders: An Integrated Developmental Approach* (New York: Brunner/Mazel, Inc., 1981).

13. Cashdan, pp. 130-131.

14. Yalom, pp. 268-272.

15. Stephanie Brown, *Treating Adult Children of Alcoholics* (New York: John Wiley and Sons, Inc., 1988), p. 241-243.

16. Stephanie Brown and Susan Beletsis,"The Development of Family Transference in Groups for the Adult Children of Alcoholics," in *Adult Children of Alcoholics in Treatment* (Deerfield Beach, FL: Health Communications, Inc., 1989), pp. 43-72. Originally published in *International Journal of Group Psychotherapy*, Winter, 1986, pp. 97-114.

17. This discussion is condensed from Timmen Cermak, "Al-Anon and Recovery," in Marc Galanter, *Recent Developments in Alcoholism, Volume 7* (New York: Plenum Publishing Corporation, 1989), pp. 91-104.

CHAPTER 4

1. Sharon Wegscheider-Cruse, *Another Chance: Hope and Health for the Alcoholic Family* (Palo Alto, CA: Science and Behavior Books, 1981), pp. 89-149.

2. Peter Steinglass, Linda Benett, Steven Wolin, and David Reiss, *The Alcoholic Family* (New York: Basic Books, Inc., 1987), pp. 176-250.

3. Steinglass, pp. 74-102.

4. Steinglass, pp. 146-175.

5. Steinglass, p. 9.

6. James Garbarino, Edna Guttman, and Janis Wilson Seeley, *The Psychologically Battered Child* (San Francisco: Jossey-Bass Publishers, 1986), p. 8.

7. These characteristics of ACAs are described in detail in Timmen Cermak, *A Primer on Adult Children of Alcoholics*, Second Edition (Deerfield Beach, FL: Health Communications, Inc., 1989), pp. 34-36.

8. Claudia Black, *It Will Never Happen to Me* (Denver: M.A.C. Printing and Publications Division, 1981), pp. 31-49.

9. Vernon E. Johnson, D.D., *Intervention: How to Help Someone Who Doesn't Want Help* (Minneapolis: Johnson Institute, 1986), p. 61.

10. *Alcoholics Anonymous*, Third Edition (Alcoholics Anonymous World Services, Inc., 1976), p. 122.

11. Vernon Johnson, *I'll Quit Tomorrow* (New York: Harper and Row, 1973), p. 30.

12. Ann Wilson Schaef, *Co-Dependence: Misunderstood—Mistreated* (Minneapolis: Winston Press, 1986), pp. 48-51.

13. Timmen L. Cermak, M.D., *A Time to Heal* (Los Angeles: Jeremy P. Tarcher, Inc., 1988), pp. 190-192.

14. Cermak, *A Time to Heal*, pp. 192-196.

15. Cermak, *A Time to Heal*, pp. 196-205.

CHAPTER 6

1. Stephanie Brown and Susan Beletsis, "The Development of Family Transference in Groups for the Adult Children of Alcoholics," in *Adult Children of Alcoholics in Treatment* (Deerfield Beach, FL: Health Communications, Inc., 1989), p. 44. Originally published in *International Journal of Group Psychotherapy*, Winter, 1986, pp. 97-114.

2. Irvin Yalom, *The Theory and Practice of Group Psychotherapy* (New York: Basic Books, Inc., 1975).

3. Yalom, p. 28.

4. Reported in Timmen Cermak and Stephanie Brown, "Interactional Group Therapy with Adult Children of Alcoholics," *International Journal of Group Psychotherapy*, Vol. 32, No. 3:375-379, 1982; reprinted in

Stephanie Brown, Susan Beletsis, and Timmen Cermak, *Adult Children of Alcoholics in Treatment* (Deerfield Beach, FL: Health Communications, Inc., 1989).

5. Yalom, p. 107.
6. Yalom, chapters 5 and 6, pp. 105-218.
7. Yalom, p. 122.

CHAPTER 7

1. Stephanie Brown, *Treating the Alcoholic: A Developmental Model of Recovery* (New York: John Wiley and Sons, Inc., 1985).
2. Fact Sheet #14, "Substance Abuse and Child Abuse," National Committee for the Prevention of Child Abuse, 332 S. Michigan Ave., Suite 950, Chicago, IL 60604, February, 1989.

BIBLIOGRAPHY

BOOKS: PROFESSIONAL

—— *Al-Anon Faces Alcoholism*, Second Edition (New York: Al-Anon Family Group Headquarters, Inc., 1984).

—— *Alcoholics Anonymous* (New York: Alcoholics Anonymous World Services, Inc., 1976).

Bean-Bayog, Margaret and Barry Stimmel, eds., *Children of Alcoholics* (New York: The Haworth Press, 1987).

Brown, Stephanie, *Treating the Alcoholic* (New York: John Wiley and Sons, Inc., 1985).

Brown, Stephanie, *Treating Adult Children of Alcoholics* (New York: John Wiley and Sons, Inc., 1988).

Cermak, Timmen, *Diagnosing and Treating Co-dependence* (Minneapolis: Johnson Institute, 1986).

Cashdan, Sheldon, *Object Relations Therapy* (New York: W. W. Norton & Company, 1988).

Cork, Margaret, *The Forgotten Children* (Ontario, Canada: General Publishing Company, 1969).

—— *Diagnostic and Statistical Manual of Mental Disorders* [DSM-III-R] (Washington, DC: American Psychiatric Association, Inc., 1987).

Doi, Takeo, *The Anatomy of Dependence* (Tokyo: Kodansha International Ltd., 1971, distributed by New York: Harper and Row).

Eth, Spencer and Robert Pynoos, *Post-Traumatic Stress Disorder in Children* (Washington, DC: American Psychiatric Press, Inc., 1985).

Garbarino, James, Edna Guttman, and Janis Wilson Seeley, *The Psychologically Battered Child* (San Francisco: Jossey-Bass Publishers, 1986).

Goodwin, Donald, *Is Alcoholism Hereditary?* (New York: Oxford University Press, 1976).

Horowitz, Mardi, *Stress Response Syndromes* (Northvale, NJ: Jason Aronson Inc., 1976).

Johnson, Vernon, *Intervention: How to Help Someone Who Doesn't Want Help* (Minneapolis: Johnson Institute, 1986).

Kohut, Heinz, *The Analysis of the Self* (Madison, CT: International Universities Press, 1971).

Kurtz, Ernest, *Not-God: A History of Alcoholics Anonymous* (Center City, MN: Hazelden, 1979).

Levin, Jerome, *Treatment of Alcoholism and Other Addictions: A Self-Psychology Approach* (Northvale, NJ: Jason Aronson Inc., 1987).

Mahler, Margaret, Fred Pine, and Anni Bergman, *The Psychological Birth of the Human Infant* (New York: Basic Books, Inc., 1975).

Masterson, James, *The Narcissistic and Borderline Disorders: An Integrated Developmental Approach* (New York: Brunner/Mazel, Inc., 1981).

Miller, Alice, *The Drama of the Gifted Child* (New York: Basic Books, Inc./ Harper Colophon Books, 1979).

Millon, Theodore, *Disorders of Personality: DSM-III, Axis II* (New York: John Wiley and Sons, Inc., 1981).

Reich, Wilhelm, *Character Analysis* (New York: Farrar, Straus & Giroux, 1949).

Rivinus, Timothy, ed., *Children of Chemically Dependent Parents: Academic, Clinical and Public Policy Perspectives* (New York: Brunner/Mazel, Inc., 1991).

Schwartz, Harvey, ed., *Psychotherapy of the Combat Veteran* (New York: Spectrum Publications, 1984).

Steinglass, Peter, *et al.*, *The Alcoholic Family* (New York: Basic Books, Inc., 1987).

Stern, Daniel, *The Interpersonal World of the Infant* (New York: Basic Books, Inc., 1985).

Vaillant, George, *Adaptation to Life* (Boston: Little, Brown and Company, 1977).

Vaillant, George, *The Natural History of Alcoholism* (Cambridge, MA: Harvard University Press, 1983).

van der Kolk, Bessel, *Psychological Trauma* (Washington, DC: American Psychiatric Press, Inc., 1987).

Vannicelli, Marsha, *Group Psychotherapy with Adult Children of Alcoholics* (New York: Guilford Press, 1989).

Wood, Barbara, *Children of Alcoholism: The Struggle for Self and Intimacy in Adult Life* (New York: New York University Press, 1987).

Yalom, Irvin, *The Theory and Practice of Group Psychotherapy* (New York: Basic Books, Inc., 1975).

BOOKS: GENERAL PUBLIC

Black, Claudia, *It Will Never Happen To Me* (New York: Ballantine, 1987).

Bowden, Julie and Herb Gravitz, *Genesis: Spirituality in Recovery from*

Childhood Traumas (Pompano Beach, FL: Health Communications, Inc., 1988).

Cermak, Timmen, *A Primer on Adult Children of Alcoholics* (Pompano Beach, FL: Health Communications, Inc., 1985).

Cermak, Timmen, *A Time to Heal* (Los Angeles: Jeremy P. Tarcher, Inc., 1988).

Gravitz, Herb and Julie Bowden, *Recovery: A Guide for Children of Alcoholics* (New York: Simon and Schuster, 1987).

Johnson, Vernon, *I'll Quit Tomorrow* (New York: Harper and Row, 1973).

Mellody, Pia, *Facing Co-Dependency* (New York: Harper and Row, 1989).

Wegscheider-Cruse, Sharon, *Another Chance: Hope and Health for the Alcoholic Family* (Palo Alto, CA: Science and Behavior Books, 1981).

INDEX

When the Johnson Institute first opened its doors in 1966, few people knew or believed that alcoholism was a disease. Fewer still thought that anything could be done to help the chemically dependent person other than wait for him or her to "hit bottom" and then pick up the pieces.

We've spent over twenty years spreading the good news that chemical dependence is a *treatable* disease. Through our publications, films, video and audio cassettes, and our training and consultation services, we've given hope and help to hundreds of thousands of people across the country and around the world. The intervention and treatment methods we've pioneered have restored shattered careers, healed relationships with co-workers and friends, saved lives, and brought families back together.

Today the Johnson Institute is an internationally recognized leader in the field of chemical dependence intervention, treatment, and recovery. Individuals, organizations, and businesses, large and small, rely on us to provide them with the tools they need. Schools, universities, hospitals, treatment centers, and other health care agencies look to us for experience, expertise, innovation, and results. With care, compassion, and commitment, we will continue to reach out to chemically dependent persons, their families, and the professionals who serve them.

To find out more about us, write or call:

The Johnson Institute
7151 Metro Boulevard
Minneapolis, MN 55439-2122
1-800-231-5165
In MN: 1-800-247-0484
or (612) 944-0511
In CAN: 1-800-447-6660

Need a copy for a friend? You may order directly.

EVALUATING AND TREATING
ADULT CHILDREN OF ALCOHOLICS
Volume One: EVALUATION
Volume Two: TREATMENT
Timmen L. Cermak, M.D.
A Johnson Institute Professional Series Book
$21.95 each volume; $37.95 set

Order Form

Please send ___ copy (copies) of **VOLUME ONE: EVALUATION** and/or ___ copy (copies) of **VOLUME TWO: TREATMENT**. Price $21.95 each or $37.95 set. Please add $3.00 shipping for the first book and $1.25 for each additional copy.

Name (please print)

Address

City/State/Zip

Attention
Please note that orders under $75.00 must be prepaid.
If paying by credit card, please complete the following:

☐ Bill the full payment to my credit card.

☐ VISA ☐ MasterCard ☐ American Express

Credit card number: _____

For MASTERCARD
Write the 4 digits below the account number: _____

Expiration date: _____

Signature on card: _____

For faster service, call our Order Department TOLL-FREE:
1-800-231-5165
In Minnesota call:
1-800-247-0484
or **(612) 944-0511**
In Canada call:
1-800-447-6660

Return this order form to:
The Johnson Institute
7151 Metro Boulevard
Minneapolis, MN 55439-2122
Ship to (if different from above):

Name (please print)

Address

City/State/Zip